REACTIONS TO CRITICAL LIFE EVENTS

Reactions to Critical Life Events
A Social Psychological Analysis

Marita R. Inglehart

New York
Westport, Connecticut
London

LIBRARY OF CONGRESS CATALOGING-IN-PUBLICATION DATA

Inglehart, Marita Rosch.
   [Kritische Lebensereignisse. English]
   Reactions to critical life events : a social psychological
analysis / Marita R. Inglehart.
     p. cm.
   Translation of: Kritische Lebensereignisse.
   Includes bibliographical references and index.
   ISBN 0–275–93875–1 (alk. paper)
   1. Life change events—Psychological aspects. 2. Cognitive
consistency. 3. Attribution (Social psychology). 4. Social
psychology. I. Title.
BF637.L53I5413   1991
302—dc20   90–27790

British Library Cataloguing in Publication Data is available.

Library of Congress Catalog Card Number: 90–27790
ISBN: 0–275–93875–1

First published in 1991

Praeger Publishers, One Madison Avenue, New York, NY 10010
An imprint of Greenwood Publishing Group, Inc.

Printed in the United States of America

The paper used in this book complies with the
Permanent Paper Standard issued by the National
Information Standards Organization (Z39.48–1984).

10 9 8 7 6 5 4 3 2 1

Copyright Acknowledgment

The author and publisher gratefully acknowledge permission from
Kohlhammer Verlag, Stuttgart, to reprint from the German-language
original edition of this work, *Kritische Lebensereignisse*.

To my father, Karl Rohr, 1923 to 1986,
and to my mother, Rita Rohr,
with love and gratitude

Contents

TABLES AND FIGURES   xi

PREFACE   xiii

ACKNOWLEDGMENTS   xv

Part I Theoretical Research on Reactions to Critical Life
        Events: The State of the Art   1

    1 A General Introduction   5

        1.1 Introduction to the Topic: Definitions   5

        1.2 The Central Questions Concerning Reactions
             to Critical Life Events   9

        1.3 Historical Overview   11

    2 Stage-Centered Theories of Reactions to Critical
       Life Events   17

        2.1 Selye's Research on Stress: The General
             Adaptation Syndrome   17

        2.2 Stage-Centered Theories of Reactions to
             Specific Events   19

        2.3 Klinger's Incentive-Disengagement Theory   22

        2.4 Stage-Centered Theories: A Final Evaluation   24

3   Lazarus: Stress, Appraisal, and Coping   27

   3.1   Lazarus' Criticism of an "Objective" Perspective in Stress Research   28

   3.2   Stress, Appraisal, and Coping   29

   3.3   Elaborating the Original Theory: Daily Hassles, Social Support, and Individual Differences   32

   3.4   A Critical Evaluation of Lazarus' Work   34

4   Cognitive Theories   37

   4.1   Seligman's Theory of Learned Helplessness   37

   4.2   Wortman's Research on Reactions to Uncontrollable Events   42

   4.3   "Seligman *or* Wortman" versus "Seligman *and* Wortman"   47

   4.4   Taylor's Theory of Cognitive Adaptation to Threatening Events   48

   4.5   A Critical Evaluation of Cognitive Theories   51

5   Theoretical Research on Reactions to Critical Life Events   55

   5.1   Theoretical Research Not Considered Thus Far   55

   5.2   A Final Evaluation of the Theories Analyzed   56

   5.3   A Theoretical Outlook   57

Part II   The Generalized Principle of Cognitive Consistency and Its Application to Reactions to Critical Life Events   61

6   The Principle of Cognitive Consistency   63

   6.1   Cognitive Consistency: A Meta-Analysis   63

   6.2   Cognitive Consistency and Reactions to Critical Life Events   70

   6.3   The Principle of Cognitive Consistency and Reactions to Critical Life Events—A Critical Evaluation   75

7   The Generalized Principle of Cognitive Consistency:
    Integrating the Principle of Cognitive Consistency
    with Hypotheses About the Attribution Process   79

    7.1   The Attribution Process: An Overview   79

    7.2   The Principle of Cognitive Consistency and
          the Process of Attribution   85

    7.3   The Generalized Principle of Cognitive
          Consistency: Summary—Evaluation—
          Implications   95

8   The Generalized Principle of Cognitive Consistency
    and Reactions to Critical Life Events: Theoretical
    Considerations, Empirical Evidence, and
    Preliminary Evaluation   103

    8.1   Theoretical Considerations and Empirical
          Evidence   103

    8.2   The Generalized Principle of Cognitive
          Consistency and Reactions to Critical Life
          Events—Preliminary Evaluation   134

Part III   The Generalized Principle of Cognitive Consistency—
           Further Implications   139

9   Social Support   141

    9.1   Social Support: An Overview   141

    9.2   The Generalized Principle of Cognitive
          Consistency and Social Support—An
          Exploration   147

10 The Generalized Principle of Cognitive
    Consistency and Individual Differences—An
    Exploration   153

    10.1   Person Variables and Reactions to Critical
           Life Events—An Overview   153

    10.2   The Generalized Principle of Cognitive
           Consistency and Person Factors—An
           Exploration   165

11 The Significance of Life Philosophies   171

11.1   Relevance of Life Philosophies in Situations
       with Critical Life Events—An Overview   171

11.2   The Generalized Principle of Cognitive
       Consistency and Life Philosophies   175

11.3   Final Evaluation of the Significance of Life
       Philosophies   178

12 The Generalized Principle of Cognitive
    Consistency and Reactions to Critical Life
    Events—Exploring Practical Implications   181

    12.1   The Generalized Principle of Cognitive
           Consistency and Reactions to Critical Life
           Events—Practical Implications for
           Counseling   181

    12.2   The Generalized Principle of Cognitive
           Consistency and Reactions to Critical Life
           Events—Practical Implications for
           Prevention   186

    12.3   Final Evaluation   187

    REFERENCES   189

    AUTHOR INDEX   213

    SUBJECT INDEX   219

Tables and Figures

Tables

2.1	Event-Specific Stage Theories: An Overview	22
2.2	Stage Theories to Critical Life Events: An Overview	25
5.1	Cognitive Theories and Reactions to Critical Life Events: An Overview	58
6.1	Meta-analysis of Theories on the Principle of Cognitive Consistency: An Overview	67
7.1	Meta-analysis of Hypotheses About the Attribution Process: An Overview	82
7.2	Meta-analyses of the Two Sets of Hypotheses and the Integrated Theory: An Overview	94
8.1	Indicators of the Amount of Reported Illness Symptoms	111
8.2	Correlations Between Post Hoc Attributions and the Amount of Tension Predicted	117
8.3	Correlations Between Importance of Event and Changes Caused by It with Amount of Tension Arising	119
8.4	Correlation Between A Priori Attributions and Predicted Effort to Reduce Tension	126
8.5	Average Rating of Expected Tension-Reduction Efforts Under Different A Priori Attributions	127
8.6	Correlations Between A Priori Attributions and Amount of One's Own Efforts Predicted for Change	128

8.7   Correlations Between One's Own Perception of
       Variability of Unexpected Events and Level of
       Control and Amount of Effort for Change   129

8.8   Field Studies Used to Test Hypotheses of
       Generalized Principle of Cognitive Consistency: An
       Overview   135

8.9   Laboratory Experiments Conducted to Test
       Hypotheses of the Generalized Principle of Cognitive
       Consistency: An Overview   136

10.1   Various Approaches to Explaining the Effects of
       Person Factors on Reactions to Critical Life Events   166

11.1   Life Philosophies in Situations with Critical Life
       Events   173

Figures

1.1   Questions an Adequate Theory of Reactions to
       Critical Life Events Should Be Able to Answer   12

7.1   Average Academic Achievement Under Various
       Levels of the Independent Variable "Degree of
       Focusing on One Possible Self"   100

7.2   Degree of Professional Involvement of Persons with
       Consistent and Inconsistent Professional Choices   101

8.1   Model 1: The Impact of "Internal versus External"
       Post Hoc Attributions on "Reported Illness
       Symptoms"   112

8.2   Average Degree of Predicted Tension in the
       Conditions "Internal" and "External Post Hoc
       Attributions"   114

8.3   Average Predicted Tension When Encountering
       Negative Inconsistent Events Under Different
       Conditions of Post Hoc Attributions   116

8.4   Model 2: Impact of "Amount of Inconsistencies" on
       "Reported Illness Symptoms"   120

8.5   Model 3: Impact of "Constant Versus Variable A
       Priori Attributions"   123

8.6   Means of Dependent Variables, "Amount of Effort
       for Direct Change" and "Amount of Effort for
       Problem Solving," Under the Independent Variable
       "Kind of A Priori Attributions"   125

Preface

When the concept of cognitive consistency was first introduced into social psychological research in the 1950s, it had enormous impact, giving rise to literally hundreds of publications. For over a decade, many of the most talented investigators in social psychology were stimulated and guided by consistency theory, which seemed to be building up a massive body of cumulative findings. A decade later, attribution theory had a similar impact. Mobilizing the best minds of that era, hundreds of studies were designed and carried out to investigate the role of attribution processes in human behavior. But by the 1970s, research on both cognitive consistency and attribution theory was dwindling. By 1990, they had become peripheral concerns to most social psychologists. This phenomenon raises the question, Is social psychology a cumulative science—or is it simply driven by transient fashions, with today's hot topics destined to sink without a trace, a decade hence?

This book was written with the conviction that social psychology *is* a cumulative science, to a far greater degree than may be immediately evident. More specifically, this book argues that cognitive consistency theory and attribution theory can be integrated into one theory, the generalized principle of cognitive consistency—and that this broader theory has important implications for much of contemporary social psychological research. In particular, it can help illuminate research on critical life events—one of the most dynamic areas of current psychological research.

Why write a book about reactions to critical life events from a social psychological perspective? The first reason was a desire to make connections between seemingly isolated pieces of research: often brilliant in conception and execution, the sheer number and variety of the investigations in this field is staggering. I tried to develop a perspective that would allow me to organize and evaluate this research. A second reason was purely theoretical. When analyzing research on the principle of cognitive consistency, it seems clear that much of life is *not solely* governed by this principle. Playing games, painting, reading novels, falling in love—so many psychological processes other than the search for consistency are involved in all of these activities that it was not surprising that researchers eventually turned away from cognitive consistency research and became concerned with other issues. At the same time I realized that there is one type of situation in a person's life where consistency is the major driving force: the situation with a critical life event. When tension arises to an extreme extent, humans try very hard to reduce it. Therefore the principle of cognitive consistency is particularly significant in situations with critical life events.

Why did I write the book the way I did? I had to find a way to make sense of huge amounts of research. My approach to this problem has been to seek basic and simple questions, the answers to which would clarify and organize the research on complex psychological phenomena. Following this approach helps to demonstrate that there is far more continuity than one might expect in the research carried out during the past 40 years on consistency and attribution theory—and that this has clear implications for current research on critical life events.

Another motivation for writing this book was to try to contribute to our understanding of what we see around us daily. Consequently, this book includes a chapter on the practical implications of these considerations and on the role of life philosophies in general. A psychologist concerned with theoretical issues may seem distant from reality. But I hope that applied working psychologists may at least find these ideas stimulating.

Acknowledgments

This book could not have been written without the support of many people both at the University of Mannheim, Germany, and at the University of Michigan.

At the University of Mannheim it was, above all, Martin Irle who encouraged me and introduced me to the world of research. I am grateful for having had the chance to work with him and thank him for his support. I also want to thank my former colleagues at the University of Mannheim, especially Dorothee Dickenberger, Dieter Frey, Volker Moentmann, and Peter Schmidt, who worked with me on the field studies described here. These field studies and the laboratory experiments could not have been conducted without the help of a number of research assistants. I want to especially thank Achim Broetz, Christine Doerner, Lydia Hammermeister, Erwin Koch, Ralph Rohrlach, Marion Rost, Susanne Schur, and Christiane Tuerner/Grosser for their help. It was a pleasure to work with them.

My work in Europe was supported by several grants from the German Science Foundation (Deutsche Forschungsgemeinschaft) as well as by a grant from the Commission of the European Community.

I started my work on "reactions to critical life events" in Mannheim and published a first monograph about my ideas in German in 1988. For the past several years, I have had the good fortune to work in the Department of Psychology at the University of Michigan. This gave me an opportunity to develop my thoughts further and led to this revised second and expanded edition of my book and its translation into English. The department of psychology at the University of Michigan and especially my colleagues in the social and the personality area provided me with a most stimulating environment. I am happy to have had the opportunity to work here and I am especially grateful for the support and encouragement of three wonderful persons, Robert Zajonc, Donald R. Brown, and Al Cain.

Numerous other colleagues stimulated me, both through their work and as role models, when I made the transition from a German university to an American university. I learned much from Toni Antonucci, Nancy Cantor, Jacquelynne Eccles, Martin Gold, Pat Gurin, James Jackson, Arie Kruglanski, Janet Landman, Mel Manis, Hazel Markus, Bill McKeachie, Richard Nisbett, Warren Norman, Linda Nyquist, Chris Peterson, George Rosenwald, Claude Steele, Joe Veroff, and Camille Wortman, all of whose work I admire. I thank them for being such fine colleagues.

The empirical work that I conducted at the University of Michigan was done with the help of some excellent research assistants and the collaboration of some outstanding graduate students. Many thanks to Debra Chesnin, Quoc Huy Do, Tuong Van Do, Liz Hudler, Julie Jarvi, Pamela Kondoff, Mimi McDonald, Daniel McIntosh, Denise Medaille, Andrew Moffit, and Rose Pacini. I really enjoyed working with them.

Danielle Hogston, Betsy Waldrop, and Karen Petticrew did a fine job on helping me with preparing this manuscript and I thank them very much.

Finally, a wholehearted thanks goes to my family, especially to my husband Ron, my son Ronald, and my two stepdaughters, Elizabeth and Rachel. I am happy and lucky to have you as my family. Thank you.

Part I

Theoretical Research on Reactions to Critical Life Events: The State of the Art

Though a relatively young discipline, psychology has already become divided into a complex system of specialized areas which have remarkably little contact with each other. Furthermore, basic research in psychology usually focuses on one specific aspect of a given area. Thus, applied research in psychology exists on its own, being loosely tied to whichever one of the psychological subdisciplines in which the given researcher was trained. As a consequence, applied psychological research often has little connection with the findings of basic psychological research.

The research on reactions to critical life events constitutes an exceptional case: it is a topic that has stimulated basic research as well as applied research and one that has been investigated by psychologists from a number of different subdisciplines. Research on critical life events provides an opportunity to bridge the gap between basic and applied research, and to enhance communication between separate areas of psychology. The present study attempts to move further in this direction.

The broad interest in reactions to critical life events has led to thousands of publications on this topic. In face of such a large body of existing literature, new research starts with two basic problems. The first is how to do justice to the voluminous research findings already available. The second problem is how to make explicit the theoretical perspective being taken and its contribution to research on critical life events.

In trying to do justice to the large body of research already conducted, I will approach the task in two phases. The first is to provide an overview of the most important theoretical considerations concerning reactions to critical life events. This comparative evaluation of theoretical research will be guided by a general frame of reference against which the various theoretical contributions are judged. This general frame of reference consists of a set of questions that, I argue, a good theory of reactions to critical life events should be able to answer.

These questions focus on explaining (1) the *energizing* component of these reactions, which determines when and how much tension or stress arises from the event, and (2) on the *structuring* component, which explains the kind of reactions that take place when critical life events occur. In the first part of this book, I will examine how adequately existing theories answer these questions.

After summarizing and evaluating the major theoretical publications in this area, I will propose a new perspective. I argue that this theory, which will be referred to as the *generalized principle of cognitive consistency*, is useful—among other things—when evaluating two groups of variable centered research findings. Particularly in the last ten years, a huge number of publications have focused on the role played by moderator variables, such as social support and personality variables, when predicting reactions to critical life events. The research on these variables will be summarized in the third part of this book. Furthermore, I suggest that it may be worthwhile—both for the sake of scientific parsimony and in order to stimulate further research—to reinterpret these findings from the perspective of the generalized principle of cognitive consistency which will be outlined in the second part of this monograph.

The second general problem that new research in this area faces is to make clear what new contribution will be made by adding yet another piece of research to an already intensively investigated field. This problem is already touched on in the subtitle of this monograph which implies that reactions to critical life events will be analyzed from a *social psychological* perspective. Specifically, in the second part of this book, I will develop a set of hypotheses which I refer to as the *generalized principle of cognitive consistency*. This principle grows out of findings from two lines of social psychological research. One line is the research on the principle of cognitive consistency (Heider 1946; Festinger 1957); the second line is the research on the process of attribution (Heider 1958; Kelley 1971a, 1971b; Weiner 1985a, 1985b). I argue that this generalized principle of cognitive consistency offers three major advantages over existing theories of reactions to critical life events. First, it is able to address all of the questions that a good theory in this area should be able to answer. Second, it offers an opportunity to reinterpret specific findings on the importance of certain variables—such as social support and individual differences—by suggesting a general theory about the underlying process involved in these situations. Third, as a general theory it may provide applied researchers with a basic understanding of the involved processes and thus may contribute to bridging the gap between basic and applied research on reactions to critical life events. This claim is elaborated in Chapter 12 of this book.

Chapter 1

A General Introduction

Three issues are raised in discussing the state of the art in theoretical research on reactions to critical life events. First, we must define three central concepts in this field of research—namely, critical life event, stress, and coping. Second, we will describe the general framework that will be used to summarize and evaluate the key theoretical contributions separately and to conduct a theoretical comparison of the available theories. Third, we will briefly review the historical development of research in this area, setting the stage to present three groups of theories.

1.1 Introduction to the Topic: Definitions

Definitions of psychological concepts often tell more about the theoretical point of view of the person defining the concept, or about current trends in psychology, than about the concept defined. To illustrate this, one need only look at the changes over time in definitions of the term *psychology* in introductory textbooks. Depending on the year a textbook was written and on the author involved, one finds psychology defined as the "scientific study of behavior," the "science of behavior and experience," or the "complete science of human experience." The shift from a predominantly behavioristic perspective in psychology to a cognitive point of view is reflected in these definitions as well as the authors' personal viewpoints.

The same holds true when we look at definitions of concepts in specific areas of research. Researchers in the field of critical life events would probably agree that the concepts that need to be defined in their research are "critical life events," "stress," and "coping." But the definitions they would provide are likely to be tied to their subjective way of thinking about these concepts. Accordingly, I will give a brief introduction on how these concepts will be used in this monograph. The definitions used by other authors will be provided in the course of evaluating their work in the following three chapters.

1.1.1 Critical Life Events

When one asks a layperson to define the concept "critical life event," one frequently gets a listing of various critical life events. Usually, the events listed are *undesired* events such as the death of a family member, the loss of employment, a serious illness, or a divorce. Psychologists by contrast, generally consider not only undesired events to be critical life events, but also positive or neutral events. One example is the well known and widely used scale for measuring the extent of life changes developed by Holmes and Rahe (1967), the Social Readjustment Rating Scale (SRRS). These authors list both negative events, such as the death of a spouse or a divorce, and positive events, such as an outstanding personal achievement or a vacation, as well as events that could be either positive or negative, such as a major change in working conditions.

A second difference between the scientific and lay concepts of critical life event concerns the degree of importance that such an event has in the life of the person involved. Laypersons tend to think of critical life events as *important* events. Events such as a change in the number of working hours, a ticket for a traffic violation, or Christmas are listed by Holmes & Rahe (1967), but they probably would not be named by laypersons.

For psychologists, critical life events include events that vary greatly in their importance and centrality for the person involved. These events include disasters such as floods, earthquakes, and tornados (Janis & Mann 1977), participation in war (Grinker & Spiegel 1945; Kaylor, King & King 1987), events in a person's private life such as the death of a spouse (Stroebe & Stroebe 1983), or having a life-threatening illness (Taylor, Lichtman & Wood 1984), chronic life stresses such as bad working conditions (Pearlin 1980), or even daily hassles (Kanner, Coyne, Schaefer & Lazarus 1981; DeLongis, Coyne, Dakof, Folkman & Lazarus 1982).

With these two issues in mind, the following definition of a critical life event will be used in connection with the generalized principle of cognitive consistency used here: A critical life event is an event that is inconsistent with that part of a person's worldview on which the person's attention is focused. A person's worldview consists of the cognitive representations of habits and expectations, wishes and fears, facts and beliefs.

This definition includes positive as well as negative events and even emotionally neutral events under the heading of critical life events. This definition does not make any explicit references to the personal importance of an event. The generalized principle of cognitive consistency will be used to explain the amount of subjective tension that arises after a critical life event has occurred, and the strengths of reactions used to reestablish consistency. In this connection, the subjective importance of events becomes an issue. But this definition conceptualizes critical life events in terms of the psychological process linked with these events, and avoids describing these events in any other way.

1.1.2 Stress

Selye, the father of stress research, claimed in 1976 that there are more than 110,000 publications on the topic of stress. This number of publications includes research on various levels of analysis. Physiological (Cannon 1929; Selye 1956) and psychological aspects of stress (Lazarus 1966) have been investigated as well as the social aspects of stress (Smelser 1963).

Furthermore, the concept of stress is even defined differently in research within a given level of analysis. The term *stress* is used to describe stimuli which produce certain stress reactions (stimulus-based definitions); it is also used to describe the reactions themselves (response-based definitions), or to describe the intervening processes (Monat & Lazarus 1985, pp. 2–3).

In view of the inconsistent ways in which the term *stress* is used, it is not surprising that some authors suggest abandoning this term completely (Hinkle 1977; Mason 1975). Other authors (Monat & Lazarus 1985) suggest using this term as a label for a whole research area and not taking into account the specific level of analysis or the precise conceptualization of a given author.

In this book I will not use the term *stress* in order to avoid confusion with the various existing connotations. Instead I argue that each critical life event leads to *tension*. This tension motivates the person to reestablish consistency in his or her worldview.

Two specific issues are of interest concerning this concept of tension. A good theory about reactions to critical life events should be able to provide answers to two questions, namely (a) when tension arises, and (b) how much tension will arise.

1.1.3 Coping

Research on the significance of stress has a long history (Cannon 1929; Selye 1936); research on the topic of coping is more recent (Coelho, Hamburg & Adams 1974; Lazarus, Averill & Opton 1974; Moos 1976). In general, the concept of coping is used to summarize all attempts by which a person tries to master a threat or a challenge, a harm, or a loss, when routine or automatic reactions are not available (Lazarus, Averill & Opton 1974; Murphy 1962, 1974; White 1974).

Some authors classify the types of coping reactions. Lazarus (1975), for example, differentiates between direct actions to change the situation, and reactions which are used to handle the emotions (palliative reactions) without changing the critical situation itself. Folkman and Lazarus (1980) refer to these two types of reactions as problem-focused and emotion-focused coping. Other authors, such as Elisabeth Kuebler-Ross (1969), are primarily interested in describing the various kinds of reactions that follow a certain critical life event and the systematic sequence in which these reactions occur. These stage centered classifications of coping reactions are usually based on observations of persons in critical life event situations. They are not derived from theoretical considerations concerning the basic psychological process behind these reactions.

I propose categorizing reactions to critical life events according to the generalized principle of cognitive consistency. In doing so, I will not employ the term *coping*, in order to avoid its diverse and potentially confusing connotations. Instead I will use two terms that are clearly connected with the underlying psychological process. Reactions to critical life events will be referred to as either *tension-reduction* reactions or as *tension-avoidance* reactions.

These two terms are deduced from consistency theoretical considerations as follows: A critical life event such as taking a new job or losing an old one leads to tension which must be reduced. It can be reduced in either of two ways. On one hand, the person can change this situation in such a way that cognitive consistency is reestablished. For example, when starting a new job with demands that are inconsistent with the person's worldview a person can take a special training course, or change his or her attitudes toward the job environment in order to reach a state of cognitive consistency. After losing one's job, the resulting tension could be reduced directly by changing one's evaluation of the job's importance, or by finding a new and more attractive job. Such reactions are directly connected with the content area in which the inconsistency occurred. They all aim at reducing the inconsistency (that is, the tension) and reestablishing cognitive consistency. We will refer to these reactions therefore as *tension-reduction reactions*.

When cognitive inconsistency arises, a second kind of reaction is also possible. A person may avoid the tension by withdrawing from that specific area and by focusing attention on a different area of life. In doing so, the existing tension is not directly reduced, but it is shut out of consciousness. This kind of reaction to a critical life event will be referred to as a *tension-avoidance reaction*.

A tension-avoidance reaction can take many forms. If a person has marriage problems, for example, one tension-avoidance reaction might be to have a relationship with a third person. Another reaction would be to devote all of one's attention to one's professional life, to one's children, or to use alcohol or drugs in order to shut out the realities of the problem. The most extreme tension-avoidance reaction is suicide.

At this point it is important to explain that our categorization of tension-reduction versus tension-avoidance reactions does not imply an evaluation. Reactions to directly reduce tension are not necessarily "good" and reactions to avoid tension are not necessarily "bad." The crucial point is to discover the conditions under which a given kind of reaction will occur, and what consequences these reactions will have for the person in the long run. The only criterion for evaluating a reaction in the framework of the generalized principle of cognitive consistency is the degree to which this reaction leads in the long run to a relatively tension-free existence.

One may be reluctant to view withdrawing from tension and shutting out of experiences as in any way positive—especially if one approaches this issue from a psychoanalytic point of view. And indeed such a withdrawal and denial of experiences could in the long run lead to a high level of tension. On the other hand, such a reaction might also allow a person to function with less tension. Imagine a woman who was abused as a child. If this woman were to think of this abuse whenever she met a man, her life would be miserable because she would be in a state of almost chronic high tension. Shutting out memories of these events in the past would lead to less tension. On the other hand, one could also imagine certain situations that would make it very difficult to shut out the original inconsistent events. If we assume that this woman were about to get married, then it is possible that this situation would evoke associations with the area of inconsistency, making tension-avoidance reactions very difficult.

Instead of evaluating these two types of reactions to critical life events, it is more important to explain the circumstances under which each of these two types of reaction is likely to occur. Furthermore, once we can predict the *general* reaction a person is likely to show—namely, a tension-reduction or tension-avoidance reaction—it is then important to be able to predict what *specific* type of tension-avoidance or tension-reduction reaction will occur. Finally, the *long term* consequences of either reaction need to be explained.

1.2 The Central Questions Concerning Reactions to Critical Life Events

The introductory remarks concerning the definitions of concepts used here, have already hinted at the questions that an adequate theory of reactions to critical life events should be able to answer. Stating these questions at the outset is useful for two reasons. First, these questions will be used to structure our review and evaluation of the existing theories in this research area and to compare the various theories. Second, these questions also provide us with specific criteria to evaluate the theoretical perspective proposed here (the generalized principle of cognitive consistency) and its contribution to explaining reactions to critical life events.

1.2.1 The Energizing Component: When Will Tension Arise and How Can It Be Predicted?

The first set of questions that a theory of reactions to critical life events should be able to answer concerns the *energizing component* in these situations.

Two questions are relevant here. First, it is important for the theory to specify under what conditions tension arises (Question 1A). If the theory states that a critical life event leads to tension (stress), then the theory must define what a critical life event is.

Second, a good theory of critical life events must offer hypotheses that explain what determines the amount of tension arising in a specific situation (Question 1B). A good theory must be able to explain why two people who encounter the same event (for example getting laid off from work), may react with drastically different amounts of tension.

1.2.2 The Structuring Component: What Kind of Reaction Will Follow?

While the first set of questions concerns the energizing component of reactions to critical life events, the second set of questions concerns the structuring component—that is, the *kind* of reactions that occur following critical life events. Once we can explain when and how much tension arises after a critical life event occurs, the next question is, what kind of reaction will the person show?

It seems useful to divide this structuring component into three questions—here referred to as question 2A, 2B, and 2C. These three questions are concerned with predicting the *general* kind of reaction, the *specific* kind of reaction, and the *long-term* consequences a person shows after a critical life event occurs.

The first question concerns the *general* kind of reaction. Question 2A inquires whether a person encountering a critical life event stays in the inconsistency-laden area and attempts to reduce the tension by directly changing the inconsistencies (a tension-reduction reaction); or whether the person withdraws from the problematic area (a tension-avoidance reaction). An adequate theory of critical life events should provide an answer to this first aspect of the structuring component.

If a theory can predict whether a person will react with tension reduction or with tension avoidance, the next problem is to predict the *specific* reaction that will take place (Question 2B). Let us assume, for example, that we were able to predict that a given person will try to directly reduce the tension arising from a divorce; at this point, we would definitely want to know which specific reaction this person is likely to use to reduce the tension directly. For example, will this person concentrate on talking about divorce with friends, or will he or she read books about problems in relationships? Conversely, if one predicts that this person is likely to avoid the tension the divorce caused, we would also want to know the specific type of reaction this person will show. Will the person immerse oneself in job related activities in order to avoid thinking about the divorce, or will the person funnel attention into a specific leisure time activity such as painting or stamp collecting? Or will the person turn to alcohol or attempt suicide in order to shut out the tension? These are very different specific reactions which could all be summarized under the general categories of tension-reduction or tension-avoidance reactions. A good theory should be able to predict which *specific* reaction a person is most likely to show.

The third aspect of the structuring component, covered by question 2C, concerns the long-term consequences. Let us assume that a theory can predict when and how much tension arises (the energizing component), and which general reaction (tension reduction or tension avoidance) and specific reaction will occur. At this point a final question arises concerning the long-term consequences. Will the person, in the long run, be relatively free or full of tension? Furthermore, what kind of reactions will the person show when new critical life events occur? Will these reactions be shaped by the experiences with the previous critical life event?

The question of the long-term consequences is of central importance for understanding the influences of a critical life event on the life of the person involved. To illustrate this, one might turn to the reactions of survivors from Nazi concentration camps. If one analyzed only the short-term reactions of these persons during the time span immediately following World War II, one would cover only part of their reactions to these experiences. One might argue that most of these persons founded families and took up some occupation or career. But in recent years reports have appeared in the media that point to the long-term consequences of these experiences for these persons. More than 40 years after the end of World War II, some of these persons—after retiring from their active job lives—have severe problems with memories of their experiences during the Holocaust. An adequate theory of critical life events should consider the long-term consequences of having encountered critical life events. Figure 1.1 presents an overview of the questions that a good theory of reactions to critical life events should be able to answer. It should be mentioned at this point that the amount of tension arising will shape the intensity of whatever reaction will be chosen in this situation.

1.3 Historical Overview

Before we use these two sets of questions as criteria to describe, evaluate, and compare existing theories concerning reactions to critical life events, let us take a brief overview of the historical development of research on this question. It will contribute to a better understanding of what we hope to accomplish in this book.

1.3.1 The Origin of Interest in Critical Life Events

Lazarus and Folkman (1984) provide an excellent summary of the origin of interest in critical life events in their monograph *Stress, Appraisal, and*

Figure 1.1
Questions an Adequate Theory of Reactions to Critical Life Events Should Be
Able to Answer

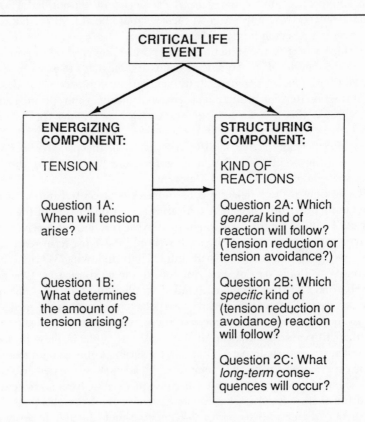

Coping. They point out that societal changes such as industrialization, World War II, and the rising divorce rate in Western industrial societies led to the early work on the significance of critical life events in many disciplines, especially sociology, psychology, and medicine.

Sociologists, for example, began to study the problem of alienation at the end of the last century (Durkheim 1897). Alienation can be interpreted as one reaction to events that are inconsistent with a person's worldview. More recently, many sociological investigations have attempted to understand the significance of catastrophes (Baker & Chapman 1962; Lucas 1969), or the significance of societal changes and the resulting stress for the persons involved.

Early medical research demonstrated a clear connection between critical life events, stress, and somatic disease (Cannon 1929; Selye 1936; Wolff 1953). This research on the connection between critical life events and somatic disease was soon supplemented by findings about the relationship between critical life events and mental disease. Early psychological research was stimulated by these findings in the area of psychopathology. Clinical psychologists realized that there was a connection between the occurrence of critical life events at one point in time and certain clinical problems observed afterwards (compare Lazarus & Folkman 1984). More recently, psychologists in other areas became interested in reactions to critical life events. Developmental psychologists realized that such events play an important role in understanding life span development. Personality psychologists began to investigate individual differences in reactions to life changes.

The psychological research can be organized in three categories. Many research papers concern only the reactions to specific events such as having cancer, the loss of employment, or bereavement. This research will be referred to as *event-centered* research. A second category of psychological research focuses on the impact certain moderating variables, such as social support or individual differences, have on reactions to critical life events. This type of research will be referred to as *variable-centered* research. Finally, a third category of research formulated theories to explain reactions to critical life events. This group of research will be referred to as *theory-centered* research.

I will briefly describe research in each of these three categories and then explain their significance for my own approach.

1.3.2 Event-Centered Research

Event-centered research covers all eventualities in life. One portion of this research concerns events that interrupt the "normal" life cycle of a person. Such events can occur in various areas of a person's life. They occur in connection with the health status of the person directly involved or of a relative (Bammer 1981; Taylor, Lichtman & Wood 1984). Such events also occur in the area of interpersonal relations, for example, in divorce or the loss of a partner through death (Stroebe & Stroebe 1983). These events can be job related, as in the loss of employment (Kasl & Cobb 1979) or coping with job demands (Dobos 1979). Moreover, a person's confrontation with a criminal act such as rape (Burgess & Holmstrom 1976, 1978, 1979) or incest (Silver, Boon & Stone 1983) as well as accidents (Bulman & Wortman 1977) all belong to this first group of event-centered studies.

A second category of event-centered research focuses on reactions to events which occur at a specific point in history (Green, Wilson & Lindy 1985; Wilson, Smith & Johnson 1985). Reactions to the experience of war (Grinker & Spiegel 1945; Kaylor, King & King 1987) and natural catastrophes (e.g. earthquakes: Cascallar, Cervantes, DeZan & Gates 1986; tornados: see Long & Richard 1986), to immigration or forced resettlement (Rosch 1985a), to surviving a concentration camp (Frankl 1985; Dimsdale 1980), or being in a nuclear catastrophe or other extreme situation (Lifton 1963) are investigated in this research.

These event-centered studies are invaluable at the exploratory phase of research. Though often merely descriptive, they point out the stress and emotional reactions the persons involved experience, and the kinds of reactions they show. These descriptions can be of tremendous importance to a reader searching for an understanding of situations which are not matters of direct personal experience to everyone. One example of such descriptive event-centered research is Rossiter's book on women in the French resistance in World War II (Rossiter 1986) or DesPres' work on survivors of concentration camps during this same period (DesPres 1976). In preparing the way for a general theory of reactions to critical life events, such descriptions of events can be extremely helpful.

Some authors of event-centered research examine the general dynamics in these specific situations. An example of such an attempt is Elisabeth Kuebler-Ross' work on reactions to death and dying (Kuebler-Ross 1969). Such authors suggest event-specific theories which may be valuable when we try to develop more general theories that explain reactions to critical life events globally. A comparison of various event-specific theories brings out the similarities and differences in reactions in different situations, which is exactly what a good general theory should be able to explain. Event-centered research can be seen as a first step on the way to a better understanding of reactions to critical life events, providing us with details on certain situations and thus contributing to formulating a theory.

When I refer to event-centered research I do not refer to the work of authors who use the investigation of reactions to a certain event to either explain their general considerations or to test their general hypotheses. An example of such research on one specific event, namely having had breast cancer, is Taylor's work on cognitive adaptation to threatening events (Taylor 1983). She used this research on this specific event to demonstrate the significance of her general theoretical argument. I will use empirical research in a similar way in this book when I present data on the reactions of immigrants to West Germany to test the general hypotheses developed in Part II of this book.

1.3.3 Variable-Centered Research

In the last ten years a good deal of research has been conducted to investigate how certain moderator variables influence reactions to critical life events. The two variables that were investigated most intensively are social support (for example, Duck & Silver 1990) and personality variables such as the Type A personality (Friedman & Ulmer 1984) or "hardiness" (Kobasa, Maddi & Courington 1981).

Such variable-centered research can be carried out from either a structural or a functional perspective. In research on the role of social support in reactions to critical life events, some studies concentrate on the structure of the social network (the size of the network, or the connections within it) while other research investigates the function of social support (Does social support buffer stress or does it have a direct effect?). In both types of studies we encounter two basic problems. One problem is that many results are closely tied to the specific event studied. The second problem is that contradictory results occur.

We need a general theory which allows us to explain the function that certain variables, such as social support or individual differences, have in the process of reacting to critical life events in general. Such a general theory should generate hypotheses that go beyond an event and situation-specific analyses of the role of these moderator variables, and it should be able to explain contradictory findings. Furthermore, it should stimulate further research.

The generalized principle of cognitive consistency provides such a general theory. Its contributions to the explanation of the role of moderator variables in reactions to critical life events are described in Part III of this book. I propose to use this general theory as a guideline for research on the significance of social support, individual differences, and life philosophies in reactions to critical life events.

1.3.4 Theoretical Considerations

Finally, there are theoretical considerations concerning reactions to critical life events. Historically, the earliest were those that stated reactions to critical life events occur in systematic stages (for example, Selye 1936). These stage theories will be summarized and evaluated in Chapter 2 of this book. The best known and most comprehensive theory on reactions to critical life events in psychological research was developed by Lazarus (for example, Lazarus & Folkman 1984). Chapter 3 will be completely devoted to his theory. The cognitive revolution in psychology gave rise to several theories based on a cognitive perspective. This work will be described in Chapter 4.

This theory-centered research on the reactions to critical life events will be summarized and evaluated in the following four chapters. The two sets of questions that a good theory in this research area should be able to answer will serve as guidelines to present and as criteria to evaluate each theory separately. Finally, these two sets of questions will be the basis for a comparison of the various theories.

Chapter 2

Stage-Centered Theories of Reactions to Critical Life Events

Stage-centered theories of reactions to critical life events developed in three phases. During the early period of stress research, Selye proposed a stage theory of reactions to noxious stimuli which he called the general adaptation syndrome (Selye 1936, 1956). The second period of stress research in the 1960s was dominated by stage-centered theories focusing on specific events. Such writers as Bowlby and Kuebler-Ross studied reactions to specific events such as the separation of a child from its mother (Bowlby 1961) or reactions to facing death and dying (Kuebler-Ross 1969), and formulated stage models to describe these reactions. Finally, in a third phase, Klinger (1975) published his incentive-disengagement theory. This theory no longer focused on reactions to specific events, but instead offered a general explanation of reactions to critical life events.

2.1 Selye's Research on Stress: The General Adaptation Syndrome

2.1.1 Selye's Theoretical Considerations

When Hans Selye died in October 1982, he had written more than 1,600 scientific articles and over 40 monographs (Malmo 1986). But even more impressive than the sheer quantity of his work, is the creativity, courage, persistence, and insight that is manifest in his writings.

His first publication introduced the concept of stress to the scientific community and was written in the 1930s (Selye 1936). In his monograph *The Stress of Life* (Selye 1956), Selye gives a vivid description of his personal struggles preceding this important publication. During his research on sex hormones, he had found that rats show systematic bodily changes when injected with various ovarian and placental extracts. The adrenal cortex of these animals became considerably enlarged; the lymphatic structure in their bodies shrank; and they developed deep bleeding ulcers. At this point, Selye hoped to make a major contribution to medical science, helping to understand the effects of hormones. These hopes were crushed when he found precisely the same somatic changes when other substances such as formalin were injected. Instead of having discovered a new hormone, he had wasted his time on the "pharmacology of dirt" as one of his professors put it when he tried to stop Hans Selye from continuing these experiments (Selye 1956, p. 32). Selye did not give up and continued his research. It was this work which launched the field of stress research.

The term *stress* is defined by Selye as the nonspecific response of the body to any demand (Selye 1956, p. 55). Stressors are the agents which lead to stress (Selye 1946, 1956). The characteristic bodily changes that he discovered in his experimental research on rats were termed the General Adaptation Syndrome. Selye postulated that every organism reacts to demands in a systematic way, with the same three stages of reaction. First, there is an alarm reaction which mobilizes the organism. The bodily changes he observed in this stage are the triad described above. If the organism survives this stage and the stress persists, this alarm reaction is followed by the stage of resistance, with distinct physiological characteristics which differ from those of the first stage. After more prolonged exposure to the noxious stimulus or demand, the organism enters a stage of exhaustion. The symptoms in this stage resemble the symptoms in the first stage. They lead to a wear and tear process of aging.

Selye's theory had three important implications. First, he postulated that the effects of stress accumulate over time. Second, he analyzed the pathological effects of stress on the body. And third, Selye concluded that stress effects are additive (compare Fleming, Baum & Singer 1984).

2.1.2 A Critical Evaluation

Selye made an invaluable contribution to stress research. He launched the research in this area and his work was of central importance in exploring the connection between stress and bodily health. From a biological-medical perspective, his work has been criticized because he postulated that there is a *general* syndrome. Mason (1975) argues that the body reacts to different noxious stimuli with different specific symptoms and not with a general syndrome. Today, psychologists and sociologists criticize Selye's quasi-mechanistic conception, which overlooks individual differences and subjective appraisal processes in reactions to stressors and the psychological processes which lead to coping with stress (see Lazarus 1975, as representative of these critiques).

Selye's theory does not stand up well in answering the two sets of questions that we propose as criteria of a good theory of critical life events. Selye did not specify precisely when stress arises and offered only general remarks concerning the amount of stress that will occur (questions 1A and 1B). The questions concerning predictions of the kind of reactions that will take place are answered only from a medical point of view; as a medical doctor, Selye was interested only in the physiological reactions of an organism. In the long run he predicts a bodily "wear and tear" process.

2.2 Stage-Centered Theories of Reactions to Specific Events

More recently, a number of researchers started from observations of reactions to specific events and developed stage-centered theories of these reactions. Such events are, for example, rape (Sutherland & Scherl 1970), miscarriage (Zahourek & Jensen 1973), becoming blind (Fitzgerald 1970), losing a spouse (Parkes 1972), having a life-threatening disease such as cancer (Gullo, Cherico & Shadick 1974), the separation or loss of a child's mother (Bowlby 1961, 1980; Horowitz 1976, 1985), bodily problems (Shontz 1965, 1975), or death and dying (Kuebler-Ross 1969). In order to illustrate the general argumentation of stage-centered approaches focusing on a specific event, let us briefly examine the two best known of these theories.

2.2.1 Bowlby: Attachment, Separation, and Loss

John Bowlby became interested in developmental psychology very early in life and especially in the problems of disturbed children (1990). After completing his medical training, he specialized in psychiatry and psychoanalysis and became a child psychiatrist. In 1946, he published a monograph in which he pointed to the significance of a child's early separation from its mother for later psychiatric problems (Bowlby 1946). When he became the director of the Department for Children and Parents of the Tavistock Clinic, he soon gathered a small research group to continue this line of research. Mary Ainsworth and Colin Murray Parkes are two of the now well-known members of this group. Bowlby (1961, 1969, 1973, 1980) clearly developed his ideas on reactions to separation or loss from one's mother, starting from a psychoanalytic perspective. But very soon he became interested in the research of developmental psychologists such as Piaget (1936, 1947) and was fascinated by the work of ethologists such as Konrad Lorenz and Robert Hinde.

In his own work, he describes how young children react with extreme despair to being separated from their mothers. This observation led him to realize the importance of attachments, and the implications of separation and loss in a person's life. He points out that attachments are of central importance in the life of humans. Initially, these attachments are to the primary caregiver, usually the mother, and later in life to other persons. If this attachment is endangered—as is the case when a child is separated from the mother—then strong reactions will occur.

Bowlby (1961, 1969, 1973) argued in his early work that these reactions follow a systematic sequence and can be organized in three stages. The reactions in the first stage are clear attempts to regain the lost object or person. Crying, anger,and protest are typical reactions in this protest phase. In the second phase, the phase of despair, the person becomes desperate, disorganized, and depressed. In the third phase, a detachment from the lost object or person takes place and the reorganization of life begins.

In 1980, Bowlby reformulated his model by postulating a fourth phase that occurs before the other three phases: a state of shock.

2.2.2 Kuebler-Ross: On Death and Dying

Elisabeth Kuebler-Ross's monograph *On Death and Dying* (1969) attempts to understand how people react to their own dying process as well as to the dying of other persons around them. Originally, she sought to discover how professionals such as nurses, doctors, or social workers could learn to provide more adequate support to persons dying in institutions. In her later work, for example in *Working It Through* (1982), she focuses her energies on conducting workshops with dying patients and persons who live with dying patients. Her work has contributed to mitigating taboos associated with dying in Western industrialized societies.

On Death and Dying provides a good idea of how a stage model is formulated and how it argues. This book is written in a descriptive way, illustrating each point with appropriate examples. It is emotionally demanding, but intellectually easy to grasp.

Kuebler-Ross (1969) describes five stages in the reaction to confronting death. The first stage is one of denial and isolation. For example, a person who is told by a surgeon that he/she has terminal cancer does not hear the message and shuts out the frightening reality. In stage two, the person is angry and aggressive toward everybody and everything. This gives way to bargaining, in stage three. The vivid example that Kuebler-Ross gives for this stage is a terminally ill woman who wants to attend her son's wedding. She manages with the help of professionals to control her pain and looks radiant when she leaves the hospital to attend the wedding. When she returns in the evening, she points out that her other son's wedding is approaching and she begins to bargain with fate to let her attend this second wedding as well. The fourth phase of reactions to dying is a phase of depression. In the fifth and last phase the person accepts the fact that he or she is going to die.

Kuebler-Ross points out that not everyone necessarily goes through all these five phases. Some persons might never, for example, experience the phase of acceptance. Her main concern was to understand the process of dying in order to help dying persons and those persons involved with them.

Considering this practical goal, her stage model might actually be helpful in several ways to those involved. It might make the reactions of dying individuals understandable in a broader framework; it might make such negatively-evaluated reactions as anger and depression acceptable; and it might even make these reactions predictable and, therefore, easier to handle.

2.2.3 Summary and Evaluation of Event-Specific Stage Theories

Some theories, for example Horowitz' theory (1976, 1985; Horowitz & Kaltreider 1980) on reactions to the loss of a loved one or Shontz' theory (1965, 1975) on reactions to bodily impairments, differ from the models just presented in one important way. These authors explicitly state that an oscillation between different phases can occur. Shontz postulates, for example, that the person involved can oscillate between retreating from a painful topic and encountering it.

Despite such differences in the predictions of reactions, these event-specific stage theories have one practical, positive aspect in common. They all communicate a positive life philosophy to the persons directly concerned or to persons indirectly involved, such as family members, friends, or nurses. This holds true in three different respects. First, all of these event-specific stage theories postulate an end result that is—at least psychologically—positive. Kuebler-Ross (1969) states that the last stage of reactions to dying is acceptance, and Bowlby (1980) points out that a detachment from the lost object or person and a reorganization of life will finally occur after a separation or loss has been experienced. This relatively optimistic outlook may help one to endure the negative stages such as depression or anger. Second, negative and unpleasant reactions such as depression are seen as a normal part of behavior (see Kuebler-Ross 1969, for example) and not as an indicator of an underlying pathology. This can help the directly involved person by letting them realize their reactions are normal, similar to those of other persons, and not a sign of mental disease. It may help the indirectly involved person to be more accepting and less judgmental about these reactions. Third, these theories may help to integrate a critical life event with one's subsequent reactions in a person's worldview. As this book argues, a person is motivated to reestablish cognitive consistency when a critical life event occurs. Certain reactions may be consistent with knowledge that a person gains through learning about stage theories. In this sense such theories may help reduce tension in certain situations shaped by critical life events.

Despite these practical advantages, these event-specific stage theories have serious theoretical drawbacks, elaborated by Silver and Wortman (1980). First, there is no clear empirical evidence of the stage-like pattern of reactions (McDaniel & Sexton 1970; Kimball 1969). Second, various event-specific stage theories make very different predictions concerning the sequence of

Table 2.1
Event-Specific Stage Theories: An Overview

Author	Bowlby (1969, 1973, 1980)	Kuebler-Ross (1969)	Shontz (1975)	Fitzgerald (1970)
Event	separation loss	death and dying	bodily impairment	becoming blind
Stages	(1980:shock) protest despair detachment	denial anger bargaining depression acceptance	shock encounter (= helpless, disorganized) retreat psychological growth	disbelief protest depression recovery

reactions (see Table 2.1 for an overview). Third, some reactions such as fear are not even mentioned in these theories, but actually do occur as part of the reactions that follow a critical life event. Fourth, none of these theories leads to precise predictions concerning the length and the intensity of given stages. Fifth, they do not help explain individual differences in reactions.

In response to the two sets of questions that an adequate theory of reactions to critical life events should be able to answer, these theories provide only very limited answers. These theories do not specify the conditions under which tension arises, since these conditions do not vary: the theories focus on reactions to one specific event. They do not generate any hypotheses concerning the amount of tension that will arise. They do describe the general reactions that will occur, but simply name a set of stages that by no means exhaust the repertoire of reactions that actually occur. Furthermore, the intensity of a certain general reaction such as anger, the duration of a reaction, or even its specific form cannot be predicted. Finally, concering long-term consequences, all event-specific stage theories describe the last stage as recovery, acceptance, or adjustment to the critical life event. This may be encouraging to those involved, but empirically it is a great oversimplification.

2.3 Klinger's Incentive-Disengagement Theory

In 1975, Klinger published a general stage-centered theory which is not concerned with reactions to specific events. As a motivational psychologist, Klinger was interested in explaining "the psychological aspects of incentive relationships" (Klinger, 1975, p. 1). The relevance of his ideas for explaining reactions to critical life events becomes evident if these events are interpreted as developments that block a person's way to reaching a given incentive. In such a case, Klinger predicts a general cycle of reactions which he calls the incentive-disengagement cycle.

Klinger (1975, 1977) starts his argument with the assumption that at each point in a person's life there are certain incentives to which the person is committed. An incentive is defined as an object or event that attracts or repels an organism. Klinger postulates that being committed to an incentive means that a certain continuing neural process takes place that somehow maintains the goal as a controlling influence on behavior. The state of being committed to a goal is called the state of "current concern." This concept describes the state between the time of commitment and the time of consummation or disengagement. It influences the person's actions, the contents of the thought processes, the readiness to react to certain stimuli, and the person's perception and memory. As soon as the person reaches the incentive (consummation), the motivational process is finished. But if the goal is blocked and the person is hindered from reaching the goal, then Klinger predicts that an orderly process of ending the commitment to the incentive will start. This process is called the incentive-disengagement cycle.

Klinger postulates that this process has five stages. In the first stage, the person tries with increased vigor to overcome the blockage and reach the goal. This first stage is called "invigoration." In some instances, these higher efforts to overcome the obstacle may actually lead to consummation. But if the obstacle cannot be overcome, then aggression will occur as the reaction that characterizes the second phase. Following this stage, Klinger (1975) predicts that persons will start to give up. This giving up takes the form of a "downswing into depression" which is the third stage in the incentive-disengagement cycle. Stage 4 is the phase of depression. In the final phase, disengagement from the incentive is reached. The person recovers and is able to make a commitment to new incentives in life.

Klinger (1975, 1977) argues that such a process has an adaptive function for the person as well as for society as a whole. If an incentive is blocked, it is functional to vigorously try to overcome the obstacle at first, because this invigoration may actually help overcome the blockage and reach the goal. But if these attempts are without success, then it will be functional for the person to stop pursuing this incentive. Depression is a stage of passivity for the person and thus is actually functional as one part of the cycle. The final recovery and disengagement from the incentive allows the person to become committed to new incentives. On a societal level, Klinger argues that such a cycle has adaptive function for population survival.

How does this theory hold up, in response to the two sets of questions an adequate theory of critical life events should be able to answer? Klinger never explicitly uses the term "critical life event," but he refers to critical life events as examples in his argument (for example, Klinger 1975, p. 15). From his perspective a critical life event can be defined as an event which is an obstacle to the person's consummation of an incentive. Klinger does not attempt to explain how much tension arises when such an obstacle occurs. He does point out that the duration and intensity of the various reactions—which could be interpreted as reflecting the amount of tension arising—depend on the importance of an incentive for the person, the degree to which positive effects are elicited by the incentive, and the relative significance of this incentive compared with other incentives. But these remarks are rather general.

Klinger's theory responds to the second set of questions, concerning the prediction of the kinds of reaction, by pointing out the five stages of the cycle as the general reactions occurring. But the prediction of specific reactions is not dealt with by this theory. Concerning the long term consequences, Klinger postulates that a disengagement from the blocked incentive will occur and a commitment to new incentives will be built up.

Klinger's theory integrates findings from very different areas of psychology and uses a genuinely new approach to organize these findings in a model of a general psychological process. Like the event-specific stage theories, Klinger's theory has some optimistic practical implications. Specific reactions such as depression are seen as functional and as part of a normal process. The outcome of the cycle is again seen in an optimistic light: The person will disengage from the blocked incentive and will build up commitment to a new incentive.

Beyond these practical considerations, some theoretical concerns need to be raised. Klinger's theory is general. It has a broader relevance than the event-specific stage theories. It does not result from observations of reactions to one specific event, but claims to present hypotheses concerning general psychological processes independent of specific conditions. This high level of generality leads to one problem: it is very difficult to test this theory empirically. This may explain why Klinger's creative approach did not generate much subsequent research.

2.4 Stage-Centered Theories: A Final Evaluation

The final evaluation of these stage-centered theories has two aspects. First, let us ask how well these theories respond to the two sets of questions an adequate theory of reactions to critical life events should be able to answer. Second, let us ask (a) whether there is evidence that reactions to critical life events *do* occur in certain stages and, assuming that they do, (b) what specific pattern these sequences have?

Table 2.2 provides an overview of the answers that these stage theories give to the questions outlined above. On the whole, these theories do not provide clear hypotheses concerning when tension will arise and what de-

Table 2.2
Stage Theories to Critical Life Events: An Overview

	Authors			
	Selye (1956)	Bowlby (1980)	Kuebler-Ross (1969)	Klinger (1977)
Question 1A: When does tension arise?	noxious stimulus	separation loss	death and dying	blocked incentive
Question 1B: Determinants of the amount of tension	not precise	not precise	no hypothesis	not precise
Question 2A: General reactions	general adaptation syndrome: alarm resistance exhaustion (physiological)	shock protest despair detachment	denial anger bargaining depression acceptance	invigoration aggression downswing depression depression disengagement
Questions 2B: Specific reactions	no hypothesis	no hypothesis	no hypothesis	no hypothesis
Questions 2C: Long-term outcome	"wear and tear"	detachment and reorganization	accepting	disengagement

termines how much tension there will be (questions 1A and 1B). They do offer hypotheses concerning what *general* reactions will occur in situations involving critical life events (see Selye 1936, 1956; Klinger 1975) or with certain specific events such as the separation from a loved person (Bowlby 1961) or dying (Kuebler-Ross 1969) (question 2A). But these hypotheses are global and do not explain the duration or the intensity of these reactions, nor do they in any way predict the specific reactions (question 2B). In regard to long-term consequences (question 2C), all of these theories except Selye's predict a positive outcome, such as adjustment or recovery. But these hypotheses are very general and do not contribute much to understanding the long-term results of encountering critical life events.

Although these stage theories do not provide adequate answers to these questions, they do raise an important issue: whether people's reactions actually *do* follow a predictable sequence. If this were the case, identifying this sequence would be a major step toward explaining the general reactions that take place.

The psychological theories presented so far are based on observations of persons involved in certain critical life events (Bowlby 1961; Kuebler-Ross 1969), or on empirical research concerning the specific issues raised (Klinger 1975). The event-specific stage theorists are not interested in testing the relevance of their theories beyond the situations on which they focus. It is not surprising, therefore, that none of these authors carried out a comprehensive test of his or her theory. Other investigators have inquired into whether reactions to critical life events follow a systematic pattern and, if so, which reactions are included in such a pattern. This work is reviewed by Silver and Wortman (1980), who conclude that different critical life events lead to different reactions. Furthermore, even the reactions to one specific event do not follow the same pattern. Anger and aggression for example occur in only 20 percent of rape victims (Notman & Nadelson 1976); less than 50 percent of those with cancer ever report anger and aggression (Peck 1972); and only about 20 percent of widowed persons report anger and aggression (Glick, Weiss & Parkes 1974).

The results from other studies also fail to support the basic assumption that there are definite stages of reactions to critical life events. Panel studies of persons with spinal injuries (Dinardo 1971; McDaniel & Sexton 1970) and persons with complicated heart operations (Kimball 1969) show that the reactions vary widely.

On the whole, the hypotheses that reactions to critical life events occur in specific stages gets little support from empirical evidence.

Chapter 3

Lazarus: Stress, Appraisal, and Coping

In 1989, R. S. Lazarus received an award from the American Psychological Association for distinguished scientific contributions. The citation that went with this award concludes that "his influences reach beyond psychology to theory, research, and application in the social and health sciences" (Lazarus 1990, p. 455). This citation gives a first impression of how influential Lazarus' work actually has been and still is. When he published his first studies of reactions to stressful stimuli, stress research was dominated by the idea that objective stressors cause predictable reactions. Nowadays, every researcher in the field of stress recognizes that subjective appraisal processes are (often) significant influences on people's reactions to stress. If Selye (1936, 1956) could be described as the founding father of stress research, then Lazarus clearly helped this research mature from its early stage to its present form.

His work can be interpreted as the bridge between the early stress research of Selye (1936, 1956) and the stage theorists just discussed on one hand; and the cognitively oriented research on critical life events of Seligman, Wortman, Taylor, and others (see Chapter 4). When Lazarus began his research in the 1960s, the dominant perspective in stress research interpreted stress as the result of encountering a noxious stimulus. His most important contribution was to point out that a given objective stimulus does not produce the same amount of stress in two different persons, or even in the same person at two different points in time. The crucial variable he introduced into research on stress and coping was the importance of cognitive appraisal. From this point on, stress was no longer seen as the objectively transformed psychological equivalent of a noxious stimulus. Instead, stress came to be viewed as the result of a subjective appraisal of a given stimulus.

Lazarus' work is interesting not only for the content of his thought and the creativity of his publications; the development of his work as a whole is exceptionally fascinating. Lazarus began by simply criticizing the old stress research (Lazarus, Speisman, Mordkoff & Davison 1962; Lazarus & Alfert 1964). He then proceeded to develop his own theory of stress, appraisal, and coping (see Lazarus & Folkman 1984, 1987, for the most comprehensive publications). Currently, he is fine tuning this theory in his research on the relevance of daily hassles (Kanner, Coyne, Schaefer & Lazarus 1981; De-Longis, Coyne, Dakof, Folkman & Lazarus 1982; DeLongis, Folkman & Lazarus 1984, 1988). Let us briefly examine each of these three groups of publications.

3.1 Lazarus' Criticism of an "Objective" Perspective in Stress Research

Lazarus' theory of reactions to critical life events developed from his criticism of what might be called the "objective" approach in stress research. His early publications (Lazarus & Alfert 1964) argued that a given objective stimulus does not produce the same amount of stress in different persons or in different situations.

In now classical experiments, Lazarus (Lazarus, Speisman, Mordkoff & Davison 1962; Lazarus & Alfert 1964; Speisman, Lazarus, Davison & Mordkoff 1964) demonstrated this point convincingly. He developed an experimental paradigm in which all subjects saw the same motion picture, namely an anthropological film about a primitive ritual having five bloody operations. The degree of stress the viewers experienced was measured (a) with physiological measures (skin resistance, heart rate), and (b) by using rating scales and a mood check list.

Lazarus demonstrated that the amount of stress experienced when watching this movie varied as a function of the situation in which the subjects were located, and as a function of individual differences, specifically in the defense mechanisms that people used when faced with stressful stimuli. The situation was manipulated by playing different soundtracks with the film. Lazarus found that when the soundtrack dramatized the bloody actions shown in the movie ("trauma track"), the indicators of stress were highest. If the soundtrack intellectualized or denied the brutality of the ritual, the subjects had significantly lower stress levels than the persons in a control condition which had no soundtrack. The extent to which various subjects used denial or intellectualization as defense mechanisms also affected the amount of stress experienced. Persons who tended to deny stress had the least stress symptoms when the movie was accompanied by the denial soundtrack. Subjects who tended to intellectualize were least stressed when the film was shown with the intellectualizing soundtrack.

These findings launched Lazarus' career as a stress researcher. From this point on, he systematically developed his own perspective on reactions to stress and coping.

3.2 Stress, Appraisal, and Coping

3.2.1 General Criticisms of Earlier Stress and Coping Research

Lazarus' own perspective can best be understood by describing some further criticisms he made of previous stress research (Lazarus & Launier 1978; Lazarus & Folkman 1984, p. 128). His critique expressed a general methodological concern about how stress research should be conducted; and, from the viewpoint of his own philosophy of science, also criticized specific aspects of the traditional stress and coping research.

His methodological argument concerns the philosophy of science traditionally held by most researchers, which he describes as interactionistic. An interactionistic approach might be described as similar to analyzing data with analysis of variance. By using this method, one investigates whether one or more variables, either alone (main effect) or together (interaction effect), influence the outcome of the dependent variable. Lazarus (Lazarus & Launier 1978) argues that a combination of this interactionist perspective with a transactionist perspective would be preferable in research on stress and coping. He argues that a transactional perspective is a pure description of the process on a cognitive phenomenological level; and that this approach can grasp stress and coping reactions in their full complexity. Thus it can complement the interactionist perspective, which is limited to focusing on only a few variables at a time.

Starting with these methodological considerations, Lazarus and Launier (1978; see also Lazarus & Folkman 1984, pp. 289ff.) then analyze problems that traditional—that is interactionistic—research encounters when studying the transaction between person and environment. The first problem is that antecedent personality variables are usually not directly measured, but that their role is inferred. A second problem is that interactionistic research is not really process oriented. This gives rise to the problem that individual changes in reactions over time cannot be considered. A third problem is that interactionistic research tends to assume linear, or one-way, cause and effect relationships; multiple causes or reciprocity of causation are not taken into account.

Lazarus and Folkman (1984) also are critical of some other specific issues in traditional stress and coping research. These issues have to do with the fact that traditional research is usually too narrowly focused. It equates coping, for example, with a mastery over the environment (Lazarus & Folkman 1984, p. 138). Lazarus and Folkman point out that many sources of stress cannot be mastered and therefore reactions that aim at accepting or ignoring the situation need to be considered also. A second issue concerned with the full complexity of the reactions is the timespan considered. Lazarus and Folkman argue that reactions need to be studied with a long-term perspective in mind and that researchers should not limit themselves to short term considerations. Furthermore, instead of focusing on a few variables, physiological, psychological, and sociological factors and their interactions should be analyzed. Moreover, coping research should not just analyze the negative outcomes of being confronted with stress such as health-related issues, but it should also consider positive effects such as the development of one's personality. Finally, they argue that coping itself should not be equated with its outcome, but that the coping process must be studied as something independent of specific outcomes.

It is interesting to see how these extensive criticisms were addressed by Lazarus in his own work. His theory of stress, appraisal, and coping attempts to overcome precisely those inadequacies that he pointed out in earlier research.

3.2.2 Stress: A Cognitive Phenomenological Perspective

In his monograph *Psychological Stress and the Coping Process* Lazarus (1966) suggests that the term *stress* constitutes an organizing concept for understanding a wide range of phenomena of great importance in human and animal adaptation. In his later writings, he warns against including too much under this general rubric and proposes limiting its meaning to the following definition: "Psychological stress is a particular relationship between the person and the environment that is appraised by the person as taxing or exceeding his or her resources and endangering his or her well-being" (Lazarus & Folkman 1984, p. 19).

This definition simultaneously captures several aspects of Lazarus' perspective. First of all, it emphasizes the importance of cognitive appraisal in stress. In keeping with his earlier research, Lazarus argues that stress is not the result of encountering an objective stimulus, but that the person's appraisal is crucial. A stimulus can be appraised as either irrelevant, benign-positive, or stressful. A stimulus appraised as irrelevant might lead to a general orienting reaction, but the person has no investment in a possible outcome in this situation. A stimulus appraised as benign-positive is likely to increase the person's subjective well-being. Stress appraisals are differentiated on a time dimension and on a quality dimension. They include harm/loss (negative event in past or present), threat (harm or loss expected in future), or challenge (a potential for gain or growth expected when encountering a negative event in the future).

A second aspect of this definition concerns the reference points in an appraisal. Appraisal can either take a person's well-being into consideration (primary appraisal) or it can take into account the resources and options a person has when encountering a given event (secondary appraisal). Lazarus argues that primary and secondary appraisal interact with each other in shaping the degree of stress and the strength and quality of one's subsequent reactions (Lazarus & Folkman 1984, p. 35). Lazarus also argues that reappraisal processes can occur when new information comes up (Lazarus & Folkman 1984, p. 38).

A third aspect of this definition is that Lazarus emphasizes the complexity of the situation as a whole, explicitly mentioning the person as well as the environment. This reflects the phenomenological perspective he takes in his research. Lazarus defends his perspective by pointing out that two negative aspects of a phenomenological approach—namely the problem of the veridicality of appraisals and the problem of circularity of arguments—are not at issue in his work. Concerning the problem of veridicality, he takes the premise in his research that appraisals are generally correlated with reality, although needs, commitments, and preferred styles of attention may influence a person's perception. In response to the problem of circularity, he points to the fact that he can identify antecedents and consequences of appraisals.

3.2.3 The Coping Process

Lazarus' second major set of considerations concerns the coping process. He defines coping as "constantly changing cognitive and behavioral efforts to manage specific external and/or internal demands that are appraised as taxing or exceeding the resources of the person" (Lazarus & Folkman 1984, p. 141).

There are four crucial differences between this definition and other conceptualizations of coping. First, this definition is process oriented, as indicated by the attribute "constantly changing." Second, it implies a distinction between coping and atomized adaptive behavior by limiting coping to reactions that take place when a person's resources are appraised as either taxed or exceeded. Third, Lazarus stresses that this definition does not confound coping with outcomes, because coping is defined as "efforts to manage" which includes much more than just outcomes. Fourth, it also does not equate coping with mastery by using the term "manage." Managing can include avoiding or accepting the stressful circumstances as well as attempts to actually master them.

Lazarus (Lazarus & Folkman 1984) categorizes coping according to the function it serves in his line of argument. Coping that aims at directly altering the problematic event is referred to as problem-focused coping. Coping that aims at regulating the emotions that occur is called emotion-focused coping. He predicts that emotion-focused coping is likely to occur when the person appraises the problem as stable, while problem-focused coping will occur when the conditions are appraised as amenable to change (Folkman & Lazarus 1980).

Lazarus explains that four different kinds of coping modes are used when a person attempts either to alter the troubled transaction or to change the emotions involved. For both of these coping efforts a person may: (a) seek information, or (b) act directly, or (c) inhibit action, or (d) react intrapsychically.

Lazarus postulates that none of these two basic ways to react is necessarily the better kind of coping. Reactions that attempt to directly alter the troubled transaction are not necessarily better than palliative reactions that aim at regulating emotions. Lazarus (Lazarus & Folkman 1984) points, for example, to the fact that a person might be so overwhelmed by emotion that a direct altering of the troubled transaction is not possible. In this situation palliative reactions might actually bring the person to the point at which he or she can finally start to think about directly altering the troubled transaction.

How does Lazarus predict which kind of reaction a person will show in a specific situation? First, he assumes that the kind of reaction is generally a result of the appraisal process. If a person, for example, believes that he or she has lots of resources and options to react with, then this will have an influence on the kind of coping behavior the person will show. More specifically, he lists four factors which influence the kind of coping reaction that is likely to occur in a given situation (Lazarus & Launier 1978, pp. 319–20). He predicts that with increasing uncertainty the seeking of information increases and direct actions decrease. He also predicts that the more an event is appraised as a serious and existential threat, the more primitive the reactions will be. Blind anger and panic, for example, might occur when a situation is appraised as life threatening. Furthermore, he argues that the more a person sees a situation as being conflict laden, the less likely the person is to directly act and the more likely the person is to use intrapsychic coping attempts. Finally, he argues that the degree to which a situation is appraised as being uncontrollable has an influence on feeling helpless and hopeless.

These statements concerning the predictions of specific reactions are quite abstract. They only convey a very general impression of the factors that need to be considered in order to make concrete predictions.

Lazarus is explicitly concerned with the long term consequences of coping. He asserts that stress and coping research should be concerned with three different areas connected with the long-term outcome (Lazarus & Folkman 1984, p. 181). These areas are the person's social functioning; the person's morale; and the person's bodily health. Lazarus discusses the relationship between cognitive appraisal, coping reactions, and the long-term outcome in each of these areas. A positive morale, for example, can depend on whether the person appraises events as a threat or as a challenge. It can also depend on the ability of the person to put negative events in a positive relationship with other things, or on appraising oneself as able to handle different demands in a situation.

3.3 Elaborating the Original Theory: Daily Hassles, Social Support, and Individual Differences

By the late 1970s, a shift in interest took place in research on stress and coping. Up to this point, the impact of major critical life events on stress and coping was at the center of attention. Suddenly, stress researchers were shifting away from this issue, moving to new topics such as the relevance of moderator variables (especially social support and individual differences) and the significance of daily hassles and uplifts. One reason for this development may be that the research on stress and coping with major critical life events had begun to stagnate. Doubts were raised about the amount of variance explained by the models developed thus far. Considering this background information, Lazarus' research in the 1980s can be interpreted as further elaborating his basic theory and as reacting to current trends in research on critical life events (DeLongis, Coyne, Folkman & Lazarus 1982; DeLongis, Folkman & Lazarus 1986; Folkman, Lazarus, Gruen & DeLongis 1986; Kanner, Coyne, Schaefer & Lazarus 1981; Lazarus & DeLongis 1983; see also Bolger, DeLongis, Kessler & Schilling 1989).

In 1977, Lazarus and Cohen divided "stressors" into three groups. They differentiated between major changes that affect large numbers of persons (for example, natural disasters and man-made catastrophes), major changes affecting one or a few persons (such as divorce or bereavement), and daily hassles. Lazarus argues that the study of stress would be too narrowly limited if "daily hassles" (little things that can irritate and distress people) were not included. In 1981, he and his coworkers (Kanner, Coyne, Schaefer & Lazarus 1981) presented the first empirical evidence that daily hassles and uplifts are actually not only good predictors of psychological symptoms, but that they are even better predictors than major life events. In later studies, the influence of daily hassles on health related symptoms such as flu, sore throat, headaches, and backaches is demonstrated (DeLongis, Folkman & Lazarus 1984, 1988) and interpreted (DeLongis, Coyne, Dakof, Folkman & Lazarus 1982) as evidence that daily hassles predict somatic health even better than life events. It seems evident from this research that daily hassles have an important influence on subjective well-being and mood (DeLongis, Folkman & Lazarus 1984; Lazarus & DeLongis 1983; Zarski 1984), but that this influence is mediated by social and individual resources (DeLongis, Folkman & Lazarus 1988; Bolger, DeLongis, Kessler & Schilling, 1989).

Daily hassles are measured with a scale that includes such items as misplacing something, being lonely, having too much to do, not getting enough sleep, or wasting time (Kanner, Coyne, Schaefer & Lazarus 1981). Lazarus (Lazarus & Folkman 1984, p. 312) finds a modest correlation of .20 between the appearance of daily hassles and life events. He interprets this correlation as indicating that the occurrence of critical life events leads to more daily hassles, but that other factors are also involved (compare also Rowlison & Felner 1988).

While the concept of daily hassles was introduced by Lazarus and his coworkers, and can thus be interpreted as a further development of his own perspective, some of his other recent research was either directly stimulated by criticisms of his work (Lazarus, DeLongis, Folkman & Gruen 1985) or is concerned with general issues in research on critical life events such as the role of social support (Dunkel-Schetter, Folkman & Lazarus 1984) and individual differences (Gruen, Folkman & Lazarus 1984). This research will be discussed later when we examine criticism of his work (3.4.2) and when the role of social support and individual differences are discussed (Chapters 9 and 10).

3.4 A Critical Evaluation of Lazarus' Work

3.4.1 A General Evaluation of His Theoretical Approach

Lazarus has devoted more than a quarter of a century to developing his theory, producing an impressive perspective on reactions to stress and coping. Besides understanding reactions to stress and coping, he has used his perspective to address problems in both basic research (see his work on emotions: Lazarus, Averill & Opton 1970; Lazarus 1982, 1984) and in applied research (see, for example, his work on the utility of different forms of therapy: Lazarus 1980). His creativity and productivity are remarkable.

His work on stress, appraisal, and coping was crucial in understanding these phenomena on a psychological level. His theory makes an impressive effort to do justice to the full complexity of the issue by taking into account all factors involved (see, especially, Lazarus & Folkman 1984, p. 305). More than any previous psychological theory, Lazarus' work has focused on explaining psychological processes that take place in such situations. A further contribution of Lazarus is that he argues that each type of reaction—whether geared to regulate emotion or to directly change the problematic circumstances or even denial—can be legitimate and functional (Lazarus 1983).

Despite these merits, his work has two basic theoretical problems. The first one is that his phenomenological perspective does not provide the clear cut predictions required for hypothesis testing in empirical research. The fact that he tries to take into account all the factors and their interactions in reactions to critical life events makes it virtually impossible to generate precise predictions. He answers the circularity argument that is frequently used against phenomenological approaches (and that can be applied to his work), by arguing that he provides antecedents and consequences for appraisal processes (Lazarus & Folkman 1984, p. 48). But by doing so, he leaves the level of phenomenological argumentation.

A good illustration of this problem is presented in Figure 10.2 in the monograph by Lazarus and Folkman (1984, p. 305). In this figure, Lazarus tries to list all the variables involved in the process. But if he were to isolate any one part of these complex relationships in order to study it in a hypothesis testing design, he would violate the idea that the full complexity of the process must be taken into consideration.

In this figure, a second basic problem in his approach becomes evident. Lazarus presents a cognitive theory. At the same time, he argues that three levels of analysis, namely the social, the psychological, and the physiological level need to be considered. Precisely at this point, the discrepancy between taking a cognitive perspective on one hand and arguing about processes on three levels of analysis on the other hand becomes strikingly evident.

Besides these two theoretical problems in Lazarus' perspective, there are problems in his empirical work. The main flaw here is a problem of confounded indicators.

3.4.2 Evaluating His Empirical Research: The Problem of Confounded Indicators

Perhaps the sharpest criticism of Lazarus' most recent considerations stems from Dohrenwend and his co-workers (Dohrenwend, Dohrenwend, Dodson & Shrout 1984; Dohrenwend & Shrout 1985). These authors argue that the indicators used in the Daily Hassles Scale (Kanner, Coyne, Schaefer & Lazarus 1981) are not really items that measure daily hassles, but are already indicators of psychological disorders. Thus, Lazarus' research has a problem of confounded measures. Items in the Daily Hassles Scale such as "Troubling thoughts about your future," "Thoughts about death," or "Trouble relaxing" are interpreted by Dohrenwend and his co-workers as indicators that a person is actually experiencing stress and having a psychological disorder, and not as items that measure daily hassles that *lead* to stress. They even provide empirical evidence of this point, by demonstrating the degree to which clinical psychologists rated each item of the Daily Hassles Scale as a symptom of a psychological disorder (Dohrenwend, Dohrenwend, Dodson & Shrout 1984).

Lazarus (Lazarus, DeLongis, Folkman & Gruen 1985) attempts to refute this criticism by claiming that the appraisal process should not and cannot be removed in the measurement of psychological stress. Therefore, Lazarus sees it as inevitable that some confounding occurs. He argues that stress should be best regarded "as a complex rubric consisting of many interrelated variables and processes rather than as a simple variable that can be readily measured and correlated with adaptational outcomes" (Lazarus et al. 1985, p. 770). This argument is consistent with Lazarus' phenomenological perspective, but it is clearly rejected by Dohrenwend (Dohrenwend & Shrout 1985).

Lazarus, DeLongis, Folkman and Gruen (1985) also provide empirical evidence that their daily hassles approach to stress and coping does not simply reflect confounding measures in this research field. For this analysis they grouped the items of the Daily Hassles Scale into three groups: namely a group of items that Dohrenwend, Dohrenwend, Dodson and Shrout (1984) had found to be confounded with stress outcome measures, one group of items that were found as not being confounded, and one group of items with ratings in between the two other groups. They then correlated the items in these three groups with measures of psychological symptoms and found quite similar patterns of relationships. They interpreted their results as an indication that hassles in general and not just the ones that clinical psychologists had rated as being an indicator of a psychological problem are good predictors of stress-related outcomes. This position is supported by more recent research (Rowlison & Felner 1988) that also demonstrates that hassles in general are good predictors of psychological symptoms.

When analyzing the debate with Dohrenwend, the clash between a phenomenological approach and a positivistic or critical rationalistic approach becomes clearly evident. The complexity of a phenomenological approach gives rise to serious difficulties when empirical evidence is sought.

3.4.3 Evaluation of the Theory's Potential to Answer the Four Questions Concerning Reactions to Critical Life Events

In response to the two sets of questions that an adequate theory of reactions to critical life events should be able to answer, Lazarus provides only partial answers. He takes up the question of when stress arises and postulates that stress is the result of cognitive appraisal (question 1A). His theory does not offer a hypothesis that would allow one to predict the amount of stress that arises in a given situation (question 1B).

Lazarus describes the general kinds of reactions that occur when stress is experienced as (a) reactions aimed at regulating emotions and (b) reactions aimed at altering the troubled situation. Both of these functions can be achieved with the help of information seeking, direct action, inhibition of action, or intrapsychic processes (question 2A). Beyond these general statements, Lazarus does not make any more specific predictions about what reactions will occur at which point (question 2B). He is clearly concerned with the long-term consequences of having encountered stress. But he only points to the general issues (morale, health, social functioning) involved in this question, remaining at an abstract global level in describing the problem (question 2C).

Chapter 4

Cognitive Theories

Cognitive theories have played a dominant role in psychological research since the 1970s, and not surprisingly, cognitive approaches have been applied to critical life events. Three such theories are discussed in this chapter.

Two of these theories, Seligman's theory of learned helplessness (Seligman 1975) and Wortman and Brehm's revision of the theory of reactance (Wortman & Brehm 1975), explicitly refer to each other. This research emerged in three stages. In the first stage, Wortman and Brehm (1975) criticized Seligman's work and integrated Seligman's hypotheses and the hypotheses of the theory of reactance (Brehm 1966, 1972). In the second stage, both groups of authors became concerned with the role of attributions. In the third stage Wortman and Seligman each developed their own ideas more fully, without reference to the other author's work. This chapter will first examine these two theories separately, and then compare them.

The third theory discussed in this chapter is Taylor's theory of cognitive adaptation to threatening events (Taylor 1983). This theory has received considerable attention for carrying a cognitive perspective to its extreme. It is a cognitive theory in its purest sense.

4.1 Seligman's Theory of Learned Helplessness

4.1.1 The Original Theory

The concept "learned helplessness" was introduced into the psychological literature in 1967 (Overmier & Seligman 1967; Seligman & Maier 1967). It was originally used to describe the reactions of dogs to uncontrollable shocks in laboratory experiments. These first two studies stimulated a large number of experiments with animals (see Klosterhalfen & Klosterhalfen 1983) as well as with human subjects (see Miller & Norman 1979). A bibliography of the research stimulated by the original theory of learned helplessness (Seligman 1972, 1975) is presented by McFerran and Breen (1978).

A typical experiment in this early research on learned helplessness has three experimental conditions ("triadic design"). The subjects in the first condition are confronted with controllable events, for example, with loud noise that can be terminated by pushing a button four times (Hiroto 1974). In a second condition, subjects are confronted with the same events as those persons in the first condition, but they cannot control the occurrence of these stimuli. In a third condition neither controllable nor uncontrollable events occur. Subsequently, the subjects in all three conditions are confronted with a different event that is controllable, for example with electric shocks that can be terminated by pushing a button.

The results of these experiments demonstrate that those subjects who, in the first phase of the experiment, were confronted with controllable events or who were not confronted with unpleasant events are able to learn the appropriate reaction in the second phase of the experiment that allows them to control the new event. The subjects who encountered uncontrollable events in the first phase of this experiment subsequently react with helplessness to the new event. They do not initiate as many attempts to solve the new task (motivational deficit); they have difficulties in learning the new task (cognitive deficit); and they tend to become depressed (emotional deficit).

Although Seligman discovered the symptoms of helplessness in animals, he argues that cognitive processes are at the heart of these phenomena (Seligman 1975). He postulates that the perception of an objective noncontingency between one's own action and the outcome in a situation alone does not lead to reactions of helplessness. The symptoms of helplessness only occur when, after having perceived noncontingencies, the person or animal forms an expectation that future actions will also be noncontingent with the outcome. This assumption that expectations—and thus cognitions—are a necessary condition for the existence of a state of learned helplessness is of central importance in Seligman's theory. It was criticized, but Maier & Seligman (1976) have demonstrated that cognitive factors are actually relevant.

When analyzing the development of Seligman's thoughts, this hypothesis about the significance of expectations moves one step away from animal research and learning theories, to explaining human behavior from a cognitive perspective. The significance of cognitive processes is even more strongly elaborated in the reformulated theory of learned helplessness (Abramson, Seligman & Teasdale 1978).

4.1.2 The Revised Theory

In 1978, Abramson, Seligman, and Teasdale reformulated the theory of learned helplessness (see also Abramson, Garber & Seligman 1980), answering two criticisms of their original theory. The first criticism was that the original theory did not offer any explanations of differences that were found in two specific situations (Bandura 1977). In both situations, a person experiences helplessness and does not expect to have any control over the outcomes; but in situation 1, the person sees that others do have control, while in situation 2, the person sees that nobody else has any control over the situation either. The original theory of learned helplessness cannot explain why persons in these two situations tend to differ in their reactions.

The second problem is that the original theory did not make specific predictions concerning the duration of helplessness effects, and of their generality versus specificity (Cole & Coyne 1977; Hanusa & Schulz 1977; Tennen & Eller 1977; Wortman & Brehm 1975).

In response to the first problem, Abramson, Seligman, and Teasdale (1978) agreed that the reactions in these two situations would be quite different. They respond to this first inadequacy of the old theory by differentiating between personal and universal helplessness. They argue that if a person assumes that he or she alone has no control over a situation, but that other relevant persons do have control, then this person experiences personal helplessness. On the other hand, this person would be in a state of universal helplessness if not only that person, but also all relevant others are believed to have no control.

This attribute "relevant" is important for predicting the consequences of these two kinds of helplessness. As an example of the importance of relevancy, Abramson, Garber, and Seligman (1980) describe a student who majors in mathematics and who fails to pass an exam in the subject. For this student, mathematics students, but not English literature students, would be relevant persons. The fact that students of English literature were unable to pass this exam would not change the person's feeling of being personally helpless, if he or she is the only student out of an entire group of math students who does not pass this exam.

Introducing this differentiation between personal and universal helplessness allows these investigators to account for different reactions to experiencing helplessness. A person in a state of personal helplessness will react by having a lower self-esteem than a person in a state of universal helplessness.

The idea that attributions may be crucial for predicting reactions to helplessness was further elaborated in response to another criticism of the original theory of learned helplessness. This criticism was that the original theory is unable to predict whether helplessness effects will occur in only one specific situation or in general and how long these effects will last. In response to this criticism, Abramson, Seligman, and Teasdale (1978) argued that the length and duration of helplessness effects depend on the kind of attributions a person makes on the dimensions global versus specific and stable versus unstable. The more globally a person attributes an event, the more general the helplessness effects will be over various situations; and the more stable rson's attributions are, the more chronic the helplessness effects will be. us, Abramson, Seligman, and Teasdale (1978) argue that helplessness ffects will be at a maximum when a person makes an internal, stable, and global attribution and at a minimum if the attribution is external, specific, and unstable.

In the reformulated theory of learned helplessness, attributions have become an essential part of the psychological process which leads to helplessness effects. Abramson, Seligman, and Teasdale (1978) argue that the attributions one makes for present and past noncontingencies are an important step between the perception of present and past noncontingency and the expectation of future noncontingency. By including attributions in this reformulated theory of learned helplessness, they can predict more precisely which kind of helplessness (personal versus universal) will occur, and how general or specific and acute or chronic the reactions will be.

4.1.3 Seligman's Recent Considerations: The Role of Attributional Styles

The work on the revised theory of learned helplessness started out in connection with research on depression. Soon after this revised theory (Abramson, Seligman & Teasdale 1978) was introduced, a further development in thinking about these phenomena followed. In this research, Seligman, Abramson, Semmel, and von Baeyer (1979) suggested that attributions might not be tied to given situations, but instead might be a function of a person's attributional or explanatory style. They found that depressed students tend to attribute failure to internal, stable, and global causes, while success is attributed to external and unstable causes. This idea led to the development of different measurement techniques for these individual differences in attributional style. In 1982, Peterson, Semmel, von Baeyer, Abramson, Metalsky, and Seligman presented the attributional style questionnaire (ASQ) as a reliable and valid paper-pencil instrument for adults. In 1984, Seligman, Peterson, Kaslow, Tannenbaum, Alloy, and Abramson introduced a version of this questionnaire for children (CASQ). And in 1983 Peterson, Luborsky, and Seligman introduced a content analytic method to supplement the questionnaire approach, called CAVE (content analysis of verbatim explanations).

The importance of attributional styles for the explanation of depression and many other behaviors such as achievement and health related symptoms has now been demonstrated in numerous publications. In 1984, Peterson and Seligman presented an impressive body of work concerning the relationship between learned helplessness, attributions, and depression. They investigated the hypothesis that an explanatory style of explaining bad events as internal, global, and stable leads to depressive symptoms (see also Seligman, Abramson, Semmel & von Baeyer 1979; Metalsky, Abramson, Seligman, Semmel & Peterson 1982). In their research with five different research strategies (cross-sectional correlational studies, longitudinal studies, experiments of nature, laboratory experiments, and case studies) they found converging support for this theory.

Besides investigating whether explanatory style is a good predictor of depression, Seligman and his colleagues also examined whether it predicts achievement-related outcomes in school children (Nolen-Hoeksema, Girgus & Seligman 1986), in life insurance sales agents (Seligman & Schulman 1986) and in college students (Peterson & Barret 1987). In all of these studies, they found clear support for the assumption that explanatory styles are crucial in predicting performance outcomes.

There is also empirical support for the assumption that a person's explanatory style affects somatic health (Rodin 1986). In a 35-year longitudinal retrospective study of Harvard alumni, Peterson, Seligman, and Vaillant (1988) found that pessimistic explanatory style predicted poor health at ages 45 and 60, even when physical and mental health at age 25 were held constant. In a prospective study, Peterson (1988) also demonstrates that those students who explain bad events with stable and global factors, subsequently experienced more days of illness and visited physicians more frequently than did students with an optimistic style of explaining bad events.

Most recently, Seligman and his co-workers have applied this concept to political phenomena (Zullow, Oettingen, Peterson & Seligman 1988). They demonstrate that the outcomes of 9 out of the last 10 presidential elections in the United States could be predicted by analyzing how pessimistic and ruminative the style of the candidates was. For Lyndon B. Johnson, they even show that changes in his explanatory style were followed by either active or passive policies. In an analysis of cultural differences of attributional styles and the consequences, they analyzed East and West Berlin newspaper reports about the 1984 Winter Olympics. They found that East German newspapers were more pessimistic than West German newspapers in their explanations of outcomes in these sports events, despite the fact that East Germans won many more medals than West Germans (24 versus 4). As one possible result of such a pessimistic style, they looked at symptoms of depression in workmen in East and West Berlin and found significantly more signs of depression in the East (Oettingen & Seligman 1990).

Despite the changes in LBJ's attributional style over the years of his presidency, Seligman clearly believes that attributional styles are reasonably stable in a person's adult life. In one study (Burns & Seligman 1989), he finds a correlation of .54 between the attributions for negative events over an average time span of 52 years.

Seligman's recent work has shifted away from simply demonstrating the helplessness phenomenon; he is concerned with elaborating the psychological process underlying these symptoms. Most recently, he has been fascinated by the importance that individual differences in attributional styles have for predicting reactions in all different parts of life.

4.2 Wortman's Research on Reactions to Uncontrollable Events

4.2.1 Wortman and Brehm's Answer to Seligman's Theory

Seligman's original hypothesis that an expectation of future noncontingencies between actions and outcomes leads to a state of helplessness (Seligman 1975), clearly contradicts Brehm's predictions in his theory of reactance (Brehm 1966, 1972). For Brehm had postulated that a person whose freedom is threatened will be motivationally aroused and invigorated to regain the threatened or lost control.

Brehm calls this motivational tension that arises when a person's freedom is threatened "reactance" (Brehm 1966). He postulates that the strength of this motivation is a function of (a) the original expectation of freedom, (b) the strength of the threat to this freedom, (c) the importance of the freedom for the person, as well as (d) the implications for the freedom of the person. He predicts that reactance motivates the person to change the evaluation of the attractiveness of the uncontrollable outcome, to attempt to engage directly in the threatened or eliminated behavior (and to restore the freedom by implication), and that it leads to the rise of hostile and aggressive feelings.

A person who behaves according to Brehm's prediction (Brehm 1966, 1972) would be active and angry; a person who behaves according to Seligman's prediction (Seligman 1975) would be passive and depressed. The contradiction between the predictions of these two theories is striking. While Seligman (1975) postulates that helplessness would occur in a situation with an expectation of no control and that this would result in cognitive, motivational, and emotional deficits, Brehm (1966, 1972) predicts exactly the opposite. He states that invigoration will occur as soon as a person's freedom is threatened, and instead of depression he postulates that anger and aggressive feelings will occur.

Wortman and Brehm (1975) analyzed this discrepancy and suggested integrating the predictions of both theories into one general theory that can explain responses to uncontrollable outcomes. They argued that each of the two theories concerns only one segment of the complete set of reactions that occur in situations with uncontrollable outcomes. They propose an integrative model that specifies the conditions under which reactance effects and helplessness effects would occur. They argue that a person will react with reactance effects as long as he or she still has some expectancy of control. This can be the case, for example, when the person experienced only a few uncontrollable events. In this situation the person might still have an expectation of control and will—according to the theory of reactance—react with enhanced efforts to regain control. But as soon as the person loses this expectation of control, helplessness effects will occur.

Wortman and Brehm (1975) were not only concerned with predicting the kind of reaction—reactance or helplessness effects—that would occur in a situation with an uncontrollable outcome. They also developed a hypothesis concerning the strength of the effects that will occur. They postulated that the higher the importance of the outcome, the stronger the attempts will be to restore the threatened freedom—or the stronger the helplessness effects would be.

This innovative integrative model (Wortman & Brehm 1975) clearly had a broader domain than either of the two original theories (Brehm 1966, 1972; Seligman 1975). The fact that it did not lead to a paradigm shift in the literature on helplessness effects is surprising. One explanation may be that Seligman and his co-workers were primarily interested in the clinical phenomena of learned helplessness (see for example, Abramson 1988). The "unclinical" reaction of trying even harder to reestablish control was not given much attention. Instead, Abramson, Seligman, and Teasdale (1978) were far more interested in clarifying their hypotheses concerning the symptoms of helplessness.

4.2.2 Critique of the Attribution Theoretical Considerations of Abramson, Seligman, and Teasdale

In 1976, Wortman investigated the relationship between causal attributions and personal control. She presented evidence that people's attributions are effected by their desire to control their environment, and raised some intriguing questions concerning the consequences of making attributions.

Having investigated the significance of attributions, it is not surprising that Wortman became interested in Abramson, Seligman, and Teasdale's reformulated theory of learned helplessness which stressed the role of attributions (Abramson, Seligman & Teasdale 1978).

In 1978, she presented five basic criticisms of the attributional analysis of the learned helplessness phenomenon (Wortman & Dintzer 1978). First, she questioned whether human beings actually do engage in attributional activity and whether there is a relationship between attributions and behavior. Second, she questioned whether the three attributional dimensions selected by Abramson, Seligman, and Teasdale (1978) are actually the most important dimensions to be considered. She argues that the controllability and foreseeability of attributions may also be important. Third, she argues that other cognitions besides expectations for future control and attributions may be relevant influences on reactions to uncontrollable events. For example, she points to the significance of finding meaning in outcomes. The fourth criticism again concerns the fact that not all human beings respond with helplessness and deficits to uncontrollable events, but that facilitated responses sometimes occur. Finally, she raises questions concerning the direction of causality between attributions, expectation, and depression. She argues that the reformulated theory of learned helplessness is circular and lacks predictive power unless the conditions under which attributions occur can be specified.

While the first three criticisms mainly concern the significance of attributions, the fourth and fifth criticism focus specifically on the theory of learned helplessness. The first three criticisms can be understood as attempts to clarify or question the significance of attributions. These criticisms and the fifth criticism are partly answered by Seligman's research on the significance of attributional styles (see for example Peterson & Seligman 1984). The fourth criticism repeats the argument that led Wortman and Brehm (1975) to suggest an integrative model. It attacks the central hypothesis of the theory of learned helplessness by pointing out that helplessness is only *one* possible reaction to uncontrollable events and that other reactions also occur.

In 1982, Silver, Wortman, and Klos published a second criticism of the reformulated theory of learned helplessness (Abramson, Seligman & Teasdale 1978) which went beyond the earlier criticisms (Wortman & Dintzer 1978). They present three criticisms which attack the central hypotheses of this theory on both the theoretical and the methodological level.

First, Silver, Wortman, and Klos (1982) question whether the performance deficits—which undoubtedly occur after uncontrollable events—are really a result of learned helplessness or whether other psychological factors such as a heightened anxiety are responsible for these effects. The second and third criticism are methodological criticisms. Silver et al. (1982) point out that the demands of the experimental situation may hinder subjects from reporting their underlying thoughts and feelings regarding the manipulations employed in these studies. Furthermore, they argue that the use of artificial laboratory experiments might not be suitable to adequately grasp the complexity of psychological phenomena such as learned helplessness.

Peterson and Seligman (1984) react to this sharp criticism by first pointing out that helplessness is a sufficient but not a necessary condition for the occurrence of deficits in connection with uncontrollable events. They argue that other factors can lead to helplessness effects as well. But they insist that helplessness is an independent and unique psychological state that is important in connection with the occurrence of uncontrollable events. Concerning the methodological criticisms, they reply that every method has certain problems; they suggest taking a multimethod approach when studying complex phenomena such as learned helplessness. They use such a multimethod approach in their own work (Peterson & Seligman 1984), investigating the learned helplessness hypothesis with five different methods. In doing so, they find converging support from the results of these various studies for the learned helplessness theory.

Downey, Silver, and Wortman (in press) go a step further in their criticisms of attributional hypotheses in the research on reactions to uncontrollable events, by presenting empirical evidence for their position. They report data from a longitudinal study of 124 parents who lost children to Sudden Infant Death Syndrome. These parents were interviewed three weeks, three months, and eighteen months after the loss and were asked about their distress, their attributions, and their thoughts about this tragic event. The results of this study support Wortman's criticisms of the relevance of attributional hypotheses in two ways. First, these authors find that by the third week, 45 percent of the parents were not concerned with attributing responsibility, and that this percentage increased over time. Second, attributional activity was not related to better adjustments in this situation. On the contrary, these investigators suggest that attributions to oneself or others might even be symptomatic of distress. They argue for moving beyond attributional explanations and towards exploring other psychological issues that might be involved in a person's vulnerability to distress following loss, and in recovery from the event.

Evaluating Wortman's combined efforts concerning the attribution adjustment issue, it seems clear that she quite appropriately pointed out contradictions and limitations to the research conducted thus far. At this stage, the challenge is to determine how these contradictions can be explained and what the exact limitations of such an approach are. One possible way of solving the contradictions might be to clarify the psychological processes of making attributions in situations with critical life events. This approach will be taken in this book, when considering the role of attributional activity and reactions to critical life events.

4.2.3 Wortman's Research on Coping with Loss

Wortman's research began with a theoretical analysis of reactions to uncontrollable events (Wortman & Brehm 1975). In a second group of publications, she reacted against research that stresses the significance of attributions (Wortman & Dintzer 1978; Silver, Wortman & Klos 1982; Downey, Silver & Wortman, in press). Her most recent publications constitute a third group of papers in which she develops a new perspective on reactions to loss (see Wortman & Silver 1987, in press; McIntosh, Silver & Wortman, under review).

These most recent publications result from an impressive group of longitudinal studies that Wortman and her co-workers have conducted during the past decade. In these studies persons who had suffered an extreme loss, such as a spinal cord injury (Silver 1982; Silver & Wortman 1987), the loss of a child to Sudden Infant Death Syndrome (Wortman & Silver 1987; Downey, Silver & Wortman, in press) or the loss of a child or spouse to a motor vehicle accident (Lehman, Ellard & Wortman 1986; Lehman, Wortman & Williams 1987; Wortman & Silver 1987, in press) were studied over long periods of time. By confronting the prevailing assumptions about reactions to loss, with the results of these studies, Wortman and Silver (1987, in press) have developed their own hypotheses concerning reactions to loss.

They start by disagreeing with some commonly shared assumptions concerning the process of mourning and coping with irrevocable loss. Specifically, they address the following five assumptions (see Wortman & Silver, in press): (a) distress or depression is inevitable; (b) distress is necessary, and failure to experience distress is indicative of pathology; (c) "working through" the loss is important; (d) recovery is expected; and (e) a resolution is reached. For each of these five assumptions they provide an overview of the literature that presents and elaborates the assumption, and the empirical evidence that contradicts it.

Wortman and Silver (1987) argue that these false assumptions shared by researchers and by the public in general, may hinder both understanding of and practical reactions to persons experiencing irrevocable loss. They suggest that instead of assuming that there is one "normal" pattern of reactions (high distress and depression in the beginning, a working through process followed by a recovery and resolution), three different patterns of reactions to loss should be considered as "normal." In their data, they find that one group of individuals actually does react as predicted in the old model. Those persons have a very strong and intense reaction immediately after the loss and adapt over time. But they also find that a second group of persons does not experience intense distress at all and that a third group of persons shows a high level of distress over a long period of time with no indications of recovery.

Concerning the suggestion that there are actually three different "normal" patterns of reactions to irrevocable loss, two issues are interesting. The first is to explain under which circumstances a given pattern of reactions will occur. The second issue is the implications this perspective has for research and for practical purposes. Silver and Wortman (1987) describe four factors as being important influences on the kind of reactions that follow an irrevocable loss. These factors are the type of relationship with the lost person (especially whether the relationship was characterized by ambivalence or dependency), the circumstances under which the loss occurred (was the death sudden, unexpected, or premature), the presence of concomitant stressors (such as chronic health ailments, or problems arising from the loss), and the availability of social support.

Concerning the implications of their new perspective, Silver and Wortman (1987, in press) argue that research should include studies of the long-term outcome and should not just focus on immediate reactions to irrevocable loss. Besides describing the implications of their perspective for future research, they are also concerned with its implications for the treatment of persons experiencing a loss, both by professionals and by persons in their support system.

Wortman's recent research (Wortman & Silver 1987, in press) is challenging and stimulating. At the same time, it is only a first step towards developing a new theory concerned with reactions to irrevocable loss. This first step is to question the prevailing assumptions and suggest alternative patterns of reactions. Worman and Silver (1987) do not attempt to explain the psychological process that leads to different reactions, but only name four different factors that may be important. Their work is provocative, providing clear evidence of the legitimacy of the questions they raise; it should stimulate future research on the psychological processes involved.

4.3 "Seligman *or* Wortman" versus "Seligman *and* Wortman"

After reading the Wortman and Brehm article published in 1975, one might well have expected that Seligman's hypothesis (Seligman 1975) would by now be fully integrated into a more general theory on which future research would be based. Surprisingly, this has not taken place.

Seligman continued his line of research by reacting to criticisms of parts of his theory. He reacted, for example, to the criticisms that his theory cannot predict differences in self-esteem, and the intensity, generality, and duration of reactions by reformulating his theory (Abramson, Seligman & Teasdale 1978). The criticisms of this reformulation—for example, criticism of the significance of attributions (Wortman & Dintzer 1978) or of the methodology used (Silver, Wortman & Klos 1982)—has been countered by Seligman by conducting an impressive volume and variety of empirical studies (Peterson & Seligman 1984) that demonstrate the role of explanatory styles in predicting health, subjective well-being, and performance.

Seligman has been very adept at using criticisms of his work as a stimulus to produce more precise predictions concerning the reactions to uncontrollable events. At the same time, by including general considerations concerning the significance of explanatory styles, he has widened the domain of reactions covered by his theory.

Wortman, on the other hand, started with a very general theory of reactions to uncontrollable events (Wortman & Brehm 1975). In her recent research (Wortman & Silver 1987, in press) she has narrowed the domain of her theoretical considerations by focusing on reactions to irrevocable losses. This new perspective is still in a developmental stage in explaining the underlying psychological processes that lead to the patterns of reactions found in her data.

A first difference between these two theories is that their development led to a reversed position in the generality of the domain of the theories. Seligman (1975) was originally only interested in clinical reactions to helplessness. His most recent research on the significance of explanatory style, covers a wide domain of reactions in very different aspects of life. Wortman, on the other hand, started with a very general theory and has limited her considerations in recent research to reactions to irrevocable loss.

Another contrast between the two approaches is that Seligman became more and more precise in his predictions concerning the kind of reactions that follow under specific conditions. Wortman, conversely, started with precise theoretical statements concerning the underlying psychological processes of certain reactions (Wortman & Brehm 1975). But in her recent work (Wortman & Silver 1987, in press) she is primarily concerned with describing general patterns of reactions and the connection between the factors involved and these general reaction patterns.

Given the potential convergence in their previous work, one wonders about the possibility of a joint research project which might be promising.

4.4 Taylor's Theory of Cognitive Adaptation to Threatening Events

4.4.1 Original Considerations

Taylor's career began with research on social cognition (1982a; Taylor, Crocker & D'Agostino 1978; Taylor & Fiske 1978; Taylor & Thompson 1982). But very early she also became interested in health-related behavior (Taylor, 1979, 1982b, 1986). This interest in cognitive processes on one hand and health-related issues on the other hand, led to the development of the theory of cognitive adaptation to threatening events (Taylor 1983).

This theory is a cognitive theory in the fullest sense of the word. It is exclusively cognitive, because it focuses on the cognitive processes that occur as reactions to threatening events.

Taylor (1983) postulates that cognitive adaptation to threatening events has three components. The first component is a search for meaning. This search focuses on both the causes of the event, and on the event's significance for the life of those involved. The second component concerns the attempts of those involved to gain a sense of mastery and control in situations with threatening events. The third component concerns the process of selfenhancement. Taylor (1983) argues that persons in situations with threatening events try to bolster their self-esteem. To do so, they compare themselves with persons in similar situations who are even worse off than they themselves. These downward social comparisons help them feel better about themselves.

After describing these three components of the cognitive adaptation to threatening events, Taylor (1983) points to two general characteristics of this process that are significant for understanding cognitive processes in general. The first issue concerns the fact that a given cognition can have very different functions under varying circumstances in the coping process. For example, an internal attribution after being raped can satisfy the person's need to answer the question, "Why did this happen?" On the other hand, this same cognition can interfere with the person's efforts to have a sense of control or to feel good about himself or herself. In different circumstances, the same attribution might not be functional for the person. Accordingly, Taylor (1983) stresses the importance of understanding the functions that specific cognitions have in the adaptation to threatening events.

The second general issue is the question of veridicality of cognitions. Taylor (1983) points out that cognitions in the adaptation process are quite frequently illusions, rather than objective representations of reality. An example would be a woman with breast cancer who believes that her breast cancer was caused by a high fat diet or a frisbee that hit her in the breast. Such a belief might satisfy her own desire to understand the cause for her disease, but it is not supported by objective medical research. If she decides to change her diet and thus gains a sense of control over the situation, this might not have an objective direct impact on her somatic health, but subjectively she might benefit by feeling better and this might enhance her health. Taylor (1983) aruges that illusions are of central importance for our wellbeing. They play a crucial role in the process of cognitive adaptation to threatening events by allowing the person to go on and function in life. These illusions might even help a person to find a new meaning in life.

4.4.2 Empirical Evidence Supporting the Theory of Cognitive Adaptation

Taylor tested her theory in three empirical studies. In her first study (Taylor 1983; Taylor, Lichtman & Wood 1984; Wood, Taylor & Lichtman 1985), she interviewed seventy-eight women with breast cancer. In her second study, she interviewed fifty-eight women who had been raped in the two years preceding the interview (Meyer & Taylor 1986). The subjects in the third study were fifty-five cancer patients (Taylor & Dakof 1988; Dakof & Taylor 1990; Collins, Taylor & Skokan, under review).

In both earlier studies she found clear evidence for her hypothesis that a search for meaning follows these threatening events. Ninety-five percent of the women with breast cancer, for example, searched for an explanation of why they had developed it (Taylor 1983). In both of these studies, attempts to gain control in these situations were correlated with a better adjustment. Both groups of women made social comparisons with other women in comparable situations. As predicted by Taylor (1983), these social comparisons were primarily directed toward women who were even worse off than themselves (Wood, Taylor & Lichtman 1985).

In Taylor's more recent publications on the role of social comparisons (Taylor & Lobel 1989; Taylor, Buunk & Aspinwall 1990), she develops her ideas about this phenomenon further. She found that social comparison processes can actually serve several functions. Downward social comparisons may be useful in helping to boost one's self-esteem; upward social comparisons on the other hand might be functional when information is sought about a "better" future.

In describing these results, Taylor again stresses the importance of understanding the function a given cognition has, instead of focusing on the
cognition's content (Taylor, Lichtman & Wood 1984). The results of these
studies support Taylor's hypothesis that if a person is able (a) to find meaning
in having experienced a threatening event, and (b) to gain a sense of control,
and (c) to maintain his or her self-esteem, then the person's subjective well-
being will be better and the person will be better able to cope with the
demands of a situation involving a threatening event.

4.4.3 The Search for Meaning and the Role of Illusions

Taylor (1983; Taylor, Wood & Lichtman 1983) offered an optimistic outlook on human beings' ability to cope with threatening events by asserting
that positive changes in beliefs will occur, and by focusing on positive adaptation. Other authors such as Wortman and her co-workers (Lehman,
Wortman & Williams 1987; Wortman & Silver 1987, in press) or Janoff-
Bulman (Janoff-Bulman & Frieze 1983; Janoff-Bulman & Timko 1986) paint
a bleaker picture. Wortman, for example, argues that severe and long-lasting
disruptions can occur in the lives of persons who have experienced such
tragic events as the loss of a spouse or child. And Janoff-Bulman points out
that negative rather than positive changes in beliefs about the self and the
world in general occur as consequences of being victimized.

In her most recent study, Taylor (Collins, Taylor & Skokan, under review)
analyzes these discrepancies between her own predictions and the work of
others. She attempts to find out (a) whether positive or negative changes in
beliefs actually do follow victimization, and (b) what the relationship is between positive or negative changes in beliefs, different kinds of coping behavior, and one's adjustment in these situations.

These two questions were investigated in the study of fifty-five cancer
patients who had experienced a diagnosis or recurrence of cancer within the
past five years (Collins, Taylor & Skokan, under review). They were asked
about the changes they had experienced in five life domains after they had
been diagnosed as having cancer, as well as questions concerning their coping
behavior and their psychological adjustment.

The results are interesting. The evidence is mixed, concerning whether
positive or negative changes in beliefs occur after victimization. The respondents did indeed report positive changes in their beliefs about activities/
priorities and about their relationships. But the changes in their beliefs about
themselves, the world in general, and their future were mixed. Although the
interviewees reported perceptions of strength and hope in these areas of life,
they also had feelings of vulnerability, mortality, and threat. Taylor (Collins,
Taylor & Skokan under review) concludes from these findings that the domain of perceptions is crucial when predictions concerning the quality of

changes in beliefs are made. She suggests that different events may lead to different changes.

Concerning the relationship between changes in beliefs, types of coping behavior, and adjustment, the results were equally complex. While negative changes in beliefs are weakly associated with low psychological adjustment, the relationship between positive changes and adjustment was mixed.

Although these results may seem discouraging, one implication of Taylor's earlier work is still quite striking. This is the notion that illusions and not objective evaluations of reality may lead to a higher level of subjective well-being (see also Taylor & Brown 1988 for a further elaboration of this point). This is an entirely new perspective on reactions to threatening events which could be described as the "world of intellectualizers." For Taylor, coping with threatening events seems to be mainly a function of reinterpreting and shaping one's thinking about the world. By presenting this new and optimistic approach, she pointed to the significance of understanding the functions that certain cognitions have and the role that illusions play in the process of cognitive adaptation. In doing so, she made a valuable contribution in calling attention to previously neglected aspects of reactions to threatening events and by stressing the importance of understanding the cognitive processes.

4.5 A Critical Evaluation of Cognitive Theories

Each of the three theories presented here is noteworthy. Seligman's theory of learned helplessness (Seligman 1975; Abramson, Seligman & Teasdale 1978; Peterson & Seligman 1984) points to the relevance of expectations of noncontingencies and the attributions made concerning these noncontingencies for predicting a person's thinking, feeling, and performance.

Wortman's earlier research (Wortman & Brehm 1975) offers a clear theoretical perspective about reactions to uncontrollable events, which integrated Seligman's hypotheses into a more general theory that explains invigoration as well as helplessness effects after experiencing an uncontrollable event. Her recent research together with Silver (Wortman & Silver 1987, in press) explores the reactions to irrevocable loss.

Taylor's theory of cognitive adaptation to threatening events (Taylor 1983) offers a cognitive analysis of the adaptation process in the truest sense of the word *cognitive*. She stimulates the reader to recognize the relativity of the objective reality and the importance of illusions for a person's subjective well-being.

What answers do these three theories give to the two sets of questions an adequate theory of reactions to critical life events should be able to answer? As we recall, these questions refer to predictions about the amount of stress arising as well as to the types of reactions that take place—general, specific, and long term—following a critical life event.

Seligman's original theory of learned helplessness (Seligman 1975) as well as his reformulated theory (Abramson, Seligman & Teasdale 1978) concerns one type of reaction that occurs in situations with critical life events. Rather than explaining which events cause such a reaction, he focuses on the cognitive basis for this reaction of helplessness. He argues that helplessness will occur if a person has an expectation of future noncontingencies and that the quality and quantity of reactions in this state of helplessness is a function of the kinds of attributions a person makes. Thus, his theory is limited to reactions of helplessness and does not make predictions about positive changes in beliefs, invigorated activities, or reactions to deny reality. Only recently, in his work on the significance of explanatory styles (see, for example, Seligman & Schulman 1986), are any effects other than helplessness considered. He is not directly concerned with predicting the amount of stress a person experiences, nor with the prediction of specific reactions or the long-term consequences of experiencing critical life events.

Wortman's work falls into two different categories. At first, she (Wortman & Brehm 1975) proposed a general theory with precise hypotheses about the kind and strength of reactions to uncontrollable events. One problem with this work is that not all critical life events are uncontrollable. A person may feel that the birth of a child is a controllable event, but nevertheless stress can occur and adaptation reactions may be necessary. The second problem is that this theory is not directly concerned with predicting the amount of stress that occurs in such a situation (a problem which tends to apply to cognitive theories in general). Finally, a third problem of Wortman's earlier work was that specific reactions as well as the long-term consequences were not considered.

In Wortman's recent work on loss (Wortman & Silver 1987, in press) she limits the domain of the hypotheses to reactions to irrevocable loss. Again she is not concerned with predicting the amount of stress that arises. She is precise in describing various general patterns of reactions to loss, but provides no explanation of why a certain pattern might occur, or which specific reaction will actually be shown. In this work she is strongly interested in long-term reactions to loss, but offers only general explanations concerning the predictions of its long term consequences.

Taylor (1983) limits her hypotheses to reactions to threatening events. She neglects the energizing aspect of this situation completely, not being concerned with predicting the amount of stress occurring. Since her main interest is to understand the cognitive processes in situations with threatening events, she limits her hypotheses concerning the general kind of reaction to this subset of all possible reactions. She is not concerned with predicting specific reactions and does not explicitly refer to the long-term consequences.

These three cognitive theories provide useful insights concerning specific aspects of reactions to critical life events, but they are not concerned with reactions to critical life events that are controllable or nonthreatening. They make no explicit predictions of the amount of stress, nor of which specific reactions will occur, after a critical life event. They provide useful insight concerning the general reaction patterns that occur.

Chapter 5

Theoretical Research on Reactions to Critical Life Events

5.1 Theoretical Research Not Considered Thus Far

The psychological research on critical life events has grown to a massive volume in recent years. The theoretical research, in contrast to variable-centered or event-centered research, is less voluminous, but still substantial. Our analysis of the theoretical research thus far has neglected three major groups of contributions: psychoanalytic approaches, theories with a developmental perspective, and theories concerned primarily with the relationship between stress and health.

Psychoanalytic approaches such as the work by Menninger (1963), Haan (1977), and Vaillant (1977) aim at understanding coping reactions. These approaches are not discussed in this book, because they include assumptions about human functioning that are difficult to investigate empirically. One such assumption is that coping responses can be seen as part of a hierarchy of responses ranging from immature or primitive coping mechanisms to mature mechanisms.

In research on reactions to critical life events, developmental issues are clearly of interest. Many critical life events are a "normal" occurrence in a person's life span. Events such as the transition from high school to college, career choice and parenthood, retirement and death are just a few examples of such experiences (see Moos 1986, for research on these topics). It is therefore not surprising that developmental psychologists have become increasingly interested in unraveling the developmental issues linked with the reactions to these life transitions. This research is not discussed here because this book focuses on the general processes involved in reactions to critical life events. Unquestionably, developmental issues are interesting and significant, but it would go beyond the scope of this book to consider them.

A tremendous amount of research has probed into the relationship between stress and health (see Friedman & DiMatteo 1989; Sarafino 1990; Snyder 1989; Taylor 1986, for overviews). This is a complex issue and a good deal of additional interdisciplinary research will be required before a clear picture evolves. This book focuses on reactions to critical life events on a psychological level. Research on the relationship between stress and somatic health is not examined because such research must consider not only psychological aspects but physiological processes as well (compare Burchfield 1985).

5.2 A Final Evaluation of the Theories Analyzed

In the introductory chapter to this book, I suggested that the various theories concerning reactions to critical life events can be evaluated by analyzing how well they answer two sets of questions about these reactions. These questions concern explaining and predicting the conditions that lead to the rise of tension and the determinants of the amount of tension arising (the energizing component); and predicting the general and specific reactions to these events, as well as the long-term consequences of experiencing such events (the structuring component).

Stage theories were discussed first. Historically, these theories were the starting point for research on stress and coping. A schematic overview of the answers that these theories give to our two sets of questions were provided in Table 2.2. As that table indicates, Selye (1936, 1956) and Klinger (1975, 1977) offer general hypotheses concerning the conditions under which stress arises or an incentive-disengagement cycle begins, while Bowlby (1961, 1969, 1973, 1980) and Kuebler-Ross (1969) are only concerned with explaining reactions to one specific event, namely death and dying or separation and loss. None of these stage theories provides precise hypotheses concerning the determinants of the amount of tension arising.

All stage theories are mainly concerned with describing the general reactions that follow a critical life event. They all postulate that these reactions occur in predictable stages. While Selye (1956) is concerned with these general reactions on a physiological level, the other theorists focus on the psychological reactions. The weakness of stage theories lies in their inability to predict the intensity and the duration of the general and specific reactions that occur. Concerning long-term consequences, Selye predicts a negative outcome, namely a "wear and tear" process, while the other stage theorists postulate positive outcomes such as acceptance and adjustment.

Stage theories have been criticized because (a) they do not include all of the reactions that occur, (b) they contradict each other in the stages they do discuss, and (c) they do not predict the intensity and duration of reactions that occur in the various stages. Furthermore, empirical research does not support the basic assumption of these theories that reactions to critical life events actually do occur in predictable patterns (compare Silver & Wortman

1980). On the whole, these theories do not provide adequate answers to the two sets of questions concerning reactions to critical life events.

An overview of the responses to these questions given by the cognitive theories discussed in Chapters 3 and 4 appears in Table 5.1. Concerning the first set of questions, Lazarus' theory (Lazarus & Folkman 1984) makes the most general statements and has the broadest domain. Wortman's earlier work (Wortman & Brehm 1975) also makes relatively global predictions about reactions to uncontrollable events. But, as noted above, critical life events are not necessarily uncontrollable. Wortman's later work (Wortman & Silver 1987) is less general and analyzes only reactions to irrevocable losses. Seligman's earlier research (Seligman 1975; Abramson, Seligman & Teasdale 1978) was solely concerned with helplessness effects that occurred when a person had an expectancy of noncontingency between input and outcome in a situation. Taylor (1983) investigated only the cognitive reactions to threatening events.

All cognitive theories have difficulty in explaining the determinants of the amount of arising tension. Lazarus (Lazarus & Folkman 1984) is mainly concerned with understanding the psychological process that leads to stress. In Wortman's earlier work (Wortman & Brehm 1975) and in Seligman's later work (Abramson, Seligman & Teasdale 1978), indirect hypotheses concerning the amount of tension that arises are made by suggesting determinants of the intensity of the occurring reactions. Taylor (1983) is not concerned with stress per se.

Concerning the predictions of the *kinds* of reactions that occur following critical life events, all of these theories present hypotheses concerning the general reactions, but they do not enable us to predict the specific reactions. The long-term consequences of having experienced a critical life event or an irrevocable loss are only mentioned by Lazarus (Lazarus & Folkman 1984) and in Wortman's most recent research (Wortman & Silver 1987, in press). Both theories remain on a very general level when speaking about long-term consequences.

Each of the theories presented thus far makes an important contribution to understanding reactions to critical life events in general, or the reactions to one specific kind of event. But none of them responds fully to our two sets of questions concerning the reactions to critical life events.

5.3 A Theoretical Outlook

In view of the creativity and productivity of the authors whose work was presented thus far, and the complexity and richness of human reactions to critical life events, the enterprise undertaken in this book is ambitious. Our goal will be to present a network of hypotheses that adequately answers the two sets of questions concerning reactions to critical life events.

The theory to be presented here, the *generalized principle of cognitive con-*

Table 5.1
Cognitive Theories and Reactions to Critical Life Events: An Overview

	Authors			
	Lazarus (1984)	Seligman (1975, 1978, 1986)	Wortman (1975, 1987)	Taylor (1983)
Question 1A: When does tension arise?	appraisal of an event as stressful	expectancy of noncontingency	1975: uncontrollable events; 1987: loss	threatening event
Question 1B: Determinants of the amount of tension	not precise	indirectly over attribution	1975: importance 1987: not precise	not considered
Question 2A: Prediction of the general kind of reaction	altering of the troubled circumstance or regulation of emotion	1975: cognitive, motivational, emotional deficit; 1978: plus self-esteem loss; 1986: general	1975: facilitation vs. helplessness, 1987; 3 reaction patterns	search for meaning; gaining a sense of mastery; self-enhancment
Question 2B: Prediction of the specific kind of reaction	no exact hypotheses	no exact hypotheses	no exact hypotheses	not considered
Question 2C: Long-term outcome	considered as important	no exact hypotheses	1975: not considered 1987: general hypotheses	no exact hypotheses but positive

* In some cases, the years following the authors' names refer to jointly authored publications.

sistency, will integrate hypotheses from the principle of cognitive consistency (Heider 1946; Festinger 1957; Rosenberg & Abelson 1960) and from the attribution process (Heider 1958; Kelley 1971a, 1971b; Weiner 1985a, 1985b). This integrative approach will be presented by first summarizing the relevant research on the principle of cognitive consistency and then discussing the research on the attribution process. We integrate these two research areas by interpreting attributional activity as a special case of activity guided by the principle of cognitive consistency. The resulting theory—the generalized principle of cognitive consistency—will be used to explain reactions to critical life events. The results of empirical studies conducted to test specific hypotheses derived from this generalized principle of cognitive consistency will then be presented.

In the final section of this book research on the significance of such variables as social support, individual differences, and life philosophies for predicting reactions to critical life events is discussed. We will demonstrate that the generalized principle of cognitive consistency offers a useful general theoretical framework that helps to reinterpret the partially contradictory results of this variable-centered research. Finally, some practical implications of this theoretical perspective will be explored.

The Generalized Principle of Cognitive Consistency and Its Application to Reactions to Critical Life Events

Our examination of the most influential theories of reactions to critical life events indicates that none of them answers *all* the questions to which an adequate theory of this topic should respond. Part II of this book proposes an alternative theory which does so—the generalized principle of cognitive consistency. This theory builds on two main streams of social psychological research: the first deals with the principle of cognitive consistency; the second explores the process of attribution.

Chapter 6

The Principle of
Cognitive Consistency

6.1 Cognitive Consistency: A Meta-Analysis

6.1.1 Introduction

Three different trends can be distinguished in social psychological research since 1950. In the fifties and early sixties research on the principle of *cognitive consistency* dominated the field. After Heider (1946) had introduced the general idea, several researchers developed their own theories of this principle of cognitive consistency. The most influential of these theories was Festinger's theory of cognitive dissonance (Festinger 1957; Zajonc 1990). In the late 1960s, research on the *attribution process* began to take over the leading role that research on the principle of cognitive consistency had previously held. Here again, Heider introduced the basic idea of the attribution process (Heider 1958). It was generalized and elaborated by Kelley (1967) and then investigated in connection with specific issues such as person perception (Jones & Davis 1965), the cognitive processes involved (Kelley 1971a, 1971b), and the consequences of making attributions (Weiner 1972). Finally, during the past decade, a general interest in *social cognition* has dominated the social psychological literature (for an overview see Fiske & Taylor 1983). This preoccupation with "cold" cognitions is now being increasingly counterbalanced by a growing interest in "hot" issues such as research on the self (see Baumeister 1986) or emotions (see Zajonc 1980, as one example).

A first glance at this development of social psychological research since 1950 might lead to the impression that social psychology is dominated by fashions. But this interpretation of development as a simple change of tastes obscures an appreciation of the evolution of social psychology in the last forty years. And the lack of such a metatheoretical analysis has unfortunate consequences for research in social psychology today. Basic social psychological research too often tends to be ahistorical and noncumulative. Its publications in most social psychological journals are highly specialized, largely variable centered, and rarely driven by a general theory. This lack of a general perspective on how humans function leaves applied research at a loss. Not surprisingly, applied research tends to develop without much connection to basic research.

It is a fascinating coincidence that two of the three major trends in social psychology were initiated by one person, Fritz Heider. Could it be more than coincidence? Is there a latent theoretical connection between the two issues Heider dealt with, the principle of cognitive consistency and the attribution process? Moreover, what was there about these issues that attracted so many of the top minds in psychology, over a period of three decades? In recent years, research in these areas has largely been abandoned. Was it all an abortive effort that led nowhere, or could this research contribute to current research? These shifts in the focus of social psychological research raise a basic question: Have social psychologists been doing science during the past four decades—or have we merely been drifting from one fashion to another? The answer is neither black nor white: fashion has played a larger role than a purist would like to admit. But it is also true that there has been a larger component of cumulative science than first meets the eye.

Chapters 7 and 8 explore these questions. They present meta-analyses of the research in these two areas. This helps us to identify the basic hypotheses concerning the general phenomena and to understand the limits of each theory. It also helps us to understand that there is an underlying connection between these two trends in social psychological research since 1950. This connection will be used to integrate these theories in one broader one, the generalized principle of cognitive consistency.

Integrating these two major sets of hypotheses serves two purposes. First, social psychological research may be able to profit by building on earlier research. Moreover, it appears that these general hypotheses make a useful contribution to applied research. The real world is complex. Predicting real-world behavior requires theories that are general enough to reflect this complexity. We will use the generalized principle of cognitive consistency developed here to explain complex reactions, namely reactions to critical life events.

After explaining the reasons for conducting a meta-analysis, the next question is how to do it. A historical overview of research on the principle of cognitive consistency helps answer this question.

Two types of research on the principle of cognitive consistency can be identified. We will refer to these as primary and secondary research. Primary research presents an original theory of the principle of cognitive consistency. Secondary research focuses on testing or elaborating the primary research.

Let us compare the hypotheses of four primary theories. The first is Heider's balance theory, the earliest publication on the topic (Heider 1946). The second is Osgood and Tannenbaum's theory of cognitive congruency which was published in 1955. These authors attempted, more than anyone else, to predict the kinds and strengths of specific reactions to occurring incongruencies; the reactions they focused on were attitude changes (Osgood & Tannenbaum 1955). The third set of hypotheses considered is Festinger's theory of cognitive dissonance (Festinger 1957), which was extremely influential, stimulating a huge amount of secondary research. Moentmann and Irle (1978) list over 800 publications on this theory up to 1977 alone. Finally, we will examine Rosenberg and Abelson's theory of consistency (1960), which made a major contribution to understanding the basic process underlying the principle of cognitive consistency.

Secondary research tests or elaborates primary research. Secondary research on the principle of cognitive consistency falls into three categories. The first category tests given aspects of one specific primary theory. The second has a primary theory as a topic and analyzes this theory in its full complexity. Irle's revision (Irle 1975) of Festinger's theory of cognitive dissonance (Festinger 1957), Cooper and Fazio's work on the theory of cognitive dissonance (Cooper & Fazio 1984; see also Scher & Cooper 1989), and Beckmann's analysis of the theory of cognitive dissonance from an action theoretical perspective (Beckmann 1984) are examples of the second category of secondary research. Finally, a third category examines the principle of cognitive consistency by comparing the hypotheses of several primary theories. The extraordinarily interesting *Theories of Cognitive Consistency: A Source Book* (Abelson, Aronson, McGuire, Newcomb, Rosenberg & Tannenbaum 1968) is the earliest example of such research. The contributions of Abelson (1983), Harary (1983), Zajonc (1983), and others in the *Personality and Social Psychology Bulletin* are more recent examples of such research.

The meta-analysis presented here (see also Rosch/Inglehart 1983; Inglehart 1987, 1988) belongs to this third category of secondary work on the principle of cognitive consistency. It will compare the hypotheses of four primary theories.

Our comparison of these theories will focus on three aspects: (1) hypotheses about the conditions under which inconsistency arises and what determines its size, (2) hypotheses that helps predict the kind of reactions that are used to reduce this inconsistency, and (3) hypotheses about the consequences of having experienced inconsistency.

6.1.2 The Determinants of Inconsistency

In comparing the theories of Heider (1946), Osgood and Tannenbaum (1955), Festinger (1957), and Rosenberg and Abelson (1960) we will first focus on their hypotheses about the conditions under which inconsistency arises; we will then compare their hypotheses concerning what determines the amount of inconsistency arising.

While Osgood and Tannenbaum's theory is explicitly narrow and tied to one domain—attitude change after incongruent information was given (Osgood & Tannenbaum 1955)—the other three theories (Heider 1946; Festinger 1957; Rosenberg & Abelson 1960) are more general.

Heider's balance theory (Heider 1946, 1958) hides the generality of its hypotheses concerning the imbalance between cognitive elements by drawing the reader's attention to a description of one specific situation, the psychology of interpersonal relations. Heider introduced the basic idea of balanced relationships in his earlier work (Heider 1946) and pointed to its generality in his later work (Heider 1958, p. 213, for example). Though he described the general phenomenon, he did not offer exact hypotheses about the psychological processes explained by this principle. Like his work on the significance of attributions (Heider 1958), his description of the principle of balance resembles a novel describing the phenomenon, although it is a clear logical analysis (compare here also Jones 1987). Heider (1946) did not specify the conditions under which imbalance occurs in general terms. Instead he limited himself to analyzing relationships between persons. He also did not define what determines the amount of tension (imbalance) arising.

In contrast to Heider's global description, Osgood and Tannenbaum (1955) are concerned with a narrow domain, the attitude change that occurs after encountering incongruency between an original attitude and new information. A second contrast is that Osgood and Tannenbaum describe precisely—with mathematical equations—how the direction of an attitude change and the size of the changes can be predicted. The amount of underlying tension due to this incongruency can be inferred indirectly by considering the amount of attitude change that results in order to reestablish a congruent situation.

Festinger's theory of cognitive dissonance (1957) has been criticized because of the imprecision of its hypothesis concerning the conditions under which dissonance occurs (compare Irle 1975). Festinger (1957) postulated that two elements are in a dissonant relation if, considering them alone, the obverse of one element would follow from the other. Festinger elaborates on this definition by giving examples but does not clarify it further. Critics pointed out that not every discrepancy between two cognitive elements will lead to dissonance, which is an argument against Festinger's general definition.

Festinger (1957, pp. 16–17) postulated that the magnitude of the dissonance will be a function of the importance of the elements. Furthermore, he suggests that the amount of dissonance between an element and the rest of the person's cognitions will depend on the proportion of relevant elements that are dissonant with the one in question. We will refer to the latter proposition as the *sum rule*.

Rosenberg and Abelson (1960) carefully define the concepts they use. They postulate that inconsistency occurs when two cognitive elements (concepts) with identical signs are believed to be negatively related, or when two cognitive elements with opposite signs are positively related. In analogy to the

Table 6.1

Meta-analysis of Theories on the Principle of Cognitive Consistency: An Overview

	Authors			
	Heider (1946 (1958)	Osgood & Tannenbaum (1975)	Festinger (1957)	Rosenberg & Abelson (1960)
Domain	general focus: interpersonal relations	attitude change	general: cognitive elements	general: cognitive elements
Conditions	general description	information= incongruent	general description	general description
Determinants of amount of tension	none	only indirectly	importance; sum rule	only indirectly
Kinds of reactions	changes in relationship or in dynamic character of one element-- direct or indirect	attitude changes	changes in behavioral, or environmental cognitive element; adding new cognitive elements	tension reduction with direct changes; "stop thinking"
Predicting which reaction	none	yes	least resistent to change	rule of least effort
End result	balance	congruence	consonance	consistency

criticism of Festinger's hypothesis about the conditions under which dissonance arises (Festinger 1957), one could argue that Rosenberg and Abelson (1960) are not sufficiently precise in explaining the occurrence of inconsistency. These authors do not attempt to explain what determines the amount of tension (inconsistency) arising.

Table 6.1 provides an overview of these four theories on the principle of cognitive inconsistency. These authors differ significantly in their hypotheses concerning the determinants of inconsistency. While Osgood and Tannenbaum's (1955) theory has a narrow domain, the other three theories are relatively general, although Heider (1946, 1958) mainly focuses on describing the psychology of interpersonal relations. All four theories have difficulty in providing a precise definition of the conditions under which inconsistency arises. Only Festinger (1957) is explicitly interested in explaining what determines the amount of tension that arises due to inconsistency.

Specifying when inconsistency arises is a central problem for these theories. It is obvious that not all *logical* discrepancies between cognitions necessarily lead to the rise of tension. For example, we all live with inconsistencies between cognitive representations of our attitudes and our behavior, without experiencing constant tension. A smoker who knows that smoking is unhealthy but smokes two packages of cigarettes a day is common. This problem can be solved by postulating that *tension* (inconsistency) *arises when an event is inconsistent with those aspects of a person's worldview that are in the person's attention*. A person's worldview is the cognitive representation of all perceived aspects of the person, the environment, and the relationship between the person and the environment.

This hypothesis has the further advantage of having a general domain. It specifies the conditions under which tension arises by introducing the component of attention.

In predicting the *amount of tension* (inconsistency) that arises, we will adopt Festinger's (1957) *sum rule* as part of the generalized principle of cognitive consistency. This rule argues that the amount of tension arising is the sum of all single inconsistencies between an element in question and other relevant elements that are dissonant with it.

6.1.3 Predicting the Reactions to Reduce Inconsistency

All four theories postulate that a person who encounters a cognitive inconsistency is motivated to reestablish consistency. The theories differ in their hypotheses about the ways that this goal is reached. Two aspects of this question are important. First, the general reactions predicted will be described. Next, we will examine the predictions of the specific reaction that will be used in a certain situation.

Heider (1946) argues that there is a tendency toward balanced states. At the same time, he is the only author who also postulates a "tendency to leave the comfortable equilibrium, to seek the new and adventurous" (Heider 1958, p. 180). He argues that this tension produced by an imbalance often has "a pleasing effect on our thinking and aesthetic feelings." Two kinds of reactions occur when imbalance exists: one may respond with (1) changes in the relationship between the involved cognitive elements or (2) changes in the dynamic character of single elements. In other words, one responds either by making direct changes or by a cognitive reorganization that restores the balance between the cognitive elements. Heider does not try to predict the specific reactions.

Osgood and Tannenbaum (1955) predict that attitude changes will occur in order to reestablish congruence. They specify precisely which attitudes will be changed, the direction of these changes, and how large they will be. They do not attempt to explain any other reaction besides attitude changes.

Festinger (1957) and Rosenberg and Abelson (Abelson & Rosenberg 1958; Rosenberg & Abelson 1960) provide more differentiated hypotheses about the various kinds of reactions that might be used to reestablish consistency. Festinger (1957) describes three kinds of reactions to reduce dissonance, namely (a) changing a behavioral cognitive element, (b) changing an environmental cognitive element, and (c) adding new cognitive elements. He states that the resistance to change of the cognitions involved determines which kind of reaction will actually occur in order to reduce dissonance. Festinger (1957) points out that the resistance to change of a cognition is mainly determined by its responsiveness to reality. Again, he elaborates these hypotheses with examples, but is not precise in explaining the hypotheses.

Rosenberg and Abelson (Abelson & Rosenberg 1958; Rosenberg & Abelson 1960) go beyond Festinger's hypotheses in two ways. First, they postulate that the tension resulting from inconsistency can be reduced not only by changing the inconsistent relationships into consistent relationships, but one may also shut out tension ("stop thinking"). This also frees the person from tension. By introducing such tension-avoidance reactions, they point out an important alternative to the direct tension-reduction reactions. The second new aspect in their theory is that they introduce the *principle of least effort*. They postulate that the tension will be reduced through that reaction that demands the least amount of effort. Festinger (1957) had pointed to the significance of resistance to change in the cognitions involved, but he remained very global in his statements. Rosenberg and Abelson (1960) present a more specific hypothesis.

The hypotheses concerning general reactions to reduce tension are summarized in Table 6.1. Rosenberg and Abelson (1960) provide the most comprehensive description of the kinds of reactions that are used to reduce tension, pointing out the distinction between reactions that directly reestablish consistency and reactions that aim at shutting out tension. In the following, the former will be referred to as *tension-reduction reactions*, and the latter will be referred to as *tension-avoidance reactions*.

In predicting the specific kind of reaction that will occur, Rosenberg and Abelson (1960) developed the *principle of least effort*, postulating that the reaction that demands the least effort will be used in order to reduce tension. This general principle allows predictions of the kind of reactions most likely to be used in situations with inconsistencies. It is therefore incorporated in our generalized principle of cognitive consistency.

6.1.4 The End Result

Each of these four theories generates hypotheses about the psychological processes that lead to the occurrence of inconsistency. They all assume that the person is motivated to reestablish consistency and describe how this goal will be reached. But they do not offer any predictions about long-term consequences of having encountered an inconsistency. They are only concerned with the reactions that take place between the occurrence of inconsistency and the moment in which this inconsistency is reduced. Heider (1946, 1958), Osgood and Tannenbaum (1955), and Festinger (1957) focus on the direct reactions of tension reduction. Rosenberg and Abelson (1960) suggest tension avoidance-reactions besides these direct reactions to reduce the tension.

These tension-avoidance reactions raise a specific problem that is part of a more general problem underlying all of these theories. The general problem is the inability of these theories to make predictions beyond the point at which consistency is reestablished. In the specific case of tension-avoidance reactions, one might argue that a consistency which is due to a tension-avoidance reaction will only exist until a new cognition leads to a resurfacing of these avoided inconsistencies. It seems therefore important to consider the long-term reactions, because it is possible that the avoided tension might be reintroduced into the situation at any later point in time.

This specific problem in turn raises a more general issue concerning (a) whether these theories can in any way explain psychological processes over time and (b) whether they reflect the complexity of human reactions.

As long as theories about the principle of cognitive consistency focused solely on direct reduction of tension as the reaction to reduce inconsistency, explaining the long-term consequences could legitimately be neglected. Ignoring what happened after inconsistency was reduced fit within the rather narrow focus of these theories, which was to explain reactions to inconsistency. But the introduction of tension-avoidance reactions shifts this focus, opening the door to broader questions—including those about subsequent steps in the process. So far, theories of cognitive consistency have not dealt with these issues.

6.2 Cognitive Consistency and Reactions to Critical Life Events

Why do we in 1990 first present an overview of the theories concerned with reactions to critical life events, and then in the same book compare theories concerned with the principle of cognitive consistency? The answer is rooted in concerns about both research areas.

What do we know about reactions to critical life events? What would we like to know about them? By comparing the answers to these two questions, the need for a more comprehensive theory in this area becomes evident. A tremendous amount of research has been carried out in this field; now it is time to pull together the empirical evidence and the theoretical ideas and create a theory that grasps the phenomenon of interest here *and* is able to come up with clear predictions. The only kind of theory that would be able to do this would be one that describes the underlying process, the driving power behind reactions to critical life events. This book argues that the driving force in situations with critical life events is the desire to reduce tension, to reduce inconsistencies. This basic assumption makes the theories of cognitive consistency highly interesting, because these theories are concerned with precisely that process which is so crucial here, the reduction of tension.

The question then is: Why did research on cognitive consistency dry out instead of being used when studying critical life events? Two factors contributed to this. The first reason was that nobody developed the general idea of the principle of cognitive consistency beyond a one-shot and situationally tied phenomenon to a process-oriented theory. In traditional consistency theoretical thinking the scenario is as follows: inconsistency arises and is reduced. I argue that this one-shot analysis does not really exhaust the theoretical possibilities. The theory could readily be generalized and could deal with a process over time. Every reduced inconsistency is just one step in a chain of reactions and provides the starting conditions for the next possible inconsistency. This idea leads to the generalized principle of cognitive consistency which better explains the complexity of reactions to critical life events.

The second reason for the drying out of consistency theoretical research is that we are not just motivated by searching for consistency. When analyzing human behavior, other aspects besides trying to establish consistency are important and need to be investigated. But there is one situation, I argue, in which this research for consistency becomes dominant: this is when a critical life event occurs. The main goal in such situations is to reduce tension. Therefore, theories of cognitive consistency become particularly central in such situations.

Our meta-analysis of the theories of cognitive consistency generated a set of hypotheses that describes the psychological processes explained by this principle of cognitive consistency. Now let us examine how these hypotheses help explain reactions to critical life events.

6.2.1 Critical Life Events Are Inconsistencies

The main assumption of this section is that critical life events are inconsistencies in a person's life. To define critical life events as events which are inconsistent with salient parts of a person's worldview, implies a direct linkage between our general hypotheses of cognitive consistency and people's reactions to critical life events. Tension arises if the person's attention is focused on that part of the worldview which is contradicted by the event that occurs.

Two things should be noted here. First, according to this definition, critical life events are not limited to unexpected or negative events. Events that one evaluates as positive (for example, winning money in a lottery or getting married) are included in this definition as well as events that are evaluated negatively (for example, losing a job or getting divorced). Expected events (such as the birth of a child) as well as unexpected events (such as being confronted with a diagnosis of cancer) can be critical life events under this definition. As long as an event is inconsistent with that part of a person's worldview on which the person's attention is focused, this event qualifies as a critical life event.

Second, this definition does not refer to the importance or subjective significance of an event. Having a flat tire, getting married, or dying of cancer can all qualify as critical life events according to this definition. The subjective importance of an event will be considered in connection with our hypotheses about the amount of tension that arises when a critical life event occurs.

6.2.2 Tension Is the Sum of the Single Inconsistencies

Having established a connection between the principle of cognitive consistency and reactions to critical life events, let us explore how this principle can answer the questions concerning reactions to critical life events presented in Part I of this book. Our first set of questions concerns the energizing component of these reactions: when will tension arise and what determines the amount of tension that arises?

According to our definition, tension arises when an event is inconsistent with that part of a person's worldview which has the person's attention. The amount of tension that arises can be predicted by using the sum rule which postulates that "the total amount of dissonance between this element and the remainder of the person's cognition will depend on the proportion of relevant elements that are dissonant with the one in question" (Festinger 1957, p. 17). It is important to bear in mind that what counts most is not the absolute number of inconsistent relations between an event and the person's worldview, but their relative proportion of all relevant relationships. To illustrate, a miscarriage can give rise to more or less tension depending on the proportion of inconsistent relations between this event and the relationships that the woman focuses on. For example, if a woman who had no career or competing interests became pregnant, we might expect her attention to be focused almost exclusively on this event. If another woman with an interesting job became pregnant, her career might take up a large amount of her attention even after she became pregnant. The amount of tension these women experience should reflect the proportion of the sum of inconsistencies that this event of a miscarriage had caused. The first woman would presumably react more strongly than the second one.

The point is that different people react to the same event with very different amounts of tension. For this reason, the "objective" importance of an event is not included in our definition of a critical life event. There is no criterion for defining the importance of an event objectively. The same event can lead to very different amounts of tension depending on the subjective relevance it has in the worldview of the person who experiences it.

6.2.3 Predicting the General Kind of Reaction to Reduce Tension

The second set of questions an adequate theory of reactions to critical life events should answer concerns the structural component of these reactions. These questions address hypotheses about the *kind of reactions* that take place when a critical life event occurs, namely about the general reactions, the specific reactions, and the long-term consequences.

Our meta-analysis of cognitive consistency theories indicates that two basic kinds of general reactions are possible. Tension can be reduced directly by changing the inconsistent relationships into consistent relationships (a tension-reduction reaction). Or tension can be shut out and thus avoided (a tension-avoidance reaction). When reacting in the second way, the person diverts attention to another part of his or her worldview.

These two types of reactions also occur in connection with critical life events. Certain reactions attempt to change the problematic issue directly (tension-reduction reactions), while other reactions to critical life events aim at shutting out tension by changing the focus of attention to another area of content (tension-avoidance reactions).

How can we predict whether a person is more likely to show a tension-reduction reaction or a tension-avoidance reaction, when a critical life event occurs? The generalized principle of cognitive consistency answers this question with Rosenberg and Abelson's principle of least effort (Rosenberg & Abelson 1960). These authors argue that tension will be reduced with that reaction that demands the least effort in this situation. We adopt this hypothesis in predicting reactions to critical life events.

These predictions of the general reactions used to reduce tension when a critical life event occurs are relatively abstract. It might seem difficult to actually apply them in specific situations. Two problems arise here. First, how can we measure the amount of effort that a certain reaction demands? This problem will be discussed in the following chapter. Second, distinguishing between tension-reduction and tension-avoidance reactions is only a first step toward predicting concrete reactions. The next question is how to predict the *specific* kind of tension-reduction or tension-avoidance reaction that will be used in a given situation.

6.2.4 Predicting the Specific Reaction: A Function of the Cognitive Availability of Alternative Reactions

In 1974, Goetz-Marchand, Goetz, and Irle examined the kind of dissonance-reduction reaction that is likely to occur in a given situation. The authors demonstrated that the *cognitive availability* of different reactions is of great significance in predicting the specific reaction a person will show. We postulate that two factors influence the cognitive availability of different reactions: (1) the amount of past experience with specific reactions, and (2) the objective availability of given stimuli associated with specific reactions at the given point in time.

6.2.4.1 Past Experience

The cognitive availability of a given type of reaction may reflect the amount of past experience the person had with this specific reaction. Past experiences include memories of oneself reacting in this specific way, as well as memories of how other persons have reacted. Especially relevant are memories of reactions of persons who are important in a person's life, such as family members and friends. Memories of these persons are numerous and tend to be evoked relatively easily. During early socialization, children learn about the world by becoming aware of the reactions of significant persons around them—parents, siblings, grandparents. A repertoire of reaction possibilities is thus learned which is cognitively available to the person when he or she is confronted with certain events later in life. Accordingly, for predicting which specific reaction is likely to take place when a given critical life event occurs, it is important to know which cognitions about past experiences are salient in this situation.

6.2.4.2 Objective Availability of Stimuli Associated with Specific Reactions

The second factor that helps to understand what is cognitively available when a certain critical life event occurs is the objective availability of certain stimuli that are associated with specific reactions.

To illustrate: A person finds out that the spouse has an extramarital relationship. This is inconsistent with this person's worldview. If the effort required to directly change this inconsistency into a consistent situation is greater than the effort to shut out the inconsistency, then the person is likely to avoid the tension by withdrawing from this problematic area. There are numerous ways in which the person can do this. One possibility would be to abuse alcohol. We argue that this possibility is more likely to be chosen if the person lives in a situation in which alcohol is objectively readily available. If the person frequently attends parties or dines in restaurants where alcohol is served, then this specific tension-avoidance reaction is more likely to occur than if alcohol is not readily available.

6.2.5 Predicting the Long-term Consequences

After discussing the predictions of the general and the specific reactions that are used to reduce tension, the predictions concerning the long-term consequences of having encountered a critical life event need to be considered. The question here is whether the principle of cognitive consistency can make predictions concerning these long-term consequences. Our theoretical meta-analysis found that the principle of cognitive consistency is only concerned with the psychological process between the moment when tension arises and the moment when it is reduced. Any consequences beyond this point are not considered. The theory needs to be developed further if one wants to use it to explain reactions to critical life events in their full complexity.

6.3 The Principle of Cognitive Consistency and Reactions to Critical Life Events—A Critical Evaluation

Defining critical life events as events that are inconsistent with that part of a person's worldview that the person's attention is focused on, enables us to use the hypotheses about the principle of cognitive consistency to predict reactions to critical life events. We argued that the *amount of tension* arising in such a situation is a positive function of the sum of single inconsistencies relative to all relationships considered. The *general* reactions to reduce tension in a situation with a critical life event are tension-reduction and tension-avoidance reactions. We predict that the reaction that demands the least effort will be used to reduce the tension. The amount of cognitive availability of certain reactions helps predict which *specific* reaction will occur. The amount of cognitive availability of certain reactions is a function of past experiences with these reactions and/or the degree to which stimuli connected with these reactions are objectively available in the person's environment. The principle of cognitive consistency does not provide hypotheses concerning the *long-term* consequences of having encountered a critical life event.

In applying the hypotheses about the principle of cognitive consistency to situations with critical life events, two problems arise. The first is that these hypotheses are so abstract that it seems difficult to predict reactions in concrete situations. This problem occurs in predicting the amount of tension arising, as well as the general and the specific reactions used to reduce tension. How can we measure the proportion of inconsistent and consistent relationships? How can the amount of effort for different reactions be measured? How can we determine which reactions are cognitively available for different persons in different situations?

The second problem has to do with the complexity of reality both at one point in time as well as over time. Situations with critical life events do not just touch on two independent and three dependent variables, as might be the case in a laboratory experiment conducted to test a hypothesis about the principle of cognitive consistency. Critical life events can shatter a person's life. This fact has two implications. First, reduction of tension may not be an easy task that can be completed in a short period of time. Second, even when the tension linked with the critical life event has been reduced, there may be long-term consequences for the person's life. The person might have reconstructed his or her worldview to such a degree that it influences all future reactions.

Can the hypotheses about the principle of cognitive consistency do justice to these problems? I argue that they can, provided that we generalize these hypotheses. Concerning the complexity of a given situation, it seems crucial to take into account the person's life philosophy and general beliefs. These metacognitions can contribute by offering an opportunity to restructure the situation in such a way that consistency in the person's worldview results. Taylor's work on the importance of the search for meaning after a critical life event occurred (Taylor 1983) can be reinterpreted as one way to reestablish consistency between the event and the rest of the person's worldview. The relevance of metacognitions such as control beliefs, or existential beliefs for establishing consistency after a critical life event occurred, will be discussed in Chapter 11.

The second problem concerns the long-term consequences of having encountered a critical life event. To illustrate, let us assume that a person gets divorced on May 10, and that this event is inconsistent with this person's worldview. Tension arises and is avoided by shifting attention to the professional part of one's life. On May 11, this person performs highly complicated computer analyses at work and shows no signs of tension connected with the divorce. The task of the principle of cognitive consistency would be fulfilled at this point. But an adequate theory of reactions to critical life events should be able to predict the long-term consequences of this divorce for the person's life.

Thus it becomes evident that in connection with critical life events, predicting long-term consequences is important. The principle of cognitive consistency does not offer relevant hypotheses about long-term outcomes. This problem can be solved by generalizing the principle of cognitive consistency. In a generalized principle of cognitive consistency, cognitive representations about the future—such as expectations, goals, possible selves, and attributions—are included as one essential part of a person's worldview. A time perspective is thereby included in our reasoning: Discrepancies between the present and the past produce the tension that leads to reactions. And each resolved inconsistency can be interpreted as the starting condition that might be inconsistent with cognitions about the future. The static principle of cognitive consistency is thus replaced by a process-oriented, generalized principle of cognitive consistency.

This generalized principle of cognitive consistency will be developed in the next chapter by integrating hypotheses about the attribution process with hypotheses about the principle of cognitive consistency.

Chapter 7

The Generalized Principle of Cognitive Consistency: Integrating the Principle of Cognitive Consistency with Hypotheses About the Attribution Process

In developing the generalized principle of cognitive consistency, we first analyzed four theories of cognitive consistency. This led to a set of hypotheses that was then used to explain reactions to critical life events. At this point, two problems became apparent: first, how to apply abstract concepts, such as the sum rule and the principle of least effort, to concrete situations; and second, how to handle the complexity of situations with critical life events. This chapter will demonstrate that by integrating hypotheses about the attribution process with the principle of cognitive consistency, we can cope with both of those problems.

To provide the background for this integrated theory, we will first analyze the work of five authors who have dealt with the attribution process. We will focus on how these authors explain (a) the conditions under which an attribution process starts, (b) the process itself, and (c) the consequences that certain attributions have. This analysis enables us to derive a set of basic hypotheses about the attribution process. We then examine the relationship between these attribution hypotheses and the principle of cognitive consistency, integrating the two sets of hypotheses into one theory: the generalized principle of cognitive consistency.

7.1 The Attribution Process: An Overview

In 1984, 92 well-known American psychologists were asked to identify those authors who had most influenced the field of psychology (Heyduk & Fenigstein 1984). Heider, Lewin, Festinger, and Asch were the only social psychologists included among the 30 most frequently named psychologists. The fact that Heider was included is truly surprising, for Heider has published relatively little in English (Harvey 1989). In the forties, he wrote one article on phenomenal causality (Heider 1944) and one article about balance theory (Heider 1946). His most famous work is *The Psychology of Interpersonal Relations*, published in 1958 (Heider 1958). Apart from these three well-known publications he published very little (see Heider 1960, 1983; Heider & Simmel 1944), but his influence on Western social psychological research since 1950 has been profound.

As we saw earlier, Heider was the researcher who introduced the idea of cognitive consistency and the concept of attributions into social psychology: astonishingly enough, one psychologist laid the foundation for two of the three main streams of research that have prevailed in Western social psychology since 1950. This point is of more than passing significance: there is a latent linkage between these two bodies of research, as we will demonstrate.

Let us now examine the work of five authors who made major contributions to understanding the attribution process. These authors are Heider (1958), Jones and Davis (1965), Kelley (1967, 1971a, 1971b), Schachter (1964), and Weiner (1972, 1985a, 1985b).

After Heider (1958) introduced the significance of the attribution process into social psychological research, Jones and Davis (1965) used this idea to develop hypotheses concerning one concrete issue, namely person perception, thus remaining close to Heider's interest in interpersonal relations. Kelley (1967, 1971a, 1971b) was the first to investigate the process of making attributions from a cognitive perspective. Schachter (1964; Schachter & Singer 1962) examined the significance of attributions for experiencing certain emotions, focusing on one specific consequence of attributions. Weiner (1972, 1985b) originally was interested in the consequences of specific attributions, especially in the achievement domain; more recently (Weiner, 1985a), he has investigated the conditions under which an attribution process gets started.

In the following, we will focus on three aspects of these author's hypotheses about the attribution process. The first question concerns the conditions under which an attribution process begins; the second question concerns the attribution process itself; and the third question concerns the consequences that follow after given attributions are made.

7.1.1 The Conditions Under Which an Attribution Process Begins

Heider (1944, 1958) assumed that a person is usually not content to simply register observations of what happens: the underlying causes are important as well. He postulated that there is a general motivation—a need for evaluation—that leads to attributional activity, but he did not provide any other insights into the conditions under which attributional activity gets started.

Jones and Davis (1965) as well as Kelley (1967) implicitly assume in their work that persons have a need to attribute causes to events and that they engage in attributional activity. But both groups of researchers are mainly interested in understanding how an attributional process develops, making no hypotheses about the exact conditions under which an attribution process begins.

Schachter (1964, 1971; Schachter & Singer 1962) developed a theory to explain the development of emotions. In it, he assumes that there is a need for evaluation whenever an arousal is perceived for which the person does not have an obvious explanation. As a consequence of this need to evaluate, an attribution process will begin. The domain of his theory is narrow and concerns only the significance of attributions for unexplainable physiological arousal. Schachter's hypotheses about the conditions under which an attribution process starts are accordingly limited to this specific situation.

Recently Weiner (Wong & Weiner 1981; Weiner 1985a) became specifically interested in the conditions under which an attribution process begins. He postulates (Weiner 1985a) that unexpected events as well as nonattainment of a goal elicit causal search. He argues that not every unexpected event leads to attributional activity, but that an attributional search is more likely when an important, unexpected event occurs. He further finds evidence for the hypothesis that information connected with the self is especially prone to elicit attributional activity. He connects his hypotheses to a general need for mastery (compare Heider 1958) and points out that it is functional for human survival to react to unexpected and negative events with heightened attention.

Earlier research either assumed that an attribution process begins because of a need for evaluation when an event occurs (compare Heider 1958) or was not concerned with this issue at all (Jones & Davis 1965; Kelley 1967). Schachter (1964) dealt with one situation in which attributions are made, those involving unexplained physiological arousal. Weiner (1985a) argues that attributional activity is elicited when events occur that are unexpected or connected with the nonattainment of a goal. Table 7.1 presents an overview of these five authors' contributions to answering the key questions about attributional activity.

7.1.2 The Attribution Process

The second aspect of attributional activity that these authors must deal with is the question, how does an attribution process unfold? Two issues are of interest here: the kinds of attributions that various authors discuss and their hypotheses about the unfolding of attributional activity itself.

Heider (1958) categorized the causes of failure or success as being located either in the person or in the environment (internal versus external attribution). Within each of these two groups of attributions, he further differentiated between causes that are variable and causes that are stable. For example, chance is described by Heider as an external variable cause, the difficulty of a task as an external stable cause, effort as an internal variable cause, and ability as an internal constant cause (Heider 1958, p. 58).

Table 7.1

Meta-analysis of Hypotheses About the Attribution Process: An Overview

| | Authors | | | | |
	Heider (1958)	Jones & Davis (1965)	Kelley (1967, 1971a, b)	Schachter (1964, 1971)	Weiner (1985a, b)
Domain	interper- sonal relations	person perception	general	emotions	achievement; general
When does it start?	need for evaluation	not speci- fied	not speci- fied	arousal	unexpected events; nonattain- ment of goal
Attribu- tional dimen- sions	internal/ external; stable/ variable	not speci- fied	not speci- fied	not speci- fied	locus; stability; controlla- bility
Process	general	tied to person perception	most elaborated	---	---
Conse- quences	inter- personal relations	intentions; traits	---	emotions	emotions; expectancy; behaviors

Heider (1958) presents a phenomenological description of the factors that are important in the reasoning process that determines which attribution is made. He was primarily interested in the psychology of interpersonal relations and, therefore, was concerned with such questions as the circumstances under which a person or something else is seen as the cause of an event. He postulated that equifinality (invariance of the ends and variability of the means) and local causality are necessary conditions for personal attributions. From his phenomenological approach to attributions, Heider (1958) does not offer any precise hypotheses about the cognitive processes involved in attributions.

Jones and Davis (1965) used Heider's (1958) considerations to explain person perception. Specifically, they were interested in clarifying how a person's intentions and personality traits are inferred in an attribution process. In their theory of correspondent inferences they examined the reasoning process that takes place here. They limit their hypotheses to person perception and do not offer any hypotheses concerning the attribution process in general.

Kelley's work (1967, 1971a, 1971b) focuses on understanding the attribution process itself. He was mainly interested in the cognitive processes that take place when attributions are made, rather than in which types of attribution exist. Unlike Heider (1958) and Jones and Davis (1965), his hypotheses analyze attributional activity in general. He emphasizes the significance of causal schemata (Kelley 1971b). He describes information processing, such as the discounting and the augmentation effects, that takes place in the attribution process. Above all, Kelley introduced a new perspective which argues that human beings process information in the same way that scientists reason in their work: the causal attributions of laypersons result from an analysis of available information that is analogous to the variance analysis a scientist uses when testing a hypothesis (see Kruglanski 1989, as a recent representative of this perspective).

Schachter's main interest was to develop a theory about emotions (Schachter 1964, 1971). Accordingly, it is not surprising that he did not analyze which types of attributions are possible nor how the cognitive process unfolds when making attributions.

Weiner (1985b) was interested in which kinds of attributions are made. He argues that attributions differ on three dimensions: the locus of attribution (internal versus external), the degree of stability of the causes, and the degree of controllability. Weiner's hypotheses about the attribution process itself are tied to Kelley's considerations (1971a, 1971b).

Let us compare the positions of these five authors concerning what attributions are made and how the attribution process unfolds. It seems clear that Weiner (1985b) provides the most comprehensive analysis of the dimensions on which attributions differ. He concludes that attributions differ in the locus, the degree of stability, and controllability that they assume. Kelley (1967, 1971a, 1971b) makes the most important contribution to understanding the attribution process itself. Using the metaphor of the person as a lay-scientist he developed an understanding of the cognitive processes that lead to specific types of attributions.

7.1.3 The Consequences of Attributions

Heider's (1958) hypotheses about the significance of attributions focus on explaining interpersonal relations, with the general consequences of making attributions. Jones and Davis (1965) focused on the significance of attributions in connection with person perception. They were interested in consequences specifically tied to this topic, investigating how intentions and personality traits are inferred from observations about others.

Kelley (1967, 1971a, 1971b) was primarily interested in the attribution process itself, rather than in the consequences of making given attributions. Schachter (1964, 1971) considers attributions as labels that are given to unspecific physiological arousal. These attributions determine the kind of emotions that result in a given situation. He does not attempt to explain the cognitive or behavioral consequences of having made attributions in general.

Weiner is centrally interested in the consequences of attributions. Initially, he studied the consequences of attributions of success and failure (Weiner & Kukla 1970). Over the years he developed his own motivational theory which he calls an attributional theory of achievement motivation and emotion (Weiner 1985b). Weiner holds that attributional activity is triggered when an unexpected, negative, or important outcome occurs. The attribution one makes on the stability dimension has cognitive consequences, influencing the expectancy of success. Attributions lead to specific emotional consequences. Weiner discusses specific emotions—such as pride, hopelessness, anger, gratitude—and explains how each of them is tied to a specific attributional pattern. He also postulates how these attributions influence actual behavior. Weiner argues the general validity of his hypotheses beyond the achievement domain, arguing that attributions of outcomes in situations are made even if these outcomes are achievement independent. But he does not explain the psychological processes connected with these achievement-independent issues explicitly.

Weiner's theory can be criticized on two points. The first concerns his hypotheses about the conditions under which attributional activity gets started. Weiner asserts that an attribution process begins when an unexpected or negative event occurs (Weiner 1985a). But attributions are also relevant when an event is positive and expected. A student does not engage in attributional activity only when he or she fails an exam: getting an A+ for a course might also be connected with an attribution. Knowing this attribution is useful for predicting the kind of reactions that follow. If the student attributes this grade to his or her intellectual brilliance, the student might feel proud, be motivated to pursue further academic endeavors, and behave accordingly. But if the student thinks that this grade was only due to having had the exams from an earlier class and unrelated to his or her abilities, the consequences will be different. In the case of an expected or a positive event, it is likely that an attribution is more readily available, so an attributional search might not be necessary. But the attribution is relevant if one wants to understand the consequences of these events.

A second criticism is that because Weiner (1985a, 1985b) ties his considerations mainly to achievement-related behavior, his hypotheses include only certain consequences. When he claims that his hypotheses apply to a broader range of events, he encounters serious problems. The emotional reactions that he has described are clearly only a few of the affective reactions that can occur: love and hate, fear and joy, envy and jealousy are some of the reactions not included in Weiner's list of emotions. Accordingly, it is difficult to apply his hypotheses to other than achievement-related events.

Furthermore, Weiner's hypotheses about the emotional consequences of encountering an unexpected event or of not attaining a goal touch only the surface of the problem; he does not suggest any underlying processes that would explain why these specific emotions result when given attributions are made.

It is significant that these theories actually *are* able to predict the consequences of given attributions. In contrast, theories of cognitive consistency do not deal with any consequences beyond the point at which consistency was reestablished. This contrast between these two sets of theories makes an attempt to integrate them particularly interesting: potentially, they are complementary.

7.2 The Principle of Cognitive Consistency and the Process of Attribution

Two types of problems are encountered when theories about the principle of cognitive consistency are used to explain reactions to critical life events. The first problem concerns the difficulty of bridging the gap between abstract concepts (such as the sum rule and the principle of least effort) and their application to concrete situations. The second problem concerns the inability of hypotheses about the principle of cognitive consistency to account for the complexity of situations with critical life events.

Two aspects are important here. First, if tension arises after a critical life event has occurred, it can be a complicated task to reorganize one's worldview in such a way that the critical life event is incorporated and cognitive consistency is reestablished. We need hypotheses that help us understand this complex process. Second, encountering a critical life event changes a person's worldview in ways which influence future behavior. To understand reactions to critical life events fully, we need to understand their long-term consequences. The hypotheses about the principle of cognitive consistency do not provide any predictions about consequences beyond the point at which cognitive consistency is reestablished.

On the other hand, research on the attribution process deals with the consequences of making certain attributions. We believe that by integrating these two sets of theories, it may be possible to generate predictions concerning the long-term consequences of experiencing a critical life event.

Furthermore, we believe that this integrative approach helps us to reconsider the methodological problem of bridging the gap between abstract concepts and concrete problems in situations with critical life events.

Before developing the generalized principle of cognitive consistency that integrates these two sets of hypotheses, let us consider some other work on the relationship between cognitive consistency and attribution research.

7.2.1 Metatheoretical Considerations of Other Authors on Integrating Consistency and Attribution Hypotheses

As noted earlier, Heider introduced both the basic idea of cognitive consistency (Heider 1946) and the idea of the relevance of attribution processes (Heider 1958) into social psychology. How did he relate the two concepts? When Harvey, Ickes, and Kidd (1976) launched their series of readers on new trends in attribution research, they asked Heider about the relationship between his balance and attribution conceptions (Heider 1976). Heider's answer is revealing. He replied, "Yes, the two are very close together: I can hardly separate them. Because attribution, after all, is making a connection or a relation between some event and a source—a positive relation. And balance is concerned with the fitting or nonfitting of relations" (Heider 1976, p. 16). In the light of this statement, it is remarkable that for the past three decades social psychological research has treated balance and attribution as two unrelated concepts, with social psychologists nearly always focusing on one of these two issues to the exclusion of the other. To be sure, Heider only provided a rough idea of the connection between these two sets of hypotheses; but this linkage has significant implications.

Before elaborating on Heider's idea, however, let us consider those few studies that explicitly dealt with the relationship between the principle of cognitive consistency and the attribution process.

In 1967, Bem suggested that his theory of self-perception can explain more parsimoniously the effects that dissonance theory claimed to explain so far, because it does not need to postulate that tension arises which has to be reduced. Bem postulates that a person observes his or her own behavior (such as getting paid either one dollar or twenty dollars for telling another subject that a certain boring experimental task is very interesting) and then concludes that he or she has certain attitudes or characteristics that cause this behavior (Bem 1967, 1972). Accordingly, he argues that attitudes are changed not because of a tension to reestablish consistency, but as a consequence of perceiving one's behavior.

Bem's research revived an interest in investigating whether there actually is a motivational tension after an inconsistency occurred (see Wicklund & Frey 1981; Markus & Zajonc 1985). Fazio and Cooper (1983; Cooper & Fazio 1984) provide the most exhaustive investigation of this question in their work. They describe three different lines of research supporting the notion that there *is* motivational tension after an inconsistency. This evidence demonstrates that (a) disssonance manipulations tend to energize dominant responses, just as arousal states are known to do, (b) physiological arousal can actually be measured after dissonance manipulations, and (c) that the state of dissonance—like the arousal involved in emotions—requires appropriate interpretation and labeling for attitude change to occur.

These conclusions stem partly from earlier research conducted by Cooper, Fazio, and Zanna (Zanna & Cooper 1974, 1976; Fazio, Zanna & Cooper 1977). These authors investigated the connection between the principle of cognitive consistency and the attribution process. Their answer to the question whether dissonance theory or self-perception theory provides the appropriate explanation is to specify the conditions under which one or the other theory explains the occurring effects. Fazio, Zanna and Cooper (1977) argue that attitude-discrepant behavior will lead to dissonance, and that attitude changes are one way to reduce this dissonance; when attitude-congruent behavior occurs, attitude change is due to a self-perception process.

Furthermore, they demonstrate that in a condition with a dissonance manipulation, attitude change will be higher if the tension cannot be attributed to external causes than when such a misattribution of arousal is possible. In this research on the misattribution of arousal paradigm, Zanna and Cooper (1974, 1976) argue that dissonance reduction and attribution processes coexist and interact.

Kruglanski also helps clarify the relationship between cognitive consistency and the attribution process (1989; Kruglanski & Klar 1987). In his theory of lay-epistemology (Kruglanski 1980, 1989), he argues that ordinary persons gain knowledge about the world by formulating hypotheses and then testing them. This epistemological process aims at establishing consistency between the cognitions involved. Accordingly, the same epistomological process is involved in cases that are explained by the principle of cognitive consistency and cases that are explained by hypotheses about the attribution process. The difference between these two groups of cases lies in their contents, and not in the cognitive process involved. Kruglanski points out that in attribution theoretical argumentation, *consistent* information is used in order to increase one's certainty of the correctness of the attribution. On the other hand, *inconsistent* information is important in consistency theoretical research.

The parallel between these considerations (Kruglanski & Klar 1987) and the work by Fazio, Zanna, and Cooper (1977) is apparent. In both instances the difference between consistency theoretical considerations and attribution theoretical argumentations is seen in the content of the cognitions involved. But it must be pointed out that Kruglanski's theory of lay-epistemology offers much more than just this statement about the difference between research based on the principle of cognitive consistency and the attribution process. Kruglanski's work offers a general theory of human information processing which is fruitful in reinterpreting specific effects in a more general framework (see, for example, Kruglanski & Freund 1983; Kruglanski 1989).

Kruglanski was the first to argue that the principle of cognitive consistency is important in dealing with *both* cognitive consistency research and attribution research. This is a crucial step toward understanding the relationship between the two theories. He also stresses the importance of the principle of cognitive consistency for understanding information processing in general.

Another innovative contribution is that Kruglanski (1980) introduces the concept of epistemological motivations as important elements of epistemological processes (see Kruglanski & Freund 1983).

I disagree with Kruglanski's view that the only difference between the principle of cognitive consistency and the attribution process is their content. Kruglanski states that attribution processes involve consistent cognitions, while consistency theories explain reactions to inconsistent cognitions. But there is clear evidence that inconsistent as well as consistent cognitions are involved in both processes. Weiner (1985a, 1985b) for example, points to the fact that attribution processes get started when events occur that are unexpected or that are connected with the nonattainment of a goal. Other authors (see Pyszczynski & Greenberg 1981; Bohner, Bless, Schwarz & Strack 1988) support this argument with empirical evidence. Such events are inconsistent cognitions and are clearly an essential part of the attribution process.

Consistent cognitions, on the other hand, do play a role in reasoning based on the principle of cognitive consistency. Festinger (1957), for example, argues that adding consistent cognitions can be one way to reduce dissonance after a decision is made. As these two examples suggest, the relationship between the attribution process and the principle of cognitive consistency is not that there are simply different contents involved. The relationship between these two sets of hypotheses needs to be clarified.

7.2.2 The Generalized Principle of Cognitive Consistency: Integrating Hypotheses About the Principle of Cognitive Consistency and the Attribution Process

As we pointed out earlier, Heider (1976) considered the balance conception and the attribution conception to be closely related. Attribution is "making a connection or a relation between some event and a source—a positive relation. And balance is concerned with the fitting or nonfitting of relations" (Heider 1976, p. 16).

This statement implies that attributional activity is one specific type of reaction explained by the principle of cognitive consistency. It aims at establishing a consistent relationship between a perceived event and its cause. This statement provides a link between the principle of cognitive consistency and the attribution process, which is the starting point for integrating these two sets of hypotheses into the *generalized principle of cognitive consistency*.

This general theory is derived by analyzing the sequence of the two processes. First, let us examine the conditions that trigger attributional activity and lead to the rise of tension due to an inconsistency. Second, we will investigate the implications of both sets of hypotheses, concerning the amount of tension arising in these situations. Finally, we will consider the kinds of reactions that occur once attributional activity is triggered or an inconsistency exists and tension needs to be reduced, analyzing predictions about the general and the specific reactions as well as the long-term consequences.

7.2.2.1 The Starting Conditions

In integrating these two sets of hypotheses, our first question concerns the conditions under which tension arises due to a cognitive inconsistency and an attribution process begins.

Our meta-analysis of four theories of cognitive consistency indicates that tension arises when an event occurs that is inconsistent with that part of a person's worldview that has the person's attention. Our meta-analysis of hypotheses about the attribution process identified Weiner's research (Weiner 1985a, 1985b) as producing the most explicit hypothesis on this question. Weiner argues that an attribution process begins when an unexpected event or an event connected with the nonattainment of a goal occurs (Weiner 1985a, 1985b).

We argued above that Weiner's formulation does not cover all situations in which attributions are involved. Even expected events and events connected with the attainment of a goal can lead to attributional activity. Following Heider's reasoning (Heider 1976, p. 16) that attribution deals with establishing consistent relations between causes and events, I argue that an attribution process is triggered when an event occurs that is inconsistent with one specific part of the person's worldview, namely with the person's assumptions about which causes lead to which effects. Attribution processes are thus used to reduce tension due to one specific inconsistency: when an event is inconsistent with a cause-effect hypothesis that is salient in this situation.

7.2.2.2 Hypotheses About the Tension Involved

Our second question concerns the tension involved in reactions explained by the principle of cognitive consistency and the attribution process. Our meta-analysis of theories of cognitive consistency pointed to the significance of Festinger's sum rule (Festinger 1957), which states that the amount of tension linked with an inconsistent event is proportional to the sum of the single inconsistencies between this event and the person's worldview, relative to the sum of consistent relationships in this situation.

At first glance it seems as if tension is not an issue in research about the attribution process. Indeed, some authors see the lack of tension in situations with attributional activity as a distinctive feature of such situations (see Bem 1967, for example). I argue that tension actually is part of the attribution process, because these activities are driven by a motivation. Two aspects are important. First, if we assume that attributional activity is triggered by a specific type of inconsistency—namely inconsistency between an event and a person's cause-effect hypothesis relating to this event—then tension *is* an issue. The sum rule can be applied here. Thus, when an event contradicts a cause-effect hypothesis, the resulting tension is a function of the sum of inconsistencies between the event and the cognitions connected with the inconsistent cause-effect hypotheses relative to all consistent relationships in this situation. The more tension arises, the more strongly the person is motivated to reduce this tension by making an attribution of the event that reestablishes consistency in the person's worldview.

Second, tension is also an issue when considering the outcome of a given attribution process and the consequences of having made a given attribution. This aspect of the attribution process is the key to moving from static thinking within the principle of cognitive consistency, to a process oriented perspective. I had argued that critical life events—unlike the inconsistencies normally produced in a laboratory setting—generally need a relatively elaborate rearranging of one's worldview in order to reestablish consistency. In this process, cognitive changes which lead to consistency in one part of the worldview may produce inconsistencies in another part of the worldview. The consequences of having made certain attributions illustrate this point. I argue that attributions are made in such a way that they are consistent with the information available in a certain situation. Accordingly, the original tension due to the inconsistency between the event and a certain cause-effect hypothesis is reduced. But at the same time the new attribution may be inconsistent with another part of the person's worldview. This rationale implies that it is a *process* of reestablishing cognitive consistency rather than a one-shot incident.

To illustrate, let us assume that a student fails an exam quite unexpectedly. Similarly, let us assume that the student is aware of having put a tremendous amount of effort into preparing for the exam, and that all the other students not only passed the exam, but even describe it as not very difficult. We argue that part of the tension in this situation stems from the inconsistency between this event and the student's cause-effect hypotheses (such as "I worked hard and therefore should have passed the exam"). Accordingly, the student searches for the reasons why he or she failed this exam. Let us assume that the outcome of this attribution process is an internal stable attribution ("My abilities in this area are low"). This attribution reduces the tension that triggered the attribution process. But at the same time, this attribution might lead to the rise of a new inconsistency, for example, between this attribution and certain aspects of the self.

This example points to a crucial feature of the integrated hypotheses of cognitive consistency and attribution: the dynamic character of the integrative model. By explicitly considering attributions, it becomes clear that each new cognition introduced into a situation in order to reduce an inconsistency, can be the source of inconsistency between this cognition and another part of the person's worldview. Instead of the static conception of the original principle of cognitive consistency which aimed only at explaining reactions between the occurrence of an inconsistent event and the point at which consistency is reestablished, this integrative model points to the dynamic character of the process.

To further clarify this process, let us consider two aspects of the attributions being made. The first aspect concerns the relation that a certain attribution has with a person's worldview. It is essential to understand with *how many* parts of the person's worldview a certain attribution is connected. Here we consider, for example, the difference between internal and external attributions, or between general and specific attributions, or between chronic and acute attributions. The second aspect of interest here is to inquire, with which point in time a resulting attribution is connected. Here we introduce the distinction between *post hoc* and *a priori attributions*.

In order to predict the amount of tension that a given attribution arouses, one must know how many cognitions of a person's worldview are relatively consistent and inconsistent with this new attribution. Direct measurements are difficult, but there are ways to indirectly estimate their relative magnitude. This indirect approach is based on the assumption that tension caused by a new attribution of a critical life event will be higher if the new attribution introduces the self as a cause into the situation rather than an external cause; if it is general rather than specific; and if it is chronic rather than acute. Let us examine these assumptions.

In his initial work on attribution Heider (1958) emphasized the difference between internal and external attributions. This differentiation is important for inferring the amount of tension in a situation. An internal attribution connects an event with that part of the person's worldview that represents the self. Clearly, the self is an extraordinarily important part of the person's worldview. It seems safe to assume that it normally takes up a larger portion of the person's cognitive representations than any other single cause. It is—by comparison with all other aspects of the person's worldview—more differentiated and more highly interconnected with other parts of the worldview (Markus & Wurf 1987). Accordingly, an internal attribution is likely to connect an event with more cognitions than an external attribution. An internal attribution of a critical life event will connect this event with the self, thus leading to the rise of more tension than will an external attribution.

Common sense explains why a general attribution of a critical life event will lead to more tension than a specific attribution, and why a chronic attribution will lead to more tension than an acute attribution. I could go on listing other attributional dimensions that might provide us with an idea of how many aspects of a person's worldview will be connected with a certain event once a certain attribution is made. What is crucial is that it is not the content itself, but the psychological process elicited by a given attribution, which influences the amount of tension triggered by an attribution.

Our next question concerns with *which* point in time an attribution is connected. Attributions can be concerned with the past. An event occurs and the person attributes it to a cause in the past ("I have skin cancer, because I used to lie in the sun a great deal"). This kind of attribution will be referred to as a *post hoc attribution*. An attribution can also link an event to the future ("I have cancer, and I am going to die from it"). These attributions will be referred to as *a priori attributions*.

This distinction is significant, for the two types of attribution predict quite different things. Post hoc attributions are relevant for predicting the *amount* of tension in a specific situation, while a priori attributions are important for predicting the *kind* of reaction used to reduce tension.

To illustrate, let us assume that Person A and Person B lose their jobs. This event is inconsistent with, among other things, their cause-effect hypotheses about what causes unemployment. The specific tension that arises due to the inconsistency between this event and the cause-effect hypothesis about unemployment will tend to be reduced in an attribution process. In this process, Person A may make an internal post hoc attribution ("I did not work hard enough lately, which is why I got fired"), while Person B makes an external post hoc attribution ("The automobile industry has been declining, so they have to let people go."). These two attributions are new cognitions in this situation and can lead to new inconsistencies between the event of losing a job and other aspects of the person's worldview. Using the sum rule together with the consideration that internal attributions are connected with more aspects of the person's worldview than external attributions, it follows that Person A should experience more tension than Person B in this situation because of the different post hoc attributions they made.

The importance of a priori attributions will be discussed in the following section in connection with considerations about the kind of reactions used to reduce tension due to inconsistency.

7.2.2.3 Predicting the General Reactions Used to Reestablish Consistency

Our analysis of theories of cognitive consistency led to the conclusion that the general reaction used to reduce tension after an inconsistency occurred can be predicted by the principle of least effort (Rosenberg & Abelson 1960). This principle states that a person will reduce tension with that reaction that demands the least amount of effort in this situation.

It is difficult to relate this abstract concept of least effort to concrete situations. How can we determine how a person might assess the relative amount of effort that given reactions might take? Integrating the two sets of hypotheses contributes to solving this question. Specifically, a priori attributions play an important role here.

A priori attributions are cause-event statements that reach into the future. They have clear implications for the reactions and outcomes relating to this event. For example, if a person assumes that an event has constant causes and cannot be changed in the future, then this implies that the reactions aimed at directly changing this event (tension-reduction reactions) will demand a tremendous amount of effort; accordingly, a tension-avoidance reaction is much more likely to occur than a tension-reduction reaction. In contrast, a person making a variable, a priori attribution would believe that the event *can* be changed and that the efforts to do so are relatively small, which enhances the likelihood that the person will engage in direct efforts to reduce the tension.

Accordingly, I argue that the a priori attributions a person makes about an event provide the link to estimates about how much effort this person thinks necessary for reducing the tension directly, or for avoiding the tension. Thus, integrating attributional considerations into the generalized principle of cognitive consistency helps solve the problem of bridging the gap between the abstract concept of least effort and concrete situations with inconsistencies. Considering a priori attributions helps us to predict which general reaction—a tension-reduction or a tension-avoidance reaction—will be used to reduce the tension.

7.2.2.4 Predicting the Specific Reactions Used to Reestablish Consistency

Attributions can help us understand which specific reaction will be used to reduce tension due to an inconsistency. I argue that the choice of a specific reaction depends on the cognitive availability of given possibilities. Cognitive availability is a function of (a) the person's earlier experiences, and/or (b) the objective availability of the means to carry out specific reactions. Attributions can help us understand which earlier experiences are cognitively available. And they can also point to aspects of the objective situation that are salient.

Again, attributions contribute to overcoming the problem of applying an abstract concept—in this case, cognitive availability—to concrete situations. Table 7.2 provides an overview of the meta-analyses of these two sets of hypotheses and the integrated theory.

7.2.2.5 Long-term Consequences

One theoretical problem pointed out in our meta-analysis of theories of cognitive consistency, was the fact that these theories do not account for long-term consequences. Having introduced tension-avoidance reactions as one way to reduce tension due to inconsistency, the long-term consequences can no longer be ignored. For once a tension-avoidance reaction has been made, subsequent events may reintroduce the avoided topic, leading to a recurrence of that tension. Furthermore, the issue of the long-term consequences is especially important when the principle of cognitive consistency is applied to situations with events that demand major reconstructions of the

Table 7.2
Meta-analyses of the Two Sets of Hypotheses and the Integrated Theory: An Overview

	A + Principle of Cognitive Consistency	B = Attribution Process	C Generalized Principle of Cognitive Consistency
Starting conditions	A event is incon- sistent with part of worldview that is in focus of attention	specific case of A: event is incon- sistent with one specific part of worldview (= cause-effect hy- pothesis)	A including B
Amount of tension	sum rule: tension = proportion of inconsistent to consistent relations of event and worldview	specific case of sum rule: tension= proportion of inconsistent and consistent re- lations between attribution and worldview; post hoc attributions	sum rule
Types of reactions to reestablish consistency	tension avoi- dance reactions; tension reduc- tion reactions	post hoc attributions; a priori attributions	A including B
Predicting reactions: general	principle of least effort	specific case of A: least effort is in- ferred from a priori attributions	A including B
specific	---	attributions con- tribute to under- stand what is cog- nitively available	cognitive availability
long term consequences	consistency reestablished	cognitive affective behavioral	dynamic pro- cess; life philosophy (beliefs, goals, pos- sible selves, values)

person's worldview for reducing the inconsistency. These reconstructions can have a clear impact on later reactions, because they are the basis for consistent thinking and actions.

Attribution research deals with the consequences of making given attributions. Attributional hypotheses contribute to explaining emotional, cognitive, and behavioral consequences by using the principle of cognitive consistency. A given attribution is made and reactions that are consistent with it are predicted to occur.

This idea is important in how the generalized principle of cognitive consistency helps predict long-term outcomes. Two aspects are involved. First, research on the consequences of certain attributions either implicitly (see Schachter 1964; Weiner 1985b) or explicitly (see Kruglanski & Klar 1987) assumes that human reactions are guided by the principle of cognitive consistency. This means that the psychological process itself is guided by this principle. Second, the content of this process and the kind of specific consequences that result for a certain person after encountering an inconsistent event can be predicted if the person's worldview is known. Here the relevance of a person's life philosophy—that is, the person's beliefs about how the world functions, his or her goals and values—becomes evident. I postulate that the long-term consequences of having encountered an inconsistent event will be those that are consistent with the person's worldview. This issue will be elaborated in Chapter 11.

7.3 The Generalized Principle of Cognitive Consistency: Summary—Evaluation—Implications

7.3.1 Summary

Let us summarize our argument thus far. In Chapter 6 our analysis of cognitive consistency theories led to a set of hypotheses capturing the essential aspects of this principle. These hypotheses provide an answer to the question of when tension due to a cognitive inconsistency arises; they suggest the sum rule for predicting the amount of tension arising and offer several hypotheses for predicting the kinds of reactions that are likely to be used to reduce the tension and reestablish cognitive consistency.

The usefulness of these hypotheses for analyzing reactions to critical life events was then investigated. Critical life events are defined as events which are inconsistent with that part of a person's worldview on which the person's attention is focused. It is argued that the *amount of tension* caused by encountering a critical life event equals the sum of the single inconsistencies between the critical life event and the single aspects of the person's worldview, relative to all the consistent relationships on which the person's attention is focused.

The *general* kind of reaction to reduce this tension is either a reaction to reduce the tension directly or a reaction that aims at avoiding the tension, and thus, at indirectly reducing it in this situation. I postulate that the tension will be reduced with that general reaction that demands the least effort. Which *specific* (tension-reduction or tension-avoidance) reaction will be used depends on the cognitive availability of various possibilities; the cognitive availability of various alternative reactions is (a) a function of prior experiences with such reactions, and (b) a function of the objective availability of stimuli related to certain reactions. *Long-term consequences* are not considered by the principle of cognitive consistency.

In using the principle of cognitive consistency to explain reactions to critical life events, two major problems arose. The first is how the abstract general concepts used in the theoretical argument (such as the sum rule, the principle of least effort, and the amount of cognitive availability) could be applied to concrete instances. The second problem concerns whether the principle of cognitive consistency is actually able to capture the complex phenomena that occur after a critical life event. It seems unlikely that a one-shot reaction could reestablish cognitive consistency in such a situation. Furthermore, even if such a process reestablishes cognitive consistency, we must consider the long-term consequences of these experiences. Again, the original principle of cognitive consistency alone does not deal with this issue. But by integrating hypotheses about the attribution process with the principle of cognitive consistency, both of these problems can be solved.

Our attempt to integrate these two major sets of hypotheses started with a meta-analysis of the attributional hypotheses of five key authors. This analysis suggested that attributions are made when an event occurs that is inconsistent with one specific part of a person's worldview, namely with cause-effect hypotheses related to this event. Starting from this assumption, we integrated attributional hypotheses with cognitive consistency hypotheses. This integrative model, the generalized principle of cognitive consistency, has three essential points.

The first is that the determinants of the rise of tension are now elaborated to include a previously neglected case: when tension is due to inconsistency between an event and one specific part of the person's worldview—a cause-effect hypothesis related to this event. The tension arising here is reduced by an attribution process in which one adopts a new cause-effect hypothesis.

The second point concerns the domain of the generalized principle of cognitive consistency. The original principle of cognitive consistency has explained information processing between the moment at which an inconsistent event occurs and the moment in which the tension due to this inconsistency is reduced and consistency is reestablished. The generalized principle of cognitive consistency has a more general domain. Unlike the static original principle of cognitive consistency, it emphasizes the *process*, the dynamic character of our reactions. If an inconsistency is reduced, one's subsequent reactions will be influenced by it. In more general terms, every change in one's worldview made to reestablish consistency at time point 1 is an antecedent that may lead to an inconsistency at time point 2.

A third aspect of this theory focuses on explaining the long-term consequences of having encountered an inconsistent event. Various authors in attribution research have investigated the consequences of attributions. They implicitly assume that the consequences are consistent with the attributions made. This can be generalized by postulating that those parts of our worldview which are related to certain reactions are relevant for understanding which reactions are made. Including cognitions related to the future such as goals, possible selves, expectations, and hopes as essential parts of the person's worldview also stresses the significance of processes over time.

Furthermore, if a person's worldview is reorganized as a consequence of having reduced tension caused by an inconsistent event, then subsequent reactions are a function of this new worldview and future reactions are influenced by this fact.

7.3.2 Evaluation

Two aspects of the generalized principle of cognitive consistency are particularly useful in explaining reactions to inconsistent events. First, inconsistent events occurring in the real world tend to cause a chain reaction, rather than just a one-shot reaction. The generalized principle of cognitive consistency brings this fact to light. It is concerned with the process unfolding in these situations. Second, although the original principle of cognitive consistency was not concerned with explaining the long-term consequences to inconsistent events, the generalized principle of cognitive consistency contributes to this issue.

These two points will be developed more fully when the implications of the generalized principle of cognitive consistency for predicting reactions to critical life events are discussed in Chapter 8. Before doing so, let us consider the significance of using theoretical comparisons in order to gain a clearer understanding of human reactions, and its implications for both theoretical and applied research in social psychology.

We developed the generalized principle of cognitive consistency by first conducting meta-analyses of the primary research on the principle of cognitive consistency and the attribution process. The initial step was to decide which primary contributions to the principle of cognitive consistency or the attribution process should be included in the analysis. We next searched for criteria—a set of questions—that would allow us to evaluate the contribution of each theory to explaining the phenomenon of interest. Each theory was then evaluated on how well it responded to this set of questions. The goal was to identify the basic hypotheses needed to analyze the phenomena of interest. Integrating these two sets of resulting hypotheses produced a more general theory.

Theoretical analyses such as these facilitate the cumulative growth of knowledge. They also help cope with the flood of publications that appears annually. Hundreds of articles are published each year in social psychology. How do social psychologists react to this situation? Apart from heroic efforts to read faster, I see three general reactions. The first is to devalue certain types of research or certain research strategies. The obvious problem is that this may hinder the recognition of significant research. A second reaction is to concentrate on one narrow aspect of research and shut out everything which is not closely tied to this issue. It is clear that specialization is essential in conducting research. But narrowly specialized studies that are not connected with general theoretical ideas are unlikely to contribute to the cumulative growth of an integrated body of knowledge. A third reaction is to approach this flood of publications with a general perspective, a "Menschenbild," which can be used as a structure to evaluate and make sense of specific findings. The generalized principle of cognitive consistency represents an attempt to develop such a perspective.

This approach has three advantages. First, only by using such a general theory is it possible to grasp a great number of specific findings and relate them to each other. Second, such a general theory also points to aspects of the problem not studied so far, but which need to be studied in the future. Third, only such a general theory can do justice to the complexity of reality. And only if we have sufficiently complex theories can we hope to arrive at theoretically founded applied social psychological research that will contribute to solving real world problems.

7.3.3 General Implications

The generalized principle of cognitive consistency has implications for basic as well as for applied psychological research.

7.3.3.1 Implications for Basic Research

In this monograph the generalized principle of cognitive consistency is used to explain reactions to critical life events. But this is not the only topic to which this generalized principle could be applied. It is relevant and useful when studying other questions as well.

Let us give two examples. The first is research on the importance of conceptions about the self for understanding academic achievement. We are going to consider how one aspect of the self, namely a person's possible selves, can be used in connection with the generalized principle of cognitive consistency to explain academic achievement (compare Markus & Nurius 1986; Inglehart, Markus & Brown 1989).

A possible self is an image, a concept or a sense of what the person might be in the future. It can be positive—an image of oneself winning the Nobel Prize—as well as negative—oneself dying of cancer. Possible selves are part of a person's worldview and they influence a person's reactions by providing the person with a goal of what the person wants to reach or wants to avoid. I argue that a person's reactions are planned in such a way that they are consistent with this goal. This basic assumption was tested in a longitudinal study of academic achievement related to certain possible selves.

This study examined whether the academic achievement of students was influenced by the degree to which they were focused on the specific possible self of becoming a medical doctor. In a longitudinal study of students in an integrated A.B.—M.D. program, the subjects responded to a questionnaire shortly before entering this program. On the basis of how many other fields besides medicine they had considered in the months before entering medical school, they were categorized as being either clearly focused on one possible self ("medicine is the only field considered"; N = 61), not so clearly focused ("one other field besides medicine was considered"; N = 31) or as unfocused ("two or more other fields were considered"; N = 18). We hypothesized that those students who were clearly focused on becoming a medical doctor would subsequently show higher achievement levels than those students who were not so clearly focused, and that the achievement of the students in the category "unfocused possible self" would be lowest. The measures of academic achievement were the students' total scores in the National Board of Medical Examination Part I (NBME-I), the total scores in the National Board of Medical Examination Part II (NBME-II), the grade point average (GPA) after the sixth year of the program, and a grade point average value for the grades up to the fifth year of the program. This last indicator of achievement ranged from 1 (GPA of 4.0–3.9) to 8 (GPA of 1.8 or less). We argued that while the achievement related actions in medical school of those students with a sharply focused possible self would be clearly consistent with this one possible self of becoming an M.D., the reactions of the other two groups would only be partly consistent with their possible selves, because they were interested in other possible selves besides becoming an M.D.

Our results support this hypothesis (Figure 7.1). Despite the fact that the three groups of students had similar ability levels when entering the program as measured by standard tests carried out on entry to the program, the medical students in the category "one professional possible self" achieved significantly better scores on the nationwide given and standardized NBME-I and NBME-II. They also had significantly higher GPAs after their fifth and sixth years of medical study than those students in the category "two professional possible selves." And these students had higher achievement levels than those in the category "three or more professional possible selves" (Manova result: $F(8/208) = 2.68$; $p = .008$).

This research used the generalized principle of cognitive consistency to

Figure 7.1
Average Academic Achievement Under Various Levels of the Independent
Variable "Degree of Focusing on One Possible Self"

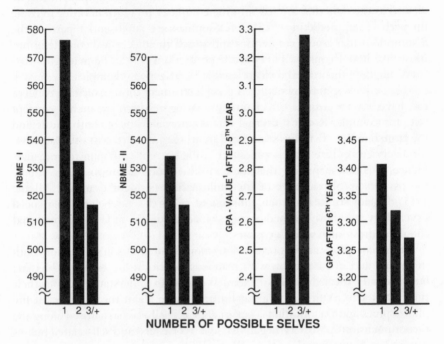

NUMBER OF POSSIBLE SELVES

[1]The GPA - values ranged from 1 (= GPA of 4.00 - 3.90) to 8 (= GPA of 1.80 and less)

predict academic achievement three to six years after a relevant component
of the self was measured. The findings point to the significance of the concept
of possible selves; they also illustrate that the generalized principle of cognitive consistency is useful in analyzing other areas besides reactions to critical
life events.

The second example is research by Inglehart, Brown, and Moore (1988)
which again analyzes reactions of medical students over a long period of time,
in this case a ten-year period. When entering the medical school program,
eighty-seven students were asked which medical specialty they would consider entering. Ten years later, when these students were practicing medicine, they responded to questions about the specialty they had actually
chosen, the number of hours they worked per week, and the balance between
family and work life they had achieved. We hypothesized that those who
were practicing in the medical specialty they originally intended to enter
(those with a consistent choice) would be working longer hours, and place
relatively heavier emphasis on work (as compared with their family) than the
students who were in the "inconsistent choice" condition. Furthermore, al-

Figure 7.2
Degree of Professional Involvement of Persons with Consistent and Inconsistent
Professional Choices

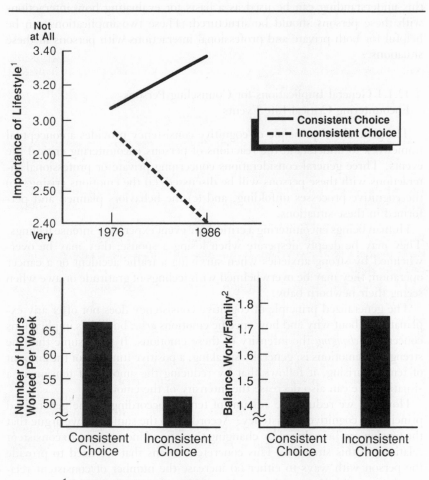

[1] 1 = "Very Much" to 5 = "None"
[2] Balance of Work and Family Life in 1986 (1 = "Work" to 3 = "Family")

though in 1976 these two groups of students did not differ in how important
lifestyle is for them, we expected that they *would* differ in their ratings ten
years later. We reasoned, according to the generalized principle of cognitive
consistency, that a consistent choice leads to reactions in which people are
more likely to spend time in this professional domain, while inconsistency
would be likelier to lead to withdrawal reactions away from the professional
domain. As can be seen in Figure 7.2, the results support our hypotheses.
Medical doctors who practiced in the specialty choice they originally con-

sidered, worked longer hours per week (66 hours versus 52 hours; $F[1,80]=14.13$; $p=.000$), spent less time with their families ($F[1,86]=5.4$; $p=.02$), and thought that lifestyle was not as important ($F[1,83]=5.39$; $p=.002$) as those medical doctors who worked in specialty choices that they originally thought they were unlikely to enter.

These two examples illustrate the applicability of the generalized principle of cognitive consistency to areas beyond critical life events. They are especially impressive because in both cases predictions were made that proved accurate over long periods of time.

7.3.3.2 Implications for Applied Social Psychology

When conducting applied social psychological research two issues are important. First, we need theories that do justice to the complexity of real life. Second, we need to understand the techniques that can be used to bridge the gap between theoretical knowledge and the concrete situation. For example, if we want to give therapy to a depressed person, we need to have a theory that explains the causes for this depression and the changes that should be achieved in the patient in order to reduce depressive symptoms. We also need to identify the concrete techniques by which these changes can be brought about.

The generalized principle of cognitive consistency is a general theory. As such it is better equipped to do justice to the complexity of these concrete issues than a narrow theory. This point is elaborated in the last chapter of this book in connection with a concrete issue, namely the prevention and counseling techniques for persons who show self-destructive withdrawal reactions such as abusing drugs or alcohol or committing suicide. The generalized principle of cognitive consistency helps clarify the psychological processes connected with these self-destructive reactions. It can also be used to analyze the psychological processes underlying different treatment approaches for these problems. Thus, the generalized principle of cognitive consistency may provide insight in applied issues connected with these problems.

Chapter 8

The Generalized Principle of Cognitive Consistency and Reactions to Critical Life Events: Theoretical Considerations, Empirical Evidence, and Preliminary Evaluation

In applying the original principle of cognitive consistency to explain reactions to critical life events, two problems emerged. First, how can we bridge the gap between theoretical reasoning and specific situations? Second, how can we predict the process of reestablishing consistency over time or explain the long-term consequences of having experienced a critical life event?

These shortcomings of the original theory can be overcome by generalizing it. The major step in doing so was to integrate it with hypotheses from the attribution literature. Thus, the generalized principle of cognitive consistency was introduced and its implications were discussed.

This chapter applies this generalized principle to explaining reactions to critical life events. The first part of this chapter presents theoretical considerations concerning these reactions, together with a body of empirical evidence that supports these hypotheses. We then make a preliminary evaluation of this attempt to explain reactions to critical life events with the generalized principle of cognitive consistency.

8.1 Theoretical Considerations and Empirical Evidence

8.1.1 Defining Critical Life Events

The linkage between the generalized principle of cognitive consistency and the specific issue of explaining reactions to critical life events is implicit in our definition of critical life events as events that are inconsistent with that part of a person's worldview on which the person's attention is focused. This definition implies that (a) positive as well as negative and neutral events constitute critical life events, and (b) the importance of an event does not determine whether an event qualifies as a critical life event or not: both daily hassles and existential threats to one's existence are included.

Furthermore, the generalized principle of cognitive consistency suggests that critical life events are frequently (though not necessarily) inconsistent with a person's cause-effect hypotheses about the event. This point has clear implications concerning the amount of tension arising and the kind of reactions chosen to reduce the tension caused by a critical life event.

Let us present empirical evidence concerning the fact that critical life events can be negative as well as positive for a person. The question whether positive as well as negative or neutral inconsistent events can cause tension is of great importance in defining the domain of the generalized principle of cognitive consistency. It is also extremely interesting in trying to unravel the significance of the need for consistency in relation to other needs we might have. One of the most intriguing questions here is whether humans give higher priority to enhancing their self-esteem or to preserving cognitive consistency (compare Steele 1988). I argue that tension arises if an event is inconsistent with that part of the person's worldview that the person's attention is focused on—even if this event is positive.

At first sight it sounds counterintuitive to think of tension as something that can be caused by a pleasurable event, such as having a date with a desirable person, winning money in a sweepstake, or getting an article accepted by the top journal in one's field. The generalized principle of cognitive consistency implies that tension *does* follow the occurrence of positive inconsistent events, and that reactions will occur to reduce this tension. This hypothesis was investigated in a field experiment (Rosch/Inglehart, Dickenberger, Irle & Moentmann 1981; Rosch/Inglehart & Schmidt 1981) as well as in two laboratory experiments (Rosch/Inglehart & Rohrlach 1981; Inglehart & Kondoff, in prep.).

In 1979, the first direct election to the European Parliament took place in the nine countries of the European Community. In the months before this election, Rosch/Inglehart, Dickenberger, Irle, and Moentmann (1981) conducted a field experiment as part of a survey of 383 persons in Mannheim, West Germany. All of these persons were eligible to vote in this election. Half of the subject (Ss) were active party members, while the other half did not belong to any part. All Ss were interviewed in their homes, and answered questions about politics in general, as well as about the European Community and the upcoming election.

Each interview had three parts. The first included questions about which party the respondents expected to win. In the second part, the participants read an essay containing information about the election plus a prediction of a well-known survey institute about the election outcome. The third part of the interview consisted of another set of questions that included the dependent variable of interest here: the Ss' evaluation of the validity of the survey institute's prediction. Answers were given on a rating scale from 1 (= not at all valid) to 10 (= very valid). We predicted that those persons whose prediction was consistent with the survey institute's prediction would evaluate the validity of the latter as higher than those whose prediction differed from the one received during the interviews—regardless of whether the discrepancy was positive (the institute predicted their preferred party would win, though they themselves had predicted that it would lose) or negative (their party was predicted to lose, though they had predicted that it would win).

By comparing the respondents' predictions about the election outcome in the first section of the interview plus their party preference, with the survey institute's predictions of the election outcome, the respondents were categorized into those who either received (1) consistent information, or (2) positively discrepant information, or (3) negatively discrepant information. The results supported our prediction. The respondents who had received consistent information rated the validity of the presented prognosis as significantly higher (mean = 6.49) than the respondents who had received positively discrepant (mean = 4.42) or negatively discrepant (mean = 3.22) information $(F (2,377) = 34.08; p = .000)$ (see Rosch/Inglehart & Schmidt 1981, p. 252).

These findings were replicated in an experiment conducted by Inglehart and Rohrlach (1981) at the University of Mannheim among ninety-six male high school students who were either fans of one specific soccer club (FC Kaiserslautern) or of other clubs. The experiment took place on a Saturday afternoon when FC Kaiserslautern played a crucial game away from home. Before the game started, all Ss answered questions about soccer and their expectations for this game. During the first 45 minutes of the game, the Ss saw entertaining movies, while the experimenters assigned half of the subjects to conditions of negatively discrepant information (the game result at half time favored the team they did not like, to a degree that they had not expected), positively discrepant information (the result favored their preferred team to a degree that they had not expected), and consistent information (the result was in the range of results they had expected). In the break, these three groups of subjects were taken to different rooms and received the manipulated half time results. They then filled out a questionnaire, were debriefed, and allowed to leave. The rest of the subjects watched another forty-five minutes of movies. At the end of the official play time, they were led into different rooms, and received either positively discrepant, negatively discrepant, or consistent information about the end result of the game. After they had filled out a questionnaire, they were debriefed, and allowed to leave.

The results of this experiment again support the hypothesis that negatively as well as positively discrepant information leads to tension that has to be reduced. We found that both positively *and* negatively discrepant information presented in the break resulted in a significant change of expectations for the end result of the game when compared with the expectations of the control group. More important than this finding is the fact that the probability with which the fans with inconsistent information believed in their own predictions was significantly lower than the probability in the condition with consistent information (positively discrepant information: 3.54; negatively discrepant information: 3.64; consistent information: 4.16; scale ranged from 1 = not at all to 5 = very probable; p = .006). Furthermore, both groups of subjects devalued their own prediction significantly (means: positively discrepant = 2.04; negatively discrepant = 1.75) when compared with the ratings of the group which had received consistent information (mean: 4.26 on a scale from 1 = not at all accurate to 5 = very accurate).

These findings were interpreted as supporting the hypothesis that positively as well as negatively discrepant information leads to the rise of tension that must be reduced. One way to reduce this tension is to devalue the discrepant information. The finding in the European Parliament Election Study that persons with a positively discrepant prediction would devalue this information is clearly counterintuitive to what common sense would let us expect. Common sense would suggest that *positively* discrepant information suits the person's preferences so well that it would be immediately accepted and valued positively. This is clearly not the case. Furthermore, when information is given that is not a prediction of a certain outcome but a clear description of an event—as was the case in the soccer fans experiment—the persons who received negatively or positively inconsistent information adjust their own expectations about future events to this information, devalue their own earlier prognosis and feel uncertain about the future. Again one might expect that receiving *positively* discrepant information might lead to a rise in the certainty of the outcome in this situation, but again the opposite is the case—which supports our basic assumption about the consequences of receiving positively discrepant information.

It is important to realize that in situations with positive critical life events, such as receiving a marriage proposal from the person we love or receiving a big research grant, tension arises that influences one's subsequent reactions.

This hypothesis was further tested in a laboratory experiment (Inglehart & Kondoff, in prep.). In this study we hypothesized that Ss who experience either a positive inconsistent event or a negative inconsistent event will perform better (be quicker and make less mistakes) in an undemanding manual task than Ss who experience a consistent event. The rationale underlying this hypothesis was the reasoning that a higher state of arousal facilitates the performance of dominant responses (compare Rosch/Inglehart 1985c).

The subjects in this experiment were undergraduates at the University of Michigan who were randomly assigned to one of three experimental conditions. In the first condition, the experimental procedures unfolded in a way that was consistent with the Ss expectations. The Ss answered a short general questionnaire and were then told to practice a certain sorting task. This task was described as an exercise for the things they would have to do in the second session of this experiment a week later. It consisted of sorting fifty index cards according to three colors and to a three digit number-letter combination written on each card. In the second condition the subjects were told that they did not need to participate in this experiment, but that they would receive full credit for coming ("positive inconsistent" condition). They were asked to fill out the short questionnaire as a legitimization for giving them the credit and to do the card sorting as an exercise for the second session a week later. The third group of subjects were told that the experiment had been delayed for about forty-five minutes and that they would have to wait. While they were waiting for the actual experiment to begin, they could fill out the short questionnaire and should do the sorting exercise for the next session a week later ("negative inconsistent" condition). All subjects were debriefed after the card sorting task and allowed to leave. The time needed to sort the cards plus the numbers of mistakes made in sorting were the dependent variables.

We predicted that the subjects in the positive inconsistent and negative inconsistent condition would sort the cards quicker and would make fewer mistakes than the subjects in the consistent condition. The results support our reasoning. While the means of the two inconsistent groups were not significantly different from each other, they did differ significantly from the means of the subjects in the consistent condition. The Ss in the inconsistent conditions sorted the cards quicker (means: 280 versus 309 seconds; F [1/114] = 3.00; p = .086) and made fewer mistakes (means: 0.62 versus 1.59 mistakes; F[1/114] = 23.9; p = .03) than the subjects in the control condition.

In this case, common sense might suggest that the subjects in the negative inconsistent condition would be displeased about having to wait forty-five minutes and that they would be less motivated to perform well. But again we find that a negative as well as a positive inconsistent event result in the same outcome when compared with the outcome in a situation with consistent information.

On the whole, these results support the assumption that positive as well as negative inconsistent events can be critical life events that produce tension. A study by Brown and McGill (1989) supports our reasoning from yet another angle. These authors looked at the "cost of good fortune." These authors showed that desirable life events lead to an increase in health-related problems for persons with low self-esteem. The fact that persons with a high self-esteem actually had better health after desirable life events occurred, points to the complexity of the subject. This finding indicates that we need to consider the amount of tension arising in a situation when a positive and a negative event occur. For persons with a positive self-image, positive events are likely to be consistent with their self-image, while for persons with a relatively negative self-image, such positive events may be inconsistent with their self-image. This tension due to inconsistencies between the self and the new event is added to the tension produced between this event and the rest of the person's worldview. Consequently, persons with a negative self-image would experience more tension when a desirable life event occurs than persons with a positive self image.

8.1.2 Predicting the Amount of Tension

An adequate theory of reactions to critical life events should be able to predict the amount of tension that arises in a situation with a critical life event. According to the generalized principle of cognitive consistency, the amount of tension following the occurrence of an inconsistent event reflects the sum of the single inconsistencies between this event and the relevant part of the person's worldview, and is inversely related to the sum of salient consistencies. In the critical evaluation of this general hypothesis we pointed out the problem of bridging the gap between this abstract hypothesis and applying it in concrete instances. I suggest three ways to solve this problem.

A first suggestion was made in discussing the role attributions play in situations with inconsistent events. We argued that a person's post hoc attributions about inconsistent events provide us with information about those parts of a person's worldview that are salient in these situations. Specifically, we postulated that internal post hoc attributions connect an event with more cognitions than external post hoc attributions, because they establish a relationship between this event and the self, which is a highly differentiated part of the person's worldview. Furthermore, general post hoc attributions relate the event to more cognitions than specific post hoc attributions, and chronic post hoc attributions lead to more cognitive connections than acute post hoc attributions.

Let us emphasize that it is not the content of attributions—that is whether they are internal, general, or chronic—but their function in relation to the person's worldview that allows us to predict how much tension arises. If a person experiences an unexpected event which is attributed internally, but is consistent with the aspects of the self to which this attribution links this event, no more tension can be expected than with an external attribution. Understanding the psychological process involved when making certain post hoc attributions is crucial for applying the sum rule correctly.

A second way to bridge the gap between abstract concepts and the concrete instances to which they are applied concerns ways to get a clearer understanding of the contents and structure of a person's worldview. Linville's work on self-complexity (Linville 1985, 1987a, 1987b) is one example of an attempt to better understand the structure of a specific part of the person's worldview.

A first crude approach to better understanding the person's worldview is to simply ask how important that part of one's worldview is, with which an event is inconsistent. We assume that the more important a given part of the person's worldview is, the more cognitions relating to it will there be. This implies that if an event is inconsistent with an important part of a person's worldview, more inconsistencies are likely to occur than if an event is inconsistent with an unimportant part of the person's worldview.

The third consideration leads away from attempts to measure the aspects of the person's worldview that are salient in these situations and points to the significance of understanding the input, namely the event side, better. When thinking about this problem of crossing the gap between the abstract concepts and concrete situations it becomes evident that in real life situations there is usually not just one single inconsistent event, but instead it is likely that a substantial cluster of inconsistent events occur. Consider a person who loses a spouse. This event "death of the spouse" can have implications for many different aspects of the surviving spouse's life. Thus, inconsistencies can arise concerning the surviving spouse's financial security, social relations, or daily routines. This suggests that we generalize the sum rule by assuming that the tension in a situation increases if the number of inconsistent events increases.

The following section presents the results of empirical research conducted in connection with these three considerations.

8.1.2.1 The Role of Post Hoc Attributions

The significance of attributions in reactions to critical life events has been extensively investigated (see Herrmann 1988, for an overview). But this research is largely descriptive and outcome oriented. This means that most research focuses on the question of which attributions (for example internal or external attributions) lead to the best adaptational outcomes in situations with critical life events such as rape, cancer, or loss of a loved one. This lack of attention to the underlying psychological processes is a clear handicap in explaining contradictory findings. Taylor (1983) for example reports that in some studies, internal attributions after rape were conducive to a good coping reaction, while in other studies external attributions led to better coping. As long as we do not understand the underlying process in such situations we cannot make sense of these contradictory findings.

By reinterpreting attributional activity as one specific case of consistency-guided information processing, we suggest a way to understand the underlying process. Specifically, it seems useful to differentiate between post hoc and a priori attributions in connection with reactions to critical life events.

Post hoc attributions are attributions of events to causes located in the past. "I lost my job, because the car industry is not doing well these days"; "I won the lottery, because I bought the ticket on Friday, the 13th"; "I was raped because I went alone to the movies after it was dark." These are just a few examples of post hoc attributions. In each case, the post hoc attribution ties the event to a part of the person's worldview. If the event is inconsistent with this part of the person's worldview, the sum of single inconsistencies will increase. Depending on the kinds of post hoc attributions a person makes,

the amount of tension following the occurrence of one and the same event
can vary quite dramatically.

In the following research we will test the hypotheses that if a negative
inconsistent event is post hoc attributed (a) internally or (b) generally, more
tension will arise than if this same event is post hoc attributed externally or
specifically. Data from a field study of reactions of Polish immigrants to West
Germany (see Rosch/Inglehart 1981, 1983, 1985a; Inglehart 1987, 1988;
Rosch/Inglehart & Irle 1983) as well as from two laboratory experiments
(Rosch/Inglehart 1985b; Inglehart 1987, under review) were used to test these
hypotheses.

The field study was conducted from December 1979 to June 1981, in
Mannheim, West Germany. In December 1979, a first group of immigrants
(N = 85) that had arrived during the previous six months was interviewed
for the first time, and followed up in three further interviews in June 1980,
December 1980, and June 1981. In order to maintain a larger sample size,
a second group of newly arrived immigrants (N = 110) was first interviewed
in June 1980, and followed up in two more interviews in December 1980
and June 1981.

Of the 195 participants, ninety-six were male and ninety-nine were female;
they ranged in age from eighteen to seventy-three years. They were first
informed about the study in a letter (both in Polish and in German). During
the week following the arrival of this letter, bilingual interviewers from the
University of Mannheim visited the immigrants and asked them to participate, being assured that the answers would be treated anonymously.

The interviews were conducted in the participants' homes, in either Polish
or German, according to the subjects' preferences.

The dependent variable "amount of tension arising" was measured in a
Likert scale with fourteen statements about bodily symptoms such as "I am
rather nervous, excited and upset," "I suffer from insomnia," or "Sometimes
my heart beats heavily." The interviews indicated on 5-point scales ranging
from 1 (= not at all) to 5 (= very much) how much they agreed with each
statement. The exact wording of these statements is provided in Table 8.1.

The degree to which the participants used internal versus external post
hoc attributions was measured by asking how much the subjects thought
that problems in six different areas of life (job, church/religion, contacts with
Germans, contacts with official agencies, family, supply with household
goods) were either internally or externally caused. The answers were given
on 5-point rating scales ranging from 1 (caused mostly by you) to 5 (completely due to external causes).

We hypothesized that the more a person attributes difficulties post hoc
internally, the more bodily symptoms will occur. This hypothesis was tested
using structural equations with latent variables (LISREL VI; Joereskog &
Soerbom 1984; see model 1 in Figure 8.1). The respondents' internal/external
attributions in six different areas of life were used as indicators of the latent

Table 8.1
Indicators of the Amount of Reported Illness Symptoms

Statements:

Sometimes I feel that I am suffering from an undetected illness.

I believe that I am more susceptible and sensitive to illnesses than most people I know.

In the last years I was mostly healthy.

My health is not optimal.

I am physically as healthy as most people I know.

Sometimes I feel I ache all over.

I perspire often, even without strain or work.

Sometimes I am dizzy in the head.

I am rather nervous, excited and upset.

I suffer from severe headaches.

Sometimes I gasp for air, even without doing heavy work.

I suffer from insomnia.

Every now and then I tremble and shudder.

Often I feel miserable, totally bad and terrible.

Legend: The answering scale reached from 1 (do not agree at all) to 5 (agree very much).

exogenous variable "amount of internal/external post hoc attributions." The fourteen answers concerning the statements about bodily symptoms of tension were used as indicators of the endogenous latent variable "amount of tension."

In order to identify model 1, the loading of the first X indicator on the latent exogenous variable and the loading of the first Y indicator on the endogenous variable are fixed to 1. In the initial estimates, no correlated errors of the indicators were taken into account, although all indicators were measured on identical scales.

The results of the LISREL analysis of model 1 show that the variable covariances predicted by this model as a whole are significantly different from the observed covariances (d.f. = 169; chi square = 483.51; p < .001;

Figure 8.1
Model 1: The Impact of "Internal versus External" Post Hoc Attributions on
"Reported Illness Symptoms"

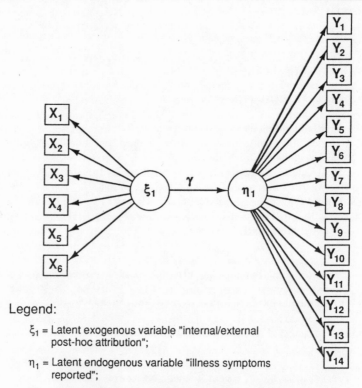

Legend:

ξ₁ = Latent exogenous variable "internal/external
       post-hoc attribution";

η₁ = Latent endogenous variable "illness symptoms
       reported";

X₁-X₆ = Indicators of the latent exogenous variable: ratings of post-hoc
         attributions for problems in six areas of life on five-point
         scales from 1 = "completely internal" to 5 = "completely external";

Y₁-Y₁₄ = Indicators of the endogenous variable: ratings of agreement
          with the fourteen statements about illness symptoms presented
          in table 7; the answers were given on five point scales
          from 1 = "do not agree at all" to 5 = "agree very much."

adjusted goodness of fit index = .866). Although model 1 does not fit the
data well, the standardized regression coefficient between the two latent
variables is in the expected direction and significant (gamma = $-.16$; d.f.
= 1; t = -3.036; p < .10). This result supports our hypothesis: the more
problems are post hoc attributed to external causes, the fewer illness symptoms are reported.

Following Bentler and Bonett's reasoning (1980), we now compare this
model 1 with a null model. This null model differs from model 1 in one
aspect: it assumes that the latent exogenous variable does not have any impact

on the latent endogenous variable (gamma = 0). All other specifications in this null model are identical with the specifications in the original model. The goodness of fit of this null model (d.f. = 170; chi square = 492.8; p = .001; adjusted goodness of fit = .0865) is significantly worse than the goodness of fit of the original model (difference in d.f. = 1; difference in chi square = 9.3; p < .001). This finding supports our theoretical argument that taking post hoc attributions into account contributes to explaining the variance in the amount of tension reported.

The lack in goodness of fit of the original model on one hand and the significant finding in regard to the theoretical model on the other hand was interpreted as indicating that the measurement model was not well specified. Therefore, the model modification indices generated by version 6 of the LISREL program were used to specify a revised model. In this revised model, correlated errors for certain indicators were taken into account. This model had a good fit (d.f. = 130; chi square = 155.39; p = .064; adjusted goodness of fit = .94) and showed a significant improvement in regard to the original model (difference in d.f. = .39; difference in chi square = 328; p < .001) (Bentler & Bonnet 1980). We interpret this finding as further support for our hypothesis.

This same hypothesis was also investigated under controlled conditions in two laboratory experiments. In the first experiment (Inglehart 1987, 1988, under review) the subjects (forty-two male and forty-five female undergraduates at the University of Mannheim, West Germany) read five different paragraphs. In each paragraph a person was described as encountering an unexpected negative event. Each of these five episodes concerned a different part of life (job, family, education, interpersonal relation, health). For example, the episode in the area of health was: "One morning, while taking a shower, Mr. M. detects a brown skin spot on his upper leg. He knows that if this spot grows it might be a first indicator of skin cancer. He observes the spot over two weeks and then decides to visit a dermatologist. This dermatologist examines the skin changes and informs Mr. M. that he must remove some material to test for cancer. He thinks it is likely that it is cancer."

The post hoc attributions were manipulated by giving the Ss information at the end of each episode about the attributions that the described person made. An example of an internal post hoc attribution is that one given in the above cases, which said: "Mr. M. immediately thinks that it is his fault that he is sick." Under the condition of an external post hoc attribution the information given was: "Mr. M. immediately thinks that cancer is an illness which is caused by environmental factors."

The subjects read each single story and afterwards indicated on an 11-point scale from 1 (= not at all) to 11 (= very much) how much they would expect the described person to be upset by the event.

As can be seen in Figure 8.2, the results are all in the predicted direction, and three of the five differences are significant. The tension predicted is

Figure 8.2
Average Degree of Predicted Tension in the Conditions "Internal" and "External
Post Hoc Attributions"

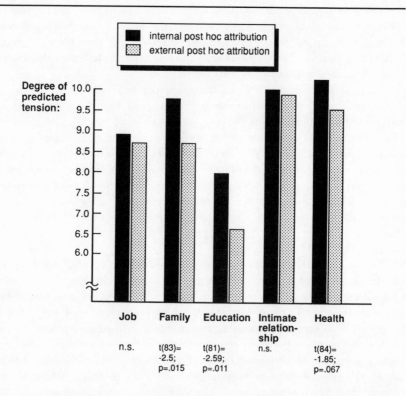

higher in the condition "internal attribution" than it is in the condition
"external attribution."

Furthermore, when the subjects were asked in the second part of this
experiment to imagine themselves in these situations, the correlation between
the Ss' degree of internal/external post hoc attributions and the amount of
resulting tension in the area of intimate relationship was in the expected
direction and significant ($r = -0.28$; $p = .002$). The correlations in the
other four areas were not significant.

This experiment was replicated with subjects from the University of Michigan (Inglehart, under review). Three changes were made from the original
study. First, in this experiment only stories in the achievement and affiliation
areas, namely stories about interpersonal relations (love and friendship) and
education/profession (job and studies) were used. The health domain was no
longer considered because this domain of life might not be of great salience
and importance for healthy undergraduates. Second, the dependent variable
"degree of tension" was now measured with four indicators ("How upset—

nervous, tense, stressed—are you?"); the answers were again given on 11-point rating scales ranging from 1 (not at all) to 11 (very much). Third, while the post hoc attributions presented in the two areas "love" and "job" were again "internal" and "external" the attributions in the areas "friendship" and "studies" were "general" and "specific post hoc attributions." This modification was introduced to test the general validity of this hypothesis.

Each subject read and evaluated one story from each of the four areas covered. The kind of post hoc (and a priori) attributions presented with each story was randomly assigned. Thirty-three subjects read the "love" story with an internal attribution, twenty-seven subjects read this story with an external attribution; thirty subjects read the "job" story with an internal attribution, and thirty-three subjects read this story with an external attribution.

As can be seen in Figure 8.3, the results concerning the influence of internal versus external post hoc attributions on the amount of tension arising clearly support our hypothesis: with an internal post hoc attribution, both in the area of "love" as well as in the area "job," the described person was evaluated as being considerably more nervous (love: 8.06 versus 6.59 [p = .053]; job: 8.43 versus 6.88 [p = .026]), more upset (love: 9.88 versus 8.67 [p = .024]; job: 9.80 versus 7.88 [p = .001]), more tense (love: 8.91 versus 7.30 [p = .022]; job: 8.83 versus 7.39 [p = .013]), and more stressed (love: 9.12 versus 7.96 [p = .065]; job: 9.50 versus 7.70 [p = .001]) about a given event than in the condition "external post hoc attribution."

The results concerning the influence of general versus specific post hoc attributions support our reasoning only partially. In the area of "friendship" the described person in the condition "general post hoc attribution" was evaluated as being significantly more nervous (N = 26/32; 6.19 versus 4.63; p = .012), significantly more tense (6.54 versus 5.50; p = .049), and significantly more stressed (6.54 versus 5.50; p = .044) than the person in the condition "specific post hoc attribution," while the difference in the dependent variable "degree to which the person is upset" is in the predicted direction, but not significant. In the area "studies," the differences between the ratings in the conditions "general" and "specific post hoc attribution" are partly in the predicted direction, but these means are not significantly different. This may be due to the fact that the type of story used describes an event that might not have much connection with the person's worldview in general.

In the second part of this experiment, the subjects were asked to imagine themselves in these situations. Their own ratings of the degree to which they thought that these events are internally versus externally caused, and generally versus specifically post hoc attributed were measured on 11-point scales ranging from 1 (internal/general) to 11 (external/specific). These subjects also indicated on 11-point scales ranging from 1 (not at all) to 11 (very much) how nervous, upset, tense, and stressed they themselves would be if such an event occurred to them. The correlations between these post hoc attri-

Figure 8.3
Average Predicted Tension When Encountering Negative Inconsistent Events
Under Different Conditions of Post Hoc Attributions

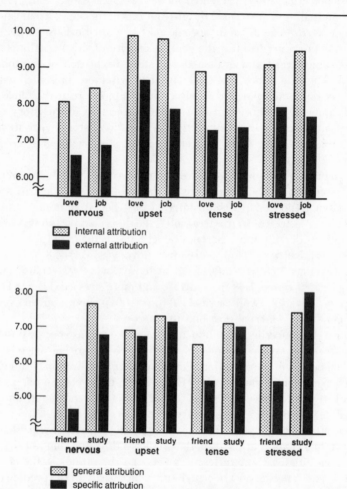

butions and the degree of tension predicted provides further support for the
relevant hypothesis. As Table 8.2 shows, the more the event in the "job"
area is attributed internally, the more tension arises; and the more the event
in the "friendship" area is attributed generally, the more tension arises. The
correlations in the other two areas are not significantly different from zero.

These results support our main hypothesis that the kind of post hoc attributions a person makes can provide valuable information about the number
of inconsistencies that exist in certain situations, and thus the amount of
tension arising.

Table 8.2
Correlations Between Post Hoc Attributions and the Amount of Tension Predicted

	Area			
	Love	Job	Friendship	Studies
		Post hoc attributions		
	internal / external	internal / external	general / specific	general / specific
Dependent Variables				
nervous	-.05	-.26 (p=.018)	-.17 (p=.10)	.08
upset	-.10	-.25 (p=.025)	-.19 (p=.08)	-.03
tense	-.09	-.22 (p=.045)	-.18 (p=.08)	.00
stressed	.03	-.29 (p=.012)	-.15 (p=.12)	.00
N	60	63	58	65

Legend: Answers to the post hoc attribution questions were given on 11-point scales (1 = internal or general to 11 = external or specific). Answers to the questions concerning the amount of tension were given on 11-point scales ranging from 1 (not at all) to 11 (very much).

One might argue that these two experimental studies have only limited external validity, because the subjects imagined themselves or another person in a situation in which an inconsistent event occurred and then evaluated how they thought another person or they themselves might react to the events. Although this procedure allows us to control the information considered, it is artificial. Therefore, an additional experiment was conducted that is one step closer to reality. This study was also designed to test the second and third consideration concerning concrete application of the abstract sum rule for predicting the amount of tension arising.

8.1.2.2 Predicting the Amount of Tension: Considering the Person's Worldview

In this experiment (Inglehart, under review), 126 undergraduates at the University of Michigan were asked to think of a positive and negative unexpected event that had happened to themselves and to describe this event. They then answered questions concerning these two events such as how this event was caused, how important it was, how many changes it had caused in their lives, and how they had reacted to it.

In this experiment, we wanted to test the second and third suggestions described above to apply the sum rule to concrete cases. In order to get a better understanding of how many cognitions of a person's worldview are related with an event, we suggested inquiring how important that part of life is for the person. We expect that the central parts of one's worldview will be rated as more important; so the more an event is rated as important, the more tension is likely to arise. We also suggested that it is helpful to get a better understanding of the input side in such a situation. This means that we should either measure how many separate inconsistent events occurred or how many separate changes a certain event demanded from the person. We expect that the more a person sees that a certain event demands changes in his or her life, the more tension should arise.

These two hypotheses were tested separately with the data from the positive event and from the negative event. The results are presented in Table 8.3. In the first part of this table, we see that the more a positive event is evaluated as important and as demanding changes in one's life, the more excited ($r = .39$; $p = .000$; $r = .26$; $p = .002$), nervous ($r = .27$; $p = .001$; $r = .15$; $p = .041$), tense ($r = .25$; $p = .002$; $r = .21$; $p = .009$), and stressed ($r = .19$; $p = .015$; $r = .19$; $p = .016$) the person is. It is interesting that for a positive event the results for the dependent variable "upset" are not significant. This may be due to the fact that the connotations of the word "upset" are affectively negative and that therefore the subjects might not see this dimension as appropriate when evaluating reactions to a positive event.

In the second part of Table 8.3, the results for the negative event are presented. The more changes a given event caused in a person's life, the more nervous ($r = .15$; $p = .05$), upset ($r = .12$; $p = .096$), tense ($r = .26$; $p = .002$), and stressed ($r = .20$; $p = .014$) the person reported having been. The more the event was evaluated as important, the more tense ($r = .14$; $p = .059$) and stressed ($r = .12$; $p = .084$) the person was. It is interesting that for the evaluations of the negative event the results for the dependent variable "excited" were not significant. The argument used above for the positive event and the use of the concept "upset," can be applied here as well. The concept "excited" may have such a positive connotation (especially for young students) that the Ss did not think it to be appropriate when describing reactions to a negative event.

Table 8.3
Correlations Between Importance of Event and Changes Caused by It with Amount of Tension Arising

Positive event

| Dependent Variables: | Ratings of | |
	importance of event	number of changes caused by event
excited	.39 (p=.000)	.26 (p=.002)
nervous	.27 (p=.001)	.15 (p=.041)
upset	-.02	-.04
tense	.25 (p=.002)	.21 (p=.009)
stressed	.19 (p=.015)	.19 (p=.016)
N	126	126

Negative event

| Dependent Variables: | Ratings of | |
	importance of event	number of changes caused by event
excited	-.10	-.006
nervous	.07	.15 (p=.050)
upset	.06	.12 (p=.096)
tense	.14 (p=.059)	.26 (p=.002)
stressed	.12 (p=.084)	.20 (p=.014)
N	126	126

Legend: Answers were given on 11-point scales ranging from 1 (not at all) to 11 (very much).

Figure 8.4
Model 2: Impact of "Amount of Inconsistencies" on "Reported Illness Symptoms"

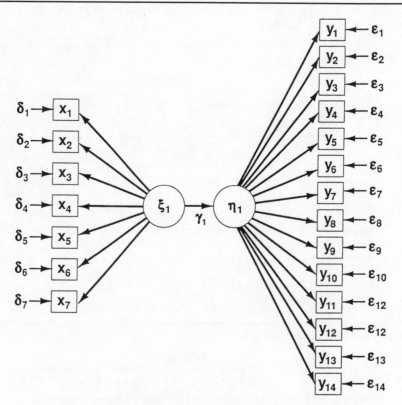

ξ_1 = Latent exogenous variable "amount of inconsistencies"

η_1 = Latent endogenous variable "illness symptoms reported"

This hypothesis about the influence of (a) the importance of an event and (b) the number of changes induced by an event, on the amount of tension arising, was also tested with data from the study of Polish immigrants to West Germany described earlier in the discussion of the influence of post hoc attributions (see Rosch/Inglehart 1983, for a more detailed description of this analysis).

This hypothesis was tested using structural equations with latent variables (LISREL VI; Joereskog & Soerbom 1984). We predict that the more inconsistencies a person encounters, the more bodily symptoms of tension will occur. (See model 2 in Figure 8.4.) The latent exogenous variable "amount of inconsistencies" was measured by seven indicators. The participants answered questions about (a) how many difficulties they encountered in seven different areas of life (job, church/religion, contacts with Germans, contacts with official agencies, family, supply with goods, education), and (b) how important these areas of life are for them. Answers were given on 5-point rating scales ranging from 1 (not at all) to 5 (very much). For each of these seven areas, the rating of the difficulties was weighted with how important this area of life was for the person by multiplying the rating of the difficulties with the ratings of the importance of each area.

The endogenous variable "amount of illness symptoms reported" was again measured with the fourteen indicators used in model 1.

The results of the LISREL analysis of model 2 show that the variable covariances predicted by this model as a whole are significantly different from the observed covariances (d.f. = 351; chi square = 351; p = .000; goodness of fit index = .754). Although model 2 has only a marginally good fit with the data, the standardized regression coefficient between the two latent variables is in the expected direction and significant (gamma = 0.29; d.f. = 1; t = 4.94; p < .10) which is interpreted as supporting the hypothesis of interest here. Again following Bentler and Bonnet's reasoning (1980), this model 2 is compared with a null model which assumes that the latent exogenous variable does not have any impact on the latent endogenous variable (gamma = 0). The goodness of fit of model 2 is significantly better than the goodness of fit of the null model, which provides clear support for our hypothesis.

In predicting the amount of tension arising, there is clear support for the sum rule. Our three suggestions help bridge the gap between this rather abstract hypothesis and concrete instances in which it is applied.

8.1.3 Predicting the General Reaction Used to Reestablish Consistency Following a Critical Life Event

According to the generalized principle of cognitive consistency, tension caused by an inconsistency between an event and the person's worldview is reduced through that reaction which demands the least effort. In general, the person can either directly reduce the tension or the person can reestablish consistency by avoiding the inconsistency.

How do we get from the abstract principle of least effort to concrete predictions concerning whether a person will show a tension-avoidance or tension-reduction reaction?

Two suggestions are made here. First, as described above, the a priori attributions that a person makes may give a rough idea of how much effort a person expects to be involved in certain reactions. Second, it may be possible to estimate the degree to which certain parts of a person's worldview are resistant to change; this would provide us with a further understanding of the amount of effort involved.

8.1.3.1 Role of A Priori Attributions in Predicting the General Kind of Reaction

The first suggestion returns to the significance of a priori attributions. One way to better understand how much effort a person perceives as needed for either reducing the tension directly or for avoiding the tension, is to measure the a priori attributions this person makes about this event.

To predict the general reaction used to reduce the tension due to a critical life event, it is necessary to know the amount of effort a tension-reduction or a tension-avoidance reaction would demand. According to the principle of least effort, the person will show that reaction that demands the least effort. A priori attributions which imply a high amount of effort for direct changes (such as a constant or a chronic a priori attribution of a negative event) are more likely to lead to a tension-avoidance reaction and are less likely to lead to a tension-reduction reaction than a priori attributions which imply less effort (such as a variable or an acute a priori attribution).

This hypothesis was tested in the study of the Polish immigrants to West Germany (see Rosch/Inglehart 1985; Inglehart 1987, under review) as well as in three laboratory experiments (Inglehart 1987, 1988, under review).

The specific case of this hypothesis tested in the field study of Polish immigrants is presented in model 3 (see Figure 8.5). This model predicts that the more problems are attributed to variable causes, the less withdrawal reactions there will be from the problem area (in this case, from contacts with West Germans). These immigrants indicated for each of eight areas of life (job, church/religion, contacts with Germans, contacts with official agencies, family, supply of goods, living circumstances, education) to what degree they perceived problems in these aspects of life as stable/variable. Answers were given on 5 point rating scales ranging from 1 (completely stable) to 5 (completely variable). These eight answers are used in model 3 as the indicators of the latent exogenous variable "amount of variable a priori attributions."

One area of life in which all the participants of this study had problems was their contacts with West Germans. One way to withdraw from these problems was to focus one's attention on one's former homeland and write more letters to Poland. Accordingly, the first indicator of the latent endogenous variable "withdrawal reactions from contacts with Germans" is the number of letters written to Poland in the two weeks preceding the interview. Another possibility for a withdrawal from contacts with West Germans was to be more engaged in the life of the Roman Catholic Church, an institution which plays an extremely important role in Polish society, but has become peripheral to West German society. A high rate of participation in the Roman Catholic Church could therefore be interpreted as withdrawal into an old, familiar behavior pattern from Poland. Accordingly, the second indicator of withdrawal behavior for this particular group, is the degree of church par-

Figure 8.5
Model 3: Impact of "Constant Versus Variable A Priori Attributions"

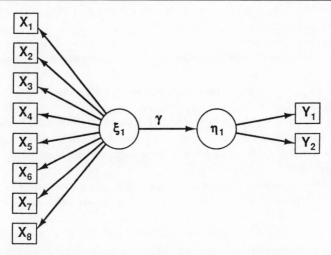

Legend:

ξ_1 = Latent exogenous variable "constant/variable attributions";

η_1 = Latent exogenous variable "withdrawal from contact with West Germans";

X_1-X_8 = Indicators of the latent exogenous variable: ratings of the constant/variable a priori attributions in eight areas of life on five-point scales from 1 = "completely constant" to 5 = "completely variable";

Y_1 = First indicator of the latent endogenous variable: number of letters written to Poland in the two weeks preceding the interview;

Y_2 = Second indicator of the latent endogenous variable: degree of participation in the life of the Catholic Church, measured on a scale from 1 = "not at all" to 5 = "very much."

ticipation. The question asked here was, "How much do you participate in the life of the church?" The answers were scored on a 5-point scale from 1 (not at all) to 5 (very much).

The results of the LISREL analysis of this model 3 show that the variable covariances predicted by this model are significantly different from the observed covariances (d.f. = 34; chi square = 160.83; $p < .011$; adjusted goodness of fit = 0.877). But again the standardized regression coefficient between the two latent variables in this model is in the predicted direction and significant (gamma = .226; d.f. = 1; t = −1.937; $p < .10$). This clearly supports our hypothesis: the more problems are attributed a priori to variable causes, the less withdrawal there will be.

Again we follow Bentler and Bonett's procedure (1980) and test this model

3 against a null model in which the latent exogenous variable does not have any impact on the latent endogenous variable (gamma = 0). The goodness of fit of this null model (d.f. = 35; chi square = 165.3; adjusted goodness of fit = .878) is significantly worse than the goodness of fit of model 3 (difference in d.f. = 1; difference in chi square = 4.7; p < .001). This finding supports the theoretical argument that taking a priori attributions into account contributes to explaining the variance of withdrawal reactions from inconsistencies.

This hypothesis about the role of a priori attributions in determining the amount of effort involved in certain reactions and thus in predicting the general kind of reaction (tension-reduction versus tension-avoidance reaction) following a critical life event was also tested in the laboratory experiments described earlier in the discussion of the role of post hoc attributions (compare Inglehart 1987, 1988, under review).

In a first experiment that was conducted at the University of Mannheim ("Story" Experiment 1), subjects read five short episodes about critical life events in five different areas of life (job, family, education, intimate relationship, health). After each episode either a constant or a variable a priori attribution was given. An example of a priori attributions in the area of health (for wording of the story, see 8.1.2) are, "Mr. M. thinks that skin cancer is fatal" (constant a priori attribution), and "Mr. M. believes that in an early stage of skin cancer, recovery is very likely" (variable a priori attribution). The dependent variable was the amount of tension-reduction attempts, which was measured with the questions "How much effort will the person make to change this event?" and "How hard will the person try to solve this problem?" The answers were given on 11-point rating scales from 1 (not at all) to 11 (very much).

We predict that under the condition of a constant a priori attribution, less tension-reduction reactions will be expected than under the condition of a variable a priori attribution. This hypothesis is clearly supported by the results (see Figure 8.6). The average degree of tension-reduction reactions for each of the two dependent variables in each of the five areas of life are higher in the condition of a variable a priori attribution than in the condition of a constant a priori attribution (job: 6.81 vs. 9.18; 6.19 vs. 8.90; result of the MANOVA analysis: $F(2,79) = 13.5$; p < .000; family: 7.03 vs. 8.67; 6.69 vs. 8.36; $F(2,78) = 5.29$; p < .007; education: 5.37 vs. 8.00; 5.63 vs. 8.46; $F(2,78) = 11.38$; p < .000; interpersonal relations: 6.68 vs. 8.20; 6.63 vs. 8.81; $F(2,81) = 9.33$; p < .0002; health: 6.74 vs. 7.33; 4.68 vs. 5.10; $F(2,84) = .39$; not significant).

These results support the suggestion that the kind of a priori attribution a person makes provides information about the amount of effort the person assumes is involved in either a tension-reduction or tension-avoidance reaction. This implies that predictions of the general reactions to critical life events are possible. But again we stress the fact that it is not the *content* of

Figure 8.6
Means of Dependent Variables, "Amount of Effort for Direct Change" and
"Amount of Effort for Problem Solving," Under the Independent Variable "Kind
of A Priori Attributions"

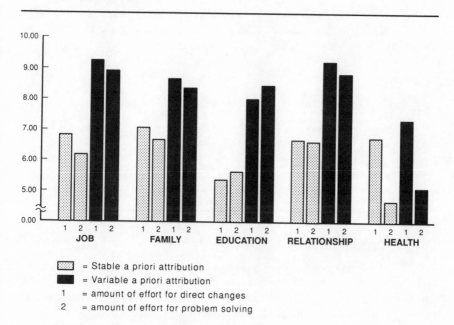

= Stable a priori attribution
= Variable a priori attribution
1 = amount of effort for direct changes
2 = amount of effort for problem solving

a given a priori attribution that contributes to our understanding, but considerations about the underlying process that is essential.

In the second part of this experiment, the subjects were asked to imagine themselves in these situations. They were then told to indicate the kind of a priori attribution they would make, how much they would try to change this event, and how much they would try to solve this problem. The correlations between the stable versus variable a priori attributions and the two indicators of efforts to reduce the tension are presented in Table 8.4. As can be seen, the more variable the a priori attributions are the more efforts to change and the more efforts to solve the problems were reported. All of these correlations are in the predicted direction and significantly different from 0.

As described in section 8.1.2, this experiment was replicated at the University of Michigan ("Story" Experiment 2). Stories from four different areas (love, job, friendship, studies) were presented and the kind of a priori attributions were manipulated. In the areas "love" and "job," the a priori attributions presented were either stable or variable; in the areas "friendship" and "studies," the a priori attributions were either chronic or acute. Three dependent variables were measured, namely the degree to which the person would try to solve the problem, the amount of effort a person would make

Table 8.4
Correlation Between A Priori Attributions and Predicted Effort to Reduce Tension

Area	Efforts to change	Problem solving
Job	.24*	.32*
Family	.20*	.20*
Education	.19*	.26*
Intimate relationship	.33**	.30**
Health	.31**	.24*

Legend: * = (p < .05); ** = (p < .01).

and the amount of work a person would perform in order to change the problematic situation. The answers were given on 11-point rating scales ranging from 1 (not at all) to 11 (very much).

A multivariate analysis for each of the four areas of life with the three dependent variables provides clear support for the present hypothesis. As Table 8.5 shows, in each of the four areas of life the amounts of predicted efforts for reducing tension are significantly higher under the a priori attribution that implies a lesser degree of effort (variable/acute), than under the a priori attribution that implies a larger amount of effort (stable/chronic).

Furthermore, when these subjects were asked in the second part of this experiment to imagine themselves in these situations and indicate how stable versus variable they would perceive this situation and how much effort for direct tension-reduction reactions they would be likely to make, further support for our hypothesis was found. As can be seen in Table 8.6, the correlations between the a priori attributions and the degree of effort predicted are all in the predicted direction.

In a third experiment ("Real Life" Experiment; for a description see 8.1.2; Inglehart, under review), this hypothesis was investigated by asking 126 undergraduates at the University of Michigan to describe a positive as well as a negative unexpected event that happened to them. After doing so they were asked to rate on 11-point scales how stable versus variable they perceived this event to be, how much control they thought they had had over it, and how much effort they had put into changing it. As Table 8.7 shows, the

Table 8.5
Average Rating of Expected Tension-Reduction Efforts Under Different A Priori
Attributions

	Area			
Dependent	Love	Job	Friendship	Studies
Variables:	Kind of a priori attributions:			
	stable vari-able	stable vari-able	chro-nic acute	chro-nic acute
try	5.83 9.10 F (1,55) = 23.6 ***	4.03 9.45 F (1,55) = 99 ***	6.66 8.17 F (1,55) = 8.4 **	5.97 8.29 F (1,55) = 45.1 ***
effort	6.28 8.87 F (1,55) = 14.1 ***	4.22 9.39 F (1,55) = 65.8 ***	6.41 7.97 F (1,55) = 7.4 **	5.97 7.85 F (1,55) = 9.1 **
work	5.79 8.97 F (1,55) = 19.5 ***	4.31 9.16 F (1,55) = 56.6 ***	6.28 7.59 F (1,55) = 4.9 *	6.06 8.06 F (1,55) = 10.0 **

Legend: The answers to the dependent variables were given on
11-point scales ranging from 1 (not at all) to 11 (very
much).
* = (p <.05); ** = (p <.001); *** = (p <.001).

more these students perceived the events as being under their control, the
more they felt confident, the more they tried to make things work out in the
future, the more effort they showed in this situation, and the more energy
they invested in this situation. The correlations between the degree to which
the subjects perceived these events as being variable was positively correlated
with the other variables of interest here, though not all of these correlations
were statistically significant.

On the whole, these results support the general hypothesis that knowing
the kind of a priori attributions a person makes about a given critical life
event provides us with a good idea of how much effort for direct tension-
reduction versus tension-avoidance reactions a given person will put forth.

8.1.3.2 Predicting the General Kind of Reaction: Considering the Resistance to Change of the Person's Worldview

The second suggestion that contributes to bridging the gap between the
abstract principle of least effort and predictions about concrete reactions in
given situations, is to try to measure or infer the resistance to change that
given cognitions have for a person. There are two ways to approach this
task. First, certain person variables may provide us with information about

Table 8.6
Correlations Between A Priori Attributions and Amount of One's Own Efforts
Predicted for Change

	Love	Job	Friendship	Studies
		Area		
		A priori attributions		
	stable / variable	stable / variable	stable / variable	stable / variable
confident	.61 ***	.61 ***	.27 *	.19 +
try	.46 ***	.40 ***	.01	.28 *
effort	.51 ***	.30 **	.10	.26 *
work	.44 ***	.36 **	.02	.27 *
N	59	63	57	65

Legend: Answers were given on 11-point scales from 1
        (stable, not at all) to 11 (variable, very much).
        + = (p <.10); * = (p < .05); ** = (p<.01);
     *** = (p <.001)

how much effort certain reactions would demand from a person. Second, collecting information about the situation a person is in will also help us understand how much effort certain reactions would demand from a person.

In the study of elections to the European Parliament (see Rosch/Inglehart, Dickenberger, Irle & Moentmann 1981; Rosch/Inglehart & Schmidt 1981), the first suggestion was used and its implications were investigated. In this study, a person variable was considered that makes it likely that given cognitions have a higher resistance to change for one group of people than for another. Active members of political parties and nonmembers of political parties were asked to participate in this study. It was assumed that for active party members, cognitions about political events (including cognitions about the impending election) have a higher resistance to change than they do for nonmembers of political parties. Accordingly, we expected that in a situation with inconsistent information about the election outcome, nonmembers and active members of political parties will show different reactions to reduce this tension. Specifically, we hypothesized that the effort to change cognitions about the election is higher for party members than for nonmembers. Accordingly, nonmembers will be more likely to reduce the tension by changing cognitions about the election than active party members, while active party

Table 8.7
Correlations Between One's Own Perception of Variability of Unexpected Events
and Level of Control and Amount of Effort for Change

	Degree of stability		Degree of control	
	Kind of event:			
	positive	negative	positive	negative
"confident"	.23 **	.15 *	.38 ***	.27 **
"try"	.04	.12 +	.40 ***	.24 **
"effort"	.07	.07	.37 ***	.18 *
"energy"	.10	.08	.35 ***	.23 **

Legend: + = (p <.10); * = (p <.05); ** = (p <. 01);
        *** = (p < .001)

Answers were given on 11-point scales ranging from 1
(stable, no control, not at all) to 11 (variable, very
much control)

members will be more likely to reduce the tension by devaluing the given prediction.

We found clear support for our hypothesis concerning the impact of this person variable "active party membership" versus "not being a member of a political party" on the way tension due to inconsistent information about the election outcome was reduced. Active party members (N = 11) who had received inconsistent information about the election outcome through an opinion poll prediction that differed from the person's own prediction of the winner, rated the validity of this information lower (mean = 1.69) on an 11-point scale (1 = not at all certain that prediction is correct to 10 = very certain) than nonmembers of a political party (N = 80) who had received inconsistent information (mean = 2.53). Moreover, both of these groups rated the validity of the prediction as lower than did party members (N = 98) and nonmembers (N = 77) who had received consistent information (means = 3.69 and 3.48). The interaction effect of a two-way analysis of variance for the two independent variables "kind of information (inconsistent/consistent)" and "party membership (yes/no)" approached significance (F(1,367) = 2.51; p = .11). Furthermore, while the nonmembers reduced the tension due to inconsistent information by downgrading the importance of the election, the active party members actually increased their ratings of the importance of this election when receiving inconsistent information, while those persons of both groups who had received consistent information did not change their evaluation of the importance of the election outcome after they received the consistent information.

We also demonstrated in two experiments that considering a person variable can contribute to making predictions according to the principle of least effort. In the experiment conducted by Rosch/Inglehart and Rohrlach (1981; for description see 8.1.1) and in a replication of this experiment by Inglehart and Schur (in prep.), fans of a given soccer club and persons interested in soccer who were not interested in this particular soccer club (the control group) participated. We predicted in both studies that the fans of a given soccer club would have a higher resistance to changing their cognitions about a game played by their preferred team than the subjects in the control group. More specifically, we expected that the fans would reduce the tension due to inconsistent information about the half time result less by changing their expectation about the end result and more by discounting the significance of the half time result, than would the control subjects. The significance of the half time result was evaluated on a 5-point scale (1 = not at all important to 5 very much important). While the fans' evaluation did not differ significantly from the control group subjects before the game started (means = 3.41 and 3.41), they were significantly lower after receiving inconsistent information (means = 3.31 and 2.46; interaction effect "time" × "fan/non-fan": $F(1,70) = 6.41$; $p = .014$). The fans were less likely to change their expectation about the end result than were the non-fans (differences in goals before game and after inconsistent information was given: 1.34 for fans, and 1.87 for non-fans; $F(1,69) = 2.77$; $p = .10$).

Both the results of this field study and those of the two experiments demonstrate how considering certain person variables can help us to get a better idea about the amount of effort a given reaction demands from a person. This is a first step toward applying the principle of least effort to a concrete situation in order to predict the general kind of reactions used to reduce tension due to an inconsistency.

The significance of considering aspects of the *situation* that given persons are in can also contribute to accomplishing this task. This will be illustrated with data from the study of the elections to the European Parliament. Interviews were conducted at three points in time before this election. We expected that the closer the election date came, the more resistant to changes the cognitions about this election would be, because the election campaign would get people increasingly interested, and would lead them to have more cognitions about it. Accordingly, we predicted that the closer the election, the less the participants would be likely to reduce tension due to inconsistent information by changing cognitions about the election (such as the importance of the election). This hypothesis was supported by the data.

These are examples of the way in which person variables on one hand and situation variables on the other hand, can help us understand the amount of effort that given reactions demand from a person.

We have demonstrated how the generalized principle of cognitive consistency can be applied to predict the general tension reduction or tension avoidance reaction to an inconsistent event. The next step is to consider how to predict specific reactions.

8.1.4 Predicting the Specific Reaction to Reduce Tension When a Critical Life Event has Occurred

Assuming that we can predict the general reaction a person will use to reduce the tension caused by a critical life event (that is, whether the tension will be reduced directly or will be shut out), the next question is how the specific reaction can be explained. For example, even if we know that a person is likely to withdraw from the problematic area and thus shut out the tension, we still do not know what specific withdrawal activity the person is likely to perform. Will he or she withdraw into alcohol abuse, or into devoting excessive time to a leisure time activity such as watching TV? Or will the person avoid the problem area by devoting energy to some other activity, such as spending time with the family or working hard on one's career? Or will the person withdraw in the most extreme possible fashion and commit suicide? There are hundreds of possible specific reactions with which tension in a given situation can be either directly reduced or avoided.

According to the generalized principle of cognitive consistency, the tension will be reduced with that specific reaction which is most cognitively available. Two factors that contribute to the cognitive availability of a given reaction are (a) prior experiences with this reaction that make this reaction salient, and (b) the objective availability of certain objects that are needed to perform this reaction.

These considerations were empirically investigated in a study of persons with one specific tension-avoidance reaction, namely in a study of male alcoholics (Rosch/Inglehart & Irle 1983). We wanted to investigate whether alcoholics had more prior experiences with other persons in their surroundings who used alcohol, and whether it had been easier for them to have access to alcohol than for members of a control group of persons.

This study was conducted with ninety-two male alcoholics (twenty to forty-five years old) and 103 control group subjects who were matched for gender, age, and educational background. All alcoholics were medically diagnosed as being alcoholics and participated in long-term therapy in a hospital. They volunteered to participate and the interviews were conducted in the hospital. The control group subjects were first contacted in a letter in which the study was described as an investigation of "reactions to problems in life." If they volunteered to participate, they were interviewed in their own homes, their offices, or at the sponsoring university.

It is interesting to note that the alcoholics reported a significantly smaller number of attempts to solve problems in the past (means: 2.83 versus 3.06 on a 5-point scale from 1 = not at all to 5 = very much), and spoke less with other persons about their problems (means: 3.16 versus 3.29; answers were given on a 5-point scale from 1 = never to 5 = always) than the subjects in the control group. The percentages of alcoholics who indicated that they spoke with their partner, their father, their mother, other family members, or friends about problems was clearly smaller than the percentage of control group subjects (partner: 53% versus 84%; father: 23% versus 27%; mother: 40% versus 47%; other family members: 49% versus 58%; friends: 64% versus 85%). Considering the fact that alcoholics report a significantly larger number of problems in all areas of life than the control group subjects, it seems clear that the degree to which they try to reduce the resulting tension directly is smaller than the degree that control group subjects show.

On the other hand, alcoholics smoke significantly more cigarettes a day (25.2 versus 8.6) and drink significantly more cups of coffee per day (6.1 versus 2.6) than persons in the control group. This is probably connected with the fact that these alcoholics are no longer drinking alcohol and may substitute the alcohol by using other substances.

In order to investigate the hypotheses that persons who show a distinct tension-avoidance reaction might do so because (a) they have prior experiences observing other persons behaving in such a way, or (b) they had stimuli in their environment that made it easy for them to perform a certain reaction, questions were asked about their family members' alcohol consumption and the alcohol consumption of their friends, as well as about the difficulties they had in getting alcohol at a time in their life when alcohol was not yet a problem for them. Rather surprisingly, the average degree to which alcoholics report that their mother or their father drank alcohol is not significantly different from the control group subjects' answers (father: 4.05 versus 4.01; mother: 2.34 versus 2.75; answers were given on 6-point scales from 1 = never to 6 = daily). This is one piece of information that seems to argue against a genetic predisposition toward alcoholism. On the other hand, the alcoholics clearly drank more alcohol together with their friends than did the control group subjects in times when alcohol was not yet a problem for them (means: 3.59 versus 2.50 on a 5-point scale from 1 = never to 5 = always). The alcoholics also reported having had fewer difficulties in getting alcohol at the time when alcohol was not yet a problem for them than control group subjects (means: 1.04 versus 1.53 on a 5-point scale from 1 = no difficulties at all to 5 = very many difficulties).

We interpret these data as preliminary evidence that it might be useful to inquire about prior experiences with certain kinds of reactions, and to take into account the objective availability of certain objects that are needed to perform specific reactions or of information provided in the environment that makes certain reactions salient to a person. Knowing a person's earlier re- actions and experiences with other persons' reactions to tension might be an excellent predictor of future reactions.

8.1.5 Predicting Long-term Consequences of Having Encountered a Critical Life Event

The last question of interest when studying reactions to critical life events is to inquire about the long-term consequences of having encountered a critical life event.

There is research on the long-term consequences of having survived being in a concentration camp (see, for example, Bergman & Jucovy 1982; DesPres 1976) and on the influences that these experiences had on the children of the concentration camp survivors (see, for example, Last & Klein 1984; Solkoff 1981). There is also a growing literature on the long-term consequences of having been in the Vietnam War (Figley & Leventman 1980; Kelly 1985). But there is very little other research available.

What can the generalized principle of cognitive consistency contribute to this issue? We argue that it is relevant in two ways. The first concerns predictions about the long-term consequences for the level of tension a person experiences. The second concerns the influence that a changed worldview can have on a person's thinking and actions.

The long-term consequences of having encountered a critical life event on the amount of tension that is carried through life is an important issue. If tension is reduced directly by reestablishing consistency, no tension would be carried over into future situations. But if tension is reduced by avoiding the inconsistency, tension is likely to reoccur later in life. A person who has been raped and shuts out this experience will encounter situations or stimuli that reintroduce the tension due to this event. Thus, unresolved inconsis- tencies will become an additional burden in situations that are related to them.

The degree to which cognitive consistency is reestablished after an incon- sistent event occurred, and its influence on the level of tension experienced later was approached in a modest way in the "real life" experiment described earlier. In this experiment 126 undergraduates from the University of Mich- igan were asked to describe a positive as well as a negative unexpected event that had happened to them in the past. The events described took place, on the average, 16.7 months before the experiment. After describing the emo- tions, cognitions, and actions at the time when the event occurred, the sub- jects were asked to rate how they felt and thought about this event at the time the study was done.

We found that the more the subjects indicated that they could make sense out of the experience of a negative event and the more they thought that it was fair and just that this negative event had happened to them, the better they felt about it (r = .20; r = .39) and the less they were upset about it (r = −.12; r = −.25). For the positive event, there is also a clear relationship between the degree to which this positive event makes sense and is fair and the degree to which the subjects feel good about it (r = .24 and r = .22).

These results are interpreted as a first indication that in order to understand the long-term tensions arising from having encountered a critical life event, we need to understand whether cognitive consistency was directly reestablished or whether there is shut out tension left over from this encounter, and under which circumstances such shut out tension is likely to be reintroduced.

There are experiences, such as having been in a concentration camp or having been tortured, that are difficult or impossible to make sense of. In this case, it is crucial to understand the role that withdrawal reactions play (see Breznitz 1985, for a more comprehensive overview of research on this issue). It is also essential to get a better understanding of the situations that trigger the reoccurrence of the old tension and the positive effects that can occur when avoidance reactions are given up (see the interesting research by Pennebaker 1989).

The second contribution that the generalized principle of cognitive consistency can make in analyzing the long-term consequences of having encountered a critical life event, concerns the fact that one's experiences can change one's worldview. According to the generalized principle of cognitive consistency, people think, plan, and act in ways that maximize the consistency between one's worldview and the new events one experiences. From this perspective, it is important to understand how a critical life event changes a person's beliefs about the world, and a person's expectations and goals (see Chapter 11 for a discussion of these issues).

8.2 The Generalized Principle of Cognitive Consistency and Reactions to Critical Life Events—Preliminary Evaluation

8.2.1 Answers to Basic Questions

The introduction to this monograph argued that an adequate theory about reactions to critical life events should be able to answer certain basic questions. First, it should define what a critical life event is. Concerning the energizing aspect of a situation involving a critical life event it should predict (a) when tension arises, and (b) what determines the amount of tension arising. Concerning the structuring aspect of such a situation, it should provide clear hypotheses about the general, and the specific reactions to a critical life event, as well as about the long-term consequences of having encountered such an event.

The generalized principle of cognitive consistency provides answers to all of these questions. As can be seen in Tables 8.8 and 8.9, data from five field

Table 8.8
Field Studies Used to Test Hypotheses of Generalized Principle of Cognitive
Consistency: An Overview

Study Number	Name	Topic	References
1	Panel study of Inteflex and Medical School students	see chapter 7: a. Possible self and and academic achievement	Inglehart, Markus & Brown, 1989
		b. Attitude changes as a way to adapt to life's inconsistencies	Inglehart, Brown & Moore, 1988
2	European Parliament Election	see 8.1.1.: a. Reactions to positive and negative inconsistent information	Rosch/Inglehart, Dickenberger, Irle & Moentmann, 1981; Rosch/Inglehart & Schmidt, 1981
		see 8.1.3.: b. Predicting the general reactions used to reduce tension	
3	Immigrants from Poland in West Germany	see 8.1.2.: a. Influence of post hoc attributions on the amount of tension	Rosch, 1981, 1983, 1985b Inglehart, 1987, 1988, under review; Rosch, Irle & Frey, 1981
		see 8.1.2.: b. Influence of the number of inconsistencies and their impact on the amount of tension	
		see 8.1.3.: c. Influence of a priori attributions on general reactions	
4	Alcoholism Study	see 8.1.4: Alcoholism - a specific tension avoidance reaction?	Rosch/Inglehart, 1983
5	Life Philosophy Study	see Chapter 11: structure and content of life philosophies	Inglehart, McIntosh & Pacini, 1990a, b McIntosh, Inglehart & Pacini, under review

Table 8.9
Laboratory Experiments Conducted to Test Hypotheses of the Generalized
Principle of Cognitive Consistency: An Overview

Experi- ment nr.	Name	Topic	References
1	"Soccer fans" experiment 1	see 8.1.1.: Positive versus negative inconsis- tent information	Rosch/Ingle- hart & Rohrlach, 1981
2	"Soccer fans" experiment 2	see 8.1.3.: resistance of change of certain reactions	Inglehart & Schur, in prep.
3	Inconsistent in- formation, arousal and task per- formance	see 8.1.1.: Positive / negative inconsistent infor- mation and task per- formance	Inglehart & Kon- doff, in prep.
4	"Story" experiment 1 Attributions and the generalized principle of cogni- tive consistency	8.1.2. / 8.1.3.: post hoc and a priori attribu- tions (a) other person (b) self ratings	Inglehart, 1987, 1988, under review
5	"Story" experiment 2	8.1.2. / 8.1.3: replication of experiment 2 (a) other person (b) self rating	Inglehart, under review
6	"Real Life" Experiment: One's experiences with unexpected events	8.1.2. / 8.1.3.: Changes and importance ratings, experienced reactions	Inglehart, under review

studies and six laboratory experiments were used to test these hypotheses
and to demonstrate the validity of our argument.

8.2.2 The Generalized Principle of Cognitive Consistency and
Reactions to Critical Life Events—Limitations

Reactions to critical life events are studied on many levels of analysis. The
perspective taken here primarily focuses on explaining reactions to critical
life events on a psychological level. Questions concerning a psychobiological
level of analysis and a sociological level of analysis are beyond the scope of
this book.

The psychological perspective taken here is a cognitive motivational theory. Motivational issues—tension and the need to reduce this tension—are considered within a cognitive framework. What implications does this generalized principle of cognitive consistency have when considering the three aspects of human reactions, namely feeling, thinking, and acting?

The domain of this theory is to explain cognitive processes. In reactions to critical life events, these cognitive issues are clearly important, although most research focuses on explaining the actions and emotions following when a critical life event occurred. The generalized principle of cognitive consistency provides hypotheses about which actions are likely to occur after critical life events, because past, present, and future actions are cognitively represented and thus fall in the domain of the generalized principle of cognitive consistency.

The last aspect of this triad—emotions—provides the greatest problems from the perspective of the generalized principle of cognitive consistency. This principle cannot do justice to the full complexity of this issue (see Zajonc 1980; Zajonc, Murphy & Inglehart 1989; as one perspective taken concerning these issues), which is one of the major challenges for contemporary psychology. But there is a certain plasticity of emotions that can be accounted for through the generalized principle of cognitive consistency. Two aspects are of interest here. First, the research on the significance of cognitions in connection with emotions must be considered (Schachter 1964, 1971; Weiner 1985b). The generalized principle of cognitive consistency is clearly relevant here. Cognitions such as knowledge and expectations concerning emotional reactions and their appropriateness in certain situations, attributions, and observations of emotional reactions in other persons can be important here. They may shape emotional experiences and emotional expression.

Second, the amount of tension arising in a situation with a critical life event is directly related to the strength of the emotion occurring. Accordingly, the hypotheses of the generalized principle of cognitive consistency that contribute to our understanding of the determinants of the tension arising and to the kind of reaction used to reduce this tension are clearly significant here.

8.2.3 The Generalized Principle of Cognitive Consistency and Its Relevance for the Interpretation of Variable-Centered Research on Reactions to Critical Life Events

In our historical overview of research on reactions to critical life events we pointed out that variable-centered research has become increasingly important in the last ten years. The general assumption underlying this research is that reactions to critical life events cannot be explained unless moderator variables such as social support or individual characteristics are considered. The generalized principle of cognitive consistency provides a useful framework in which this research can be reinterpreted, and future research can be stimulated. In the following chapter this principle is used to reinterpret the results of research on the significance of social support and of individual differences. The role of the specific, general, and existential beliefs will be analyzed in Chapter 11. In the last chapter, we examine the potential contribution of the generalized principle of cognitive consistency for applied research.

Part III

The Generalized Principle
of Cognitive Consistency—
Further Implications

Part II of this book was devoted to developing the generalized principle of cognitive consistency and demonstrating its utility in explaining reactions to critical life events. Part III explores some further implications of this theory for the general domain of reactions to critical life events. Chapters 9 and 10 are an attempt to demonstrate that it may be fruitful to use this theory when explaining the impact of social support and individual differences on reactions to critical life events. The role of a person's life philosophy in situations with critical life events will be investigated in Chapter 11. The practical implications of the generalized principle of cognitive consistency for counseling and prevention in connection with critical life events will be discussed in the last chapter of this book. This chapter demonstrates that this principle can be useful as a theoretical framework to guide applied work.

Chapter 9

Social Support

By May 1987, about 21,000 persons had died of AIDS in the United States and 36,000 persons had the disease. At the same time, there were official estimates that between 1.5 and 2 million people were already infected with the AIDS virus and that as many as fifty percent of these persons would actually come down with AIDS in the near future (Walker 1987). The lives of these *directly* confronted persons will be changed dramatically, and so will the lives of their relatives and friends, who are indirectly confronted with this event. Thus, a complex and often delicate process of giving and receiving social support begins to develop.

Before we discuss the implications of the generalized principle of cognitive consistency for understanding this process, a brief introduction to this topic will be given. It would be beyond the scope of this chapter to provide a detailed review of this research, but we will present a short overview, with particular attention to the positive and negative aspects of giving and receiving social support in situations with critical life events.

9.1 Social Support: An Overview

9.1.1 A General Introduction

Social interactions are clearly a topic of interest for social psychologists. Nevertheless, social support—which can be interpreted as one kind of social interaction—has never been a central interest of social psychologists. Helping behavior, on the other hand, became a widely studied subject after the famous Kitty Genovese murder occurred (Darley & Latane 1968), in which a young woman was slaughtered while a large number of her neighbors observed what was going on, but did not help her. This shocking incident stimulated much research on helping behavior. But most of this research is concerned with short-term interactions between two strangers in concrete situations, such as an emergency. The far more common domain of helping behavior among family members and friends in everyday life and with critical life events was, until recently, a neglected topic in social psychology. Recently, Duck and Silver (1990) demonstrated that there might be fruitful cooperation between social support researchers and social psychologists concerned with interpersonal relationships. But up to now, social support research has developed in relative isolation from mainstream social psychological research.

This may be due to the fact that the dominant methodology used in social psychology is still the laboratory experiment, which is not well suited to investigating the topic of social support. Another reason may be that social support first became interesting to epidemiologists and sociologists who investigated its effect on physical and mental health.

The first empirical study of social support was Durkheim's famous research on suicide (Durkheim 1897; Engl. ed. 1951). He found that persons who are part of stable groups such as families, religious communities, or organizations are less likely to attempt or commit suicide than persons without such social networks (Durkheim 1897; Engl. ed. 1951). Although this study became famous, it did not open up the research on social support to a significant extent. Before 1977, there were only one or two citations listed in the Social Science Citation Index per year. But after 1977 the number of publications on this topic increased rapidly. By 1982, there were about fifty citations annually under this index term.

This rapid increase in the number of publications is largely due to the publications of two extremely influential publications in 1976. Cassel (1976) described how social support can protect a person against stress-induced diseases. And Cobb (1976) presented some quite striking research showing that social support in crisis situations can protect a person against a wide variety of physical symptoms.

It seems that the time was right for these two publications in two ways. Stress and its consequences had by then become a prominent research topic (see Selye 1956). Moreover, research on the significance of social networks (Litwak & Szelenyi 1969), of social disorganization (Leighton 1963), and on the significance of a basic human need for social relationships (Maslow 1968) has received considerable attention. Building on these two research areas, research on the role of social support in stressful situations followed quite logically. (For a more detailed overview of early research on social support, see Henderson 1984.)

Let us consider what social support research is actually about. It includes the presence of littermates, contacts with family members, friends and acquaintances, and membership in church and community organizations. Gottlieb (1981) organizes these various studies by proposing that support can be investigated on three levels: macro, mezzo, and micro level. On a macro level of support, such global aspects as the degree of community integration are considered. Research on the mezzo level focuses on the number of persons or contacts that provide a person with social support. And research on the micro level considers the process of receiving support, specifically whether the person actually perceives to receive social support. This variety of topics covered provides some idea of how diverse research on social support has become.

One often cited definition of social support was suggested by Cobb (1976), who defines social support as information that leads the subject to believe that he/she is cared for and loved, estimated and valued, and/or that he/she belongs to a network of communication and mutual obligations. A later definition is given by House (1981). He defines social support as the flow between people of emotional concern, instrumental aid, information, or appraisal.

The ways in which social support is measured are as varied as the definitions of social support (see Cohen & Syme 1985). This makes a comparison of research on social support difficult. One might classify the methods into those that try to measure the structure of social networks and those that try to measure the function that social support has. Researchers in the first category investigate such factors as the size, reciprocity, durability, and frequency of social networks. Research in the second category focuses on the functions of social support; investigating, for example, whether social support has a buffering effect between stress and outcome variables such as health and subjective well being, or whether it has a direct impact on stress or on these outcome variables.

9.1.2 General Research Findings

Research on social support got started when the results of longitudinal studies demonstrated that being part of a social network seemed beneficial to a person's health. Let us briefly review two empirical studies of this significance of social support: the panel studies by Berkman and Syme (1979) and by House, Robbins, and Metzner (1982).

Berkman and Syme (1979) reported the results of a study of 2,229 men and 2,496 women between thirty and sixty-nine years old who lived in Alameda County, California. In 1965, these persons answered a questionnaire concerning their health and health-related behavior. In 1974, Berkman and Syme analyzed the mortality rate of these participants. Four possible kinds of social support (marriage, contacts with friends, membership in a church community, and in other organizations), were summarized in a Social Network Index. The influence of social support on the mortality rates of the participants could be clearly demonstrated. This finding held up even when the researchers controlled for age and a range of self-reported health behaviors and health status variables. Persons with a low Social Network Index in 1965 had a much higher probability (30 to 300 percent higher) of having died in the nine years following these interviews.

The critics of this study argued that those persons with less social support might have already been in bad health in 1965, and that this might have led to less social support at this earlier point. This alternative explanation could not be ruled out, because Berkman and Syme had no objective measures of the participants' health status in 1965.

This alternative explanation was investigated by James House and his colleagues (House, Robbins & Metzner 1982) in an analysis of panel data from the Tecumseh Community Health Study. Between 1967 and 1969, 1,322 men and 1,432 women of Tecumseh, Michigan, participated in detailed medical examinations and tests, as well as in self-report interviews and questionnaires. In 1979, the mortality status of this sample was determined. Again the findings clearly demonstrated the significance of social support for living longer. However, in this study the results were stronger and more significant for men than for women.

These two studies as well as numerous other prospective studies summarized by House, Landis, and Umberson (1988) investigated the role of social support for a person's health status in general and independently of whether a specific critical life event had occurred or not. Numerous other studies were conducted to explore the effects of social support in stressful situations, and especially its effect on a person's physical health (see Cohen & Syme 1985, as an example) and mental health (Lin & Dean 1984; Lin, Dean & Ensel 1986) in such situations.

This research can be grouped in three categories. One body of research focuses on structural aspects of a person's social network such as its size, density, or homogeneity, and how these quantitative characteristics influence a person's adjustment. Another type of research analyzes the functional aspects of a social support situation (see Cohen & Wills 1985, for an overview). The central issue here is whether social support acts like a buffer between the stress occurring and bodily and/or psychological symptoms, or whether it has a main effect on the amount of stress occurring or the health status of the person in general. The conclusion that Cohen & Wills (1985) drew in their review of the literature, is that both effects occur and that future research should investigate the precise processes underlying these effects. The third type of research focuses on the perception of social support as one global issue. Pierce, Sarason, and Sarason (1990) provide an excellent summary and critical evaluation of these three groups of studies.

9.1.3 Social Support and Critical Life Events—Positive and Negative Aspects

In February 1985, an article was published entitled "What price friendship? The darker side of social networks" (Turkington 1985). This article was indicative of a shift in the dominant perspective taken in research on the effects of social support. While earlier research had primarily focused on the positive effects of receiving social support, a more differentiated outlook began to develop. The research began to focus on the negative as well as the positive effects of receiving and of giving social support.

Three aspects of this research will be discussed here. First, research on the negative consequences of giving social support will be presented. Second, the negative consequences for the person receiving social support will be discussed. Third, one strategy taken when investigating effects of social support was to study under which conditions which effects will occur. This strategy stimulated research on the effects of certain person variables such as the degree to which a person has an internal versus external locus of control (Lefcourt, Martin & Saleh 1984) or is hardy (Kobasa & Puccetti 1983), and on the effects of certain situation factors such as the amount of stress or daily hassles in given situations (DeLongis, Folkman & Lazarus 1988).

Concerning the first aspect (the effects of giving social support), it is helpful to consider how stressful it is for a person to see their relative or friend experience a critical life event, such as dying of AIDS. Accordingly, these human beings experience tension already. Giving social support is then one component in a situation already full of tension.

Therefore, it is not surprising that we find empirical evidence that giving social support either in a situation with chronic stress, such as to a person with Alzheimer's disease (Casky & Gates 1988; Zarit, Reever & Bach-Peterson 1980), or in a situation with a critical life event, such as to a person who has cancer (Ward & Leventhal 1986; Northouse & Wortman, in press), has negative effects for the support-giving person.

Dunkel-Schetter and Wortman (1981, 1982) describe two relevant problems. The first has to do with the fact that the indirectly involved person may feel helpless. It is difficult to imagine how one can help when a friend is dying of AIDS or cancer. One may not know what to do, what behavior would be helpful, or what is expected. And even if one knows what needs to be done, one may find it extremely difficult to act on this knowledge (Lehman, Ellard & Wortman 1986). These feelings of helplessness influence a person's health and subjective well-being and they have a clear impact on the person's reactions. A helpless person is likely to engage in tension-avoidance reactions, which may mean that the person withdraws from contact with the directly involved person and does not give social support.

The second problem that Dunkel-Schetter and Wortman (1981, 1982) describe concerns the fact that seeing a close friend or family member go through a situation with a critical life event may make the indirectly involved person feel vulnerable. Observing one's best friends getting divorced or dying of cancer is likely to evoke one's own anxieties concerning divorce or death. This increases the existing tension in such a situation.

In an analysis of the negative consequences of giving social support, the cost factor should not be forgotten. Kessler and McLeod (1985; see also Kessler, McLeod & Wethington 1986) in their analysis of gender differences in mental health suggest that it tends to be women who pay the costs of giving social support and thereby drain themselves emotionally. Other researchers (Hobfoll 1986; Antonucci & Akiyami 1987) support these arguments with further empirical evidence. Research on the burnout of health professionals (see Maslach 1978) also seems connected with this issue. It becomes increasingly clear that giving social support can have negative effects for the care giving person (see also LaGaipa 1990).

The second aspect of recent research on social support is concerned with the negative effects of receiving social support. While earlier research primarily focused on the negative effects of not getting enough social support (see, for example, Coates, Wortman & Abbey 1979), there is a growing literature on the negative effects of getting social support. Cohen & Wills (1985) suggest that negative effects of receiving social support primarily occur when there are network conflicts. Other studies show that negative effects for the person receiving social support can even occur when no network conflicts exist. Wortman and Lehman (1985) describe well-intended attempts to give social support that can have negative effects when they are excessive, inappropriate, or given at an inappropriate time (compare also Maddison & Walker 1967). Coyne, Wortman, and Lehman (1985) point especially to the negative effects of overinvolvement of spouses and family members. In these instances, receiving social support can demonstrate to a person that he/she is dependent and powerless, and that the relationship is unbalanced. This can lead to feelings of loss of control and helplessness which are detrimental to the person's own attempts to adjust in difficult situations (compare Wortman & Conway 1985).

Finally, social support can also be tied to specific expectations that the receiving person has to live up to, and which can be a further stressor for the person receiving the support. Turkington (1985) describes how single, young mothers with a lower socio-economic status may feel pressured to perform according to the expectations of their families who give social support to them.

Given empirical evidence that social support has positive as well as negative effects for the person giving as well as receiving it, the question arises, How can we explain which effects social support has in a given situation? This is the third issue discussed.

A variable-centered approach to this issue consists of two groups of studies: the first concerns person factors that might moderate the effects of social support, while the second concerns situation factors.

Studies on the role of person variables investigate a number of different factors. Lefcourt, Martin, and Saleh (1984) demonstrate that persons with an internal locus of control benefit more from social support than persons with an external locus of control. Kobasa and Puccetti (1983) find that persons with a low value on the "hardiness" scale have more health problems when they receive a high amount of social support than when they do not get much social support. Hobfoll, Nadeler, and Leiberman (1986) point to the significance of a person's level of self-esteem as a moderating variable when social support is given. Gender differences are investigated as well: on the whole, women seem to suffer more from giving social support than men (Kessler, McLeod & Wethington 1986; see also Hobfoll 1986, for an overview of the literature on stress, social support, and women). Age is another important factor that can moderate the effects of receiving social support (see Antonucci 1985).

Studies that focus on the role of situation variables are equally varied. Some studies investigate whether the effects of social support are a function of the amount of stress or daily hassles in a situation. Lootens and Strube (1985) found for example that in a situation with a high level of stress the person's psychological well-being can be lower when a lot of social support is given than when less social support is given. These authors suggest that this may be due to the fact that a high level of social support can place an additional burden on the person in a situation which has already a high stress level.

Other research investigates whether the effects of social support depend on the causes that led to the stress. House (1981) demonstrates, for example, that the effects of social support depend on (a) which causes led to a high level of stress (for example, work stress due to an overload of work, or role conflicts), and (b) who gives social support (colleagues, supervisor, or family members). Dakof and Taylor (1990) describe how the person's perception of receiving support differs according to who gives social support (spouse, other family member, friend, physician, nurse, acquaintance, other person with cancer; see also Taylor & Dakof 1988).

This listing of studies of the effects of social support in interaction with other factors could be continued. At the end of such a listing we might be impressed with the variety of factors investigated, but it would be difficult to use this research to come to concrete predictions for given situations, because there are too many specific aspects that have not yet been studied. Instead of trying to consider each variable that might be important here, we suggest finding a theory that could shed light on the underlying psychological processes in these situations. Let us investigate whether the generalized principle of cognitive consistency can be useful here.

9.2 The Generalized Principle of Cognitive Consistency and Social Support—An Exploration

9.2.1 General Considerations

Exactly how can we use the generalized principle of cognitive consistency to explain the effects of receiving social support?

The starting point is to recall that all our social relationships are cognitively represented. Past experiences with social interactions, the present status of our relationships, as well as expectations for the future are all part of our worldview. These cognitions are consistently organized. Receiving and giving social support introduces new cognitions into our worldview that may or may not be consistent with our old worldview. The generalized principle of cognitive consistency can help clarify two issues here. First, it can help answer the question of whether receiving social support in a situation with a critical life event is likely to increase or decrease the amount of tension that is already there; and second, it can help to clarify how receiving social support influences the kind of reaction chosen to reduce this tension.

In the following sections the implications of the generalized principle of cognitive consistency for explaining these effects on the person receiving social support are elaborated. But we argue that these considerations also can be used, conversely, to explain the effects on the person giving social support.

9.2.2 Social Support and the Amount of Tension

When a critical life event occurs, tension arises. The research on the effect of social interactions in general and specifically of receiving social support in such a situation on the level of tension was discussed earlier (see Lieberman 1982, for an overview). Social support can lead to both a decrease and an increase in tension in such situations. The interesting question then is to explain precisely which effect social support will have on the level of tension that arises.

Two separate aspects must be considered when answering this question, for social support has both *content specific* effects on the tension level and it also has *content unspecific* effects.

Receiving social support introduces cognitions into the person's worldview whose contents are of central importance for understanding whether the social support increases or decreases the tension level. These cognitions are concerned with the problematic event, and with the social relationship with the person giving social support.

To illustrate, let us imagine that a fifty-year-old man has a heart attack and is rushed to the hospital. His twenty-year-old son is phoned and immediately returns home. He provides his father with social support by trying to get all the information possible about the father's condition, by being emotionally reassuring, and by taking over responsibilities for the house and car. In this situation, the son's social support can decrease the father's tension. The son does things the father would worry about if they were not taken care of. After a few days, the doctors decide to perform an angioplasty. It works and the father can leave the hospital. Arriving home, tension arises between the father, who wants his son to behave in the old familiar way, and the son who holds on to the new style of interaction.

This example should illustrate two important points when we try to understand the effect that receiving social support has on the level of tension a person experiences. First, at different points in time different parts of a person's worldview are salient. In the emergency situation, a different part of the person's worldview is salient than after one has recovered. Accordingly, we need to understand which part of a person's worldview is confronted with the newly introduced cognitions.

Second, the sum of single inconsistencies relative to the sum of consistencies can be changed by receiving social support. Accordingly, we need to understand the relation that receiving social support has with that part of the person's worldview that is salient at this point. Receiving social support can decrease the tension globally by shifting the person's attention to a part of the worldview that has fewer or no inconsistencies ("I am so lucky that my son loves me"); it can also change inconsistencies to consistencies ("I was worried about the . . . and my son took care of it") or introduce consistent cognitions ("My son says I am basically in good shape and that is true"). Receiving social support can increase tension by introducing new inconsistencies ("I am the father and have to take care of my son and not let him take care of me"), or by reintroducing old and shut out inconsistencies ("My father and grandfather died of heart attacks and I knew . . ."). Receiving social support can also influence the level of tension by making consistent or inconsistent aspects of the self salient ("I am a strong person; I can cope with everything" versus "Now I am old; my son has to take care of me").

To summarize these content specific considerations of the effects of receiving social support on the level of tension, it can be said that according to the generalized principle of cognitive consistency it is important to understand how receiving social support changes the sum of inconsistencies relative to the sum of consistencies at given points in time. This can happen either by shifting one's attention to another part of one's worldview, by introducing consistent cognitions, or by changing inconsistent to consistent cognitions.

The second effect of receiving social support on the level of tension is content unspecific. This aspect has to do with the way the receiving person uses the social support as a way to change the inconsistencies into consistencies. This issue has two interesting aspects, namely the function of opening up a person's handling of these inconsistencies, and the person's ventilation of the inconsistencies.

Encountering a critical life event and then shutting out the tension caused by it can be effortful if stimuli in the person's surrounding reintroduces the old inconsistencies. Pennebaker (1985) describes vividly the positive effects that starting to address formerly shut out inconsistencies can have. Receiving social support from friends or family members can provide the person with a chance to start working on inconsistencies instead of trying to unsuccessfully shut them out.

The second content unspecific effect that receiving social support can have on the level of tension arising has to do with ventilating the inconsistencies (Dunkel-Schetter & Wortman 1981). Ventilation can be illustrated when we think of conversations with persons who experienced a critical life event. Frequently, these persons repeat over and over what had happened. A person giving social support might be astonished and even annoyed that the directly involved person tells exactly the same details again and again and might wonder why the person does this.

With the generalized principle of cognitive consistency in mind, two things are worth considering when thinking about the function of ventilation. First, by going through the events again and again, the person might be able to reconcile separate aspects with each other and thus establish consistencies. The version of the story one tells may become reality. Second, the person may be unable to shift attention to another part of the worldview and thus procrastinate by speaking about this incident. But having another person listen might have a positive influence on the person's self-esteem and contribute to shifting attention to a less tension loaded part of the person's worldview.

Receiving social support can have content specific as well as content unspecific effects on the amount of tension arising in a situation with a critical life event. When we observe sensitive persons giving social support, we notice that they unconsciously do exactly what the generalized principle of cognitive consistency suggests. They try to point out consistencies in the situation, or they distract the person's attention from the tension loaded part of the worldview. With the generalized principle of cognitive consistency in mind we are able to understand the psychological processes of receiving social support in different situations, and its implications over time.

9.2.3 Social Support and Reaction Used to Reduce It

Receiving social support cannot only influence the amount of tension arising in a situation with a critical life event; it can also have an impact on the kind of general and specific reactions used to reduce the tension. The generalized principle of cognitive consistency can help us understand the psychological processes underlying these effects.

According to the generalized principle of cognitive consistency, one will reduce the tension due to an inconsistency with that general reaction that demands the least amount of effort. Receiving social support can provide the person with resources that make certain ways to react less effortful. It may also influence how much effort a person perceives as necessary for certain reactions.

Social support can have a direct influence on how much effort a certain reaction demands. Let us assume that a person accidentally destroys a car. One kind of social support in such a situation would be material support, such as money from one's parents. Another kind of social support would be informational support, such as from a friend who happens to know about a good buy in a used car. Social support could thus influence the amount of effort perceived as necessary to reduce the tension directly by buying another car. Receiving social support can therefore have a direct effect on the decision whether a tension-reduction or a tension-avoidance reaction is more likely to occur by influencing the amount of effort that these reactions would demand from the person.

Social support can also indirectly influence the amount of effort perceived as necessary for either a tension-reduction or a tension-avoidance reaction by making the person more confident about his or her abilities. If receiving social support makes the person believe that he or she is incompetent, then the likelihood of a tension-avoidance reaction is increased. There is support in the literature that criticism in situations with critical life events is detrimental for the person and leads to less adaptive reactions (see Janis 1983; Manne & Zautra 1987). On the other hand, positive social support can make the person aware that he or she is able to reduce the tension directly. In this case, the effort for a tension-avoidance reaction might seem as relatively higher and the person is more likely to directly reduce the tension.

The generalized principle of cognitive consistency also includes hypotheses about the specific tension-reduction or tension-avoidance reactions. It postulates that the person will use that specific reaction that is most cognitively available. At this point, social support again can play a crucial role by explicitly introducing resources and options into the situation that would not be available otherwise. It can thus change the objective availability of stimuli that are associated with certain reactions. Social support can also make past experiences with certain reactions more salient.

The generalized principle of cognitive consistency helps clarify the effects that receiving social support has on the kind of reaction used to reduce tension. For it helps us understand how the received social support influences the amount of effort perceived as necessary for certain reactions. It is also important to understand which reactions become cognitively available when social support is provided. From the perspective of the generalized principle of cognitive consistency, we no longer focus on whether social support has positive or negative effects for the person giving or receiving it. Instead we try to understand the function that social support has in given situations. The effects of social support are thus no longer analyzed separately, but are now seen as one aspect of the process of reacting to critical life events.

Chapter 10

The Generalized Principle of Cognitive Consistency and Individual Differences—An Exploration

Research on individual differences and the personality is a world of its own. Four basic perspectives can be distinguished (compare, e.g., Endler & Edwards 1982). There are proponents of (a) a psychoanalytic perspective (Freud 1959), (b) traditional personality research (trait theoreticians; Allport 1966; Cattell 1946; Guilford 1959), (c) a social approach (Dewey & Humber 1951; Mead 1934; Mischel 1968, 1973, 1985; Rotter 1954), and (d) an interactionist approach (Endler & Magnusson 1976; Endler 1982; Endler & Edwards 1982). While the first two groups of researchers focus solely on the person—that is on intrapsychic processes in given individuals and personality traits—supporters of a social learning theory stress the importance of the situation and its significance for the explanation of individual reactions. Interactionists assume that individual behavior is the result of the interaction between person and situational factors.

All four of these approaches are represented in research on the role of person variables in situations with critical life events. This chapter starts with an overview of this research, and will then use the generalized principle of cognitive consistency to clarify the role of person variables in situations with critical life events.

10.1 Person Variables and Reactions to Critical Life Events— An Overview

No topic in research on critical life events has stimulated as many publications in recent years as research on person variables and their significance as moderators between stress and outcome reactions. A multitude of different concepts has been introduced and investigated. Let us briefly review the most extensively studied concepts.

10.1.1 The Type A Behavior Pattern

Research on the role of Type A behavior patterns in reactions to critical life events and stress dates back to the 1950s (Friedman & Rosenman 1959). This concept is not only well known to lay persons, but has also been investigated by specialists in psychology (see Wright 1988), epidemiology, and medicine. Its implications for coronary artery disease are well documented, although not undisputed (compare Matthews 1988; Friedman & Booth-Kewley 1988).

The Type A behavior pattern was first described in 1959 by two physicians, Friedman and Rosenman, who published the results of a study of patients with coronary artery disease (see also Rosenman, Friedman, Strauss, Wurm, Kositchek, Hahn & Werthessen 1964; Rosenman, Brand, Jenkins, Friedman, Strauss & Wurm 1975). They found that heart attack patients had distinctive behavior patterns: they were competitive, multiphasic (tending to do several things at once such as watching TV and reading), achievement-oriented, had a sense of time urgency and impatience, and were easily aroused, hostile, or angry. One can readily imagine what such a behavior pattern does to a person's arteries: such persons frequently become upset, which increases the pressure on the arteries; this leads to wear and tear and can ultimately result in heart attacks (see Friedman & Ulmer 1984; Matthews 1982; Wright 1988, for overviews).

The Type A behavior pattern is primarily measured with the Structured Interview (SI) (Friedman & Rosenman 1974) and the Jenkins Activity Scale (JAS) (Jenkins, Rosenman & Friedman 1967; Jenkins, Zyzanski & Rosenman 1976; Jenkins & Zyzanski 1980). The Structured Interview allows the researcher to challenge subjects and thus measure both their expressive style (nonverbal and emotional) and the verbal responses (compare Friedman & Booth-Kewley 1987). The Jenkins Activity Scale is a self-report, paper-and-pencil questionnaire. Newer research (Wright 1988) attempts to develop more differentiated measures. The JAS has been used in numerous countries to investigate the connection between a person's behavior patterns and coronary artery disease (see Goldband, Katkin & Morell 1979; Derogatis 1982, as overviews). Other scales used to measure Type A behavior patterns are the Bortner Scale (Bortner 1969; Bass 1984) and the Framingham Type A Scale (Matthews 1982).

Psychological research on the Type A behavior pattern falls into two groups (Glass 1977; Matthews 1982). The first group investigates the impact of the Type A behavior pattern on various aspects of a person's behavior, such as subjective well-being (Strube, Berry, Goza & Fennimore 1985; Lootens & Strube 1985), reactions to uncontrollable events (Brunson & Matthews 1981), success and failure (Musante, McDougall & Dembroski 1984), and post-failure performance (Strube, Boland, Manfredo & Al-Falaij 1986).

The second group of studies investigates the psychological mechanism that explains the effects of the Type A behavior pattern. Some authors (Brunson & Matthews 1981; Glass 1977; Matthews 1979) argue that Type A persons, far more than Type B persons, react with learned helplessness to uncontrollable events. Strube (1990) argues against this explanation and points out (a) that this hypothesis is not supported in all studies, (b) that the success orientation of Type A persons is inconsistent with reactions of helplessness, and (c) that Type A persons are not more depressive than Type B persons. His own explanation is called the "self-appraisal model"; it argues that Type A persons are more motivated to evaluate their own abilities than Type B persons. Therefore, if Type A persons encounter failure or loss of control, then they become more uncertain about their own abilities and employ Type A behavior to obtain diagnostic information about their own abilities. Most recently, the role of emotional distress in connection with Type A behavior pattern and coronary heart disease were studied (Suls & Wan 1989).

These explanations go beyond Friedman and Rosenman's original hypothesis (Friedman & Rosenman 1959). They reflect the trend in contemporary personality research to move away from rigid personality traits and instead to develop theories about the underlying psychological processes.

Research on the Type A behavior pattern is still struggling with problems of measurement and conceptualization (Friedman & Booth-Kewley 1988), as well as with the problem of working out the practical implications (see Matthews & Haynes 1986; Snyder & Houston 1988; Wright 1988).

10.1.2 Control

The control issue is central to the work of numerous authors (see Bandura 1977, 1982; Rodin & Langer 1977; Rodin 1986; Baltes & Baltes 1986; Thompson 1981). This issue was studied in connection with several key terms in situations with critical life events. Here we will discuss three groups of studies, namely (a) Rotter's locus of control construct (Rotter 1966; Lefcourt 1981, 1983a, 1984), (b) on internal or external control beliefs in general (see for example Folkman 1984), and (c) on control issues connected with Kobasa's "hardiness" construct (1979, 1982a, 1982b).

10.1.2.1 Internal Versus External Locus of Control

In 1966, Rotter introduced the concept of internal versus external locus of control into psychological literature, giving rise to a tremendous amount of subsequent research on this construct (for an overview see Lefcourt 1981, 1983a, 1984). Rotter (1954) developed this idea in the framework of an interactionistic personality theory. Subsequently, he became far better known for his internal versus external locus of control construct than for his original theory (see Rotter 1989). In a recent publication, Rotter (1990) presents his own ideas on why the concept of internal versus external locus of control has stimulated so much research. He argues that its success is linked with the fact that it is (a) precisely defined, (b) embedded in a broader theoretical perspective, (c) has an accompanying measurement instrument, and (d) that its first publication was done in the Psychological Monographs which provided a much better basis for presenting a careful analysis of this research than a single journal article would have done.

In research on reactions to critical life events, locus of control has been investigated intensively. The central question is whether an internal or an external locus of control is more beneficial when a critical life event occurs. Lefcourt (1983b) gives an excellent overview of this research, concluding that an internal control belief will generally be more useful in a stressful situation than an external locus of control (see also Thompson 1981; Parkes 1984).

There are methodological questions whether the original locus of control scale is a reliable and valid instrument (see Lefcourt 1981, for example). But there seems to be agreement that a person's control beliefs have an impact on the degree of stress experienced and the kinds of coping reactions that take place when a critical life event occurs.

10.1.2.2 Control Beliefs—A General Consideration

Some studies on the effects of general control beliefs (see Folkman 1984, for an overview) report contradictory findings concerning which kind of control beliefs are more beneficial. In some of these studies, persons with internal control beliefs experience more stress and/or cope less well than persons with external control belief. Folkman (1984) suggests that these contradictions can be explained if the influence of specific contexts is taken into account. Using Lazarus' theory of stress, appraisal, and coping (see Lazarus & Folkman 1984) as a theoretical framework, she reconsiders the influence of control beliefs in situations with critical life events. This leads to some interesting insights into the psychological processes linked with the effects of control beliefs. For example, Folkman (1984) points out that a personal control locus can simultaneously have very different psychological functions: a person with an internal control belief may not only feel good about having control and being able to do something, but he or she may also expect that costs arise from having control which may increase the stress level.

Although Folkman (1984) only offers a phenomenological analysis of the psychological processes involved, her analysis suggests that it would be useful to integrate control beliefs into a broader theory that explains psychological reactions to critical life events. We follow this suggestion using the generalized principle of cognitive consistency to explore the role of control beliefs in situations with critical life events.

10.1.2.3 Hardiness

In 1979, Kobasa introduced the concept of "hardiness" into the discussion of person factors in stressful situations. She identified two groups of middle

and upper level executives who had had comparably high degrees of stressfu
life events in the three years preceding this study. One group stayed relatively
healthy despite experiencing these stressful events, while the second group
became sick. Kobasa (1979) demonstrated that the two groups differed significantly in the degree to which they were "hardy." High stress/low illness
managers compared to high stress/high illness managers were characterized
by having a strong commitment to themselves, an attitude of vigor toward
the environment, a sense of meaningfulness, and an internal locus of control.
Hardiness was thus defined as having three components, namely a commitment, a control, and a challenge component.

Originally, Kobasa (1979) used several existing scales to measure hardiness.
These scales were the Internal versus External Locus of Control Scale (Rotter
1966), several scales of the Alienation Test (Maddi, Kobasa & Hoover 1979),
subscales of the Personality Research Form (Jackson 1974), and the California
Life Goals Evaluation Schedule (Hahn 1966). The results of her first study
(Kobasa 1979) led to a short version of the Hardiness Scale (Kobasa 1982a,
1982b).

Kobasa's basic hypothesis is that hardy persons—that is persons who have
internal control beliefs, who interpret changes as a challenge, and who have
a high commitment to life—stay healthier when stress occurs than persons
who are low in hardiness. This hypothesis has been supported by the results
of numerous studies (Kobasa 1982a, 1982b; Kobasa, Maddi & Kahn 1982;
Kobasa, Maddi & Courington 1981; Kobasa, Maddi & Puccetti 1982; Kobasa
& Puccetti 1983; Kobasa, Maddi & Zola 1983).

Kobasa's work was criticized in three ways. Methodological criticism of
the Hardiness Scale's validity and utility (Funk & Houston 1987) cast doubts
on the quality of the research instrument. Furthermore, some empirical
studies could not replicate the finding that hardiness had a stress-buffering
effect (see, for example, Singer & Rich 1985), or came up with more differentiated results (see, for example, Schlosser & Sheeley 1985, who found that
the component of challenge has no significance for women; Hull, Van Treuren & Virnelli 1987). Finally, Kobasa was also criticized on theoretical
grounds. Lazarus and Folkman (1985, p. 212) argue, for example, that Kobasa's statements about the impact of hardiness on a person's health status
(Kobasa 1979; Kobasa & Puccetti 1983) contain implicit assumptions about
the coping process: Kobasa implies that hardiness leads to a specific kind of
coping and that this kind of coping has an impact on a person's health status.
Considering these indirect assumptions, which Kobasa never explicitly investigated, led Lazarus and Folkman (1985) to emphasize the importance of
directly studying the coping process in order to understand the effects of
stress on a person's health status. Another theoretical explanation for the
influence of hardiness in stressful situations was presented by Rhodewalt
and Zone (1989). They argue that the negative affectivity of nonhardy persons
(and not the stress resilience of hardy persons) may explain the differences

\ groups. Roth, Wiebe, Fillingim, and Shay (1989) argued
\ influence the occurrence or subjective interpretation of
 but that it does not have a moderator effect when pre-
.. health status.

..neralized principle of cognitive consistency offers an alternative
..oretical explanation for the effects described by Kobasa (1979, 1982b).
We argue that persons high on hardiness may encounter fewer inconsistencies
between their outlook and the demands of the environment than those low
in hardiness. Being a middle or upper level manager with an internal control
belief, a high commitment to one's job, and a positive attitude toward changes
is likely to be consistent with the demands of the business environment,
which rewards persons who take initiative and live up to their potential in
competitive settings. Being hardy may also go with a tendency to directly
reduce tension due to inconsistencies, instead of making avoidance reactions,
because hardy persons may estimate the efforts for direct tension-reduction
reactions to be lower than do less hardy persons. This again is a behavior
that tends to be rewarded in business settings.

This explanation has two implications. First, it accounts for the contradictory finding that the hardiness hypothesis does *not* hold up when tested
with college students (Singer & Rich 1985) and female staff nurses (Rich &
Rich 1985). The environment of college students and staff nurses does not
make demands that correspond to the person variables of the hardiness scale
nearly as closely as does the managerial environment. Accordingly, hardiness
is much less relevant to the health status of students and nurses. This explanation stresses the significance of understanding the psychological mechanism underlying the hardiness/health status relationship. It also follows
Lazarus and Folkman's suggestion (1985) to investigate the role of this variable
in the context of a broader theory about reactions to critical life events.

10.1.3 Styles

Another group of person factors can be summarized under the heading
"styles." This concept assumes that people develop strategies to react to the
environment in general and to critical life events in particular. These strategies may focus on evaluating events, as is the case when attributional styles
are used. They may also concern the kinds of reactions chosen in general
(see, for example, blunting versus monitoring as two coping styles when
threatening events occur; Miller 1988). Styles can also be specific behavioral
strategies that tend to be used in anxiety provoking situations such as defensive pessimism (see Norem & Cantor 1986a, 1986b).

10.1.3.1 Attributional Styles

Research on attributional styles ties together considerations about the significance of control in critical life events and hypotheses about the strategies
used to evaluate and react to these events.

In the chapter on cognitive theories (see, especially, 4.1.2 and 4.1.3), we pointed out that Seligman and his coworkers introduced attributions as crucial factors into the revised theory of learned helplessness (Abramson, Seligman & Teasdale 1978). Later, they generalized these ideas in their considerations of attributional or explanatory styles.

In the revised theory of learned helplessness, Seligman (Abramson, Seligman & Teasdale 1978) argued that people who react to negative outcomes with a generalized tendency to attribute these outcomes to internal, stable, and global factors would be more helpless and more depressed than those who tend to make external, unstable, and specific attributions. The specific connection between certain types of attributions and depression was investigated by numerous researchers. Robins (1988) lists eighty-seven studies that test this hypothesis. While some authors (for example Peterson & Seligman 1984) find clear support that these three attributional dimensions are relevant for predicting depression, others postulate that they do not have great relevance (see, for example, Coyne & Gotlib 1983), or that only one or two of the three dimensions are relevant (see Robins 1988).

In more recent research, Seligman and his coworkers analyzed the role of attributional styles on behavior in general (Seligman & Schulman 1986; Peterson 1986; Nolen-Hoeksema, Girgus & Seligman 1986). They found that a person's attributional style affects a number of behaviors and even a person's general health status (see 4.1.3 for a more detailed overview of this research).

In view of the contradictory findings concerning the impact of attributional style on depression (see Robin 1988) and on coping in general (see Herrmann 1988), one wonders whether a general theory about reactions to critical life events can help us understand these contradictory findings. The generalized principle of cognitive consistency suggests that attributions may decrease or increase the amount of tension a person experiences when a critical life event occurs. They may also influence the kind of general and specific reactions a person uses to reduce the tension due to an inconsistent life event by (a) providing the person with information about the amount of effort involved in certain reactions, and (b) making certain reactions cognitively more available. By analyzing the role of attributions in the psychological process that unfolds after a critical life event has occurred, we may begin to understand their significance.

10.1.3.2 Coping Styles

Coping styles—as conceptualized by Miller (1980, 1981, 1987, 1988)—are individual predispositions to reactions to threatening information. Specifically, Miller (1988) differentiates between monitors and blunters. Other authors use the concept of coping styles in different ways (compare for example Hamilton & Fagot 1988). Miller distinguishes between the degree to which a person seeks out and monitors information about threat, and the degree to which a person distracts oneself from and psychologically blunts threatening information. She measures these two coping styles with a self-report scale, the Miller Behavioral Style Scale (Miller 1987). This scale consists of four stress-evoking and uncontrollable scenes, each of which is followed by eight statements about ways to cope with these events. Four of the statements describe monitoring and four statements describe blunting behavior. Miller demonstrates that a person's scores on this scale are unrelated to demographic variables and to trait measures such as repression-sensitization, depression, anxiety, and Type A behavior pattern (Miller & Brody 1985; Miller, Lack, & Asroff 1982; Miller & Mangan 1983; Miller & Mischel 1986).

The effects of these coping styles on reactions to threatening information were demonstrated in several laboratory experiments (see Miller 1987) and in field studies on health-related behavior (see, for example, Miller, Brody & Summerton 1988; Miller 1989). Miller (1988) finds, for example, that high monitors come to physicians with less severe medical problems than low monitors, but that they report equivalent levels of discomfort, dysfunction, and distress compared with low monitors. During the week following a visit to a physician, high monitors expressed less symptom improvement in both physical and psychological problems than did low monitors. They demanded more tests, information, and counseling during their visit, but demanded a less active role in their own care than low monitors.

Although Miller (1987, 1988) argues that dispositional differences in coping style are an important moderator of actual coping strategies in adverse situations, she recognizes that there are situational constraints on the degree to which a person seeks out or blunts information. She found for example less distraction from threatening information if the threat was highly probable, long or imminent, or if there was a high level of threat.

The generalized principle of cognitive consistency leads us to inquire what causes people to develop a given coping style, and what consequences this style has for a given way of reacting to threatening information. Concerning the first question, we suggest that blunting and monitoring can be interpreted as specific forms of tension-avoidance and tension-reduction reactions, respectively. According to the principle of least effort used to predict whether a person is more likely to directly reduce tension or to avoid tension, one would predict that (due to prior experiences) high monitors have generalized expectations that the costs of shutting out threatening events are higher than the costs of coping with them, while high blunters have learned that the costs of direct tension-reduction reactions are higher than the costs of tension-avoidance reactions. An investigation of the socialization experiences of high monitors and high blunters would enable us to test this interpretation.

It seems important to investigate the consequences of having a given coping style. The generalized principle of cognitive consistency might contribute to understanding the psychological process involved. The amount of tension arising is a function of the amount of threatening information considered.

The kind of reaction used to reduce the tension depends on the amount of threatening information considered, because this has an impact on the amount of effort perceived for certain reactions. The kind of information considered also influences what becomes cognitively available—which in return influences which specific reaction will be used to reduce the tension.

These remarks suggest that research on coping styles might profitably be approached from the perspective of a general theory about reactions to critical life events.

10.1.3.3 Defensive Pessimism

Seeking out information or blunting information can take many forms. One style of reacting to situations that are risky (because they present the possibility of failure and potential threats to self-esteem) is defensive pessimism, a construct introduced by Norem & Cantor (1986a, 1986b; Cantor, Norem, Niedenthal, Langston & Brower 1987).

People using the strategy of defensive pessimism have low expectations in risky situations, although prior experiences in similar situations may have not been negative. An example of a defensive pessimist is a straight A student who expects to fail coming exams and tells friends that the best he or she can hope for might be a C minus.

Although there is evidence that this strategy influences outcomes (see Norem & Cantor 1986a, 1986b; Cantor et al. 1988), there are still some open questions. For example, little is known about how common this strategy is, what the situational constraints are that make this strategy likely, what its possible long-term effects are, or what consequences such a strategy may have on other aspects of life. The results of the initial studies on this concept suggest that it would be worthwhile to investigate these questions.

10.1.3.4 Optimism/Pessimism

While the defensive pessimism research focuses on one specific strategy to manage anxiety in risky situations (Norem & Cantor 1986a, 1986b), the dispositional optimism/pessimism dimension is defined as a generalized expectancy about one's future life outcomes (Carver & Scheier 1987; Scheier & Carver 1985, 1987; Strack, Carver & Blaney 1987). It is measured with a brief self-report scale, the Life Orientation Test (LOT).

Carver and Scheier (1987) argue that dispositional optimism has a clear impact on how well and in what manner people cope with stress. This hypothesis was investigated in laboratory experiments in which people imagined themselves in stressful situations and then described how they think they would react. While optimists used an active problem-focused coping style, pessimists were more likely to focus on feelings of distress and become immersed in those feelings. This hypothesis was also tested in field studies in such settings as giving birth to a child, going through an alcoholism rehabilitation program or having bypass surgery. The results of these studies (Carver & Scheier 1987; Scheier & Carver 1985, 1987; Strack, Carver & Blaney 1987; Scheier, Matthews, Owens, Magovern, Lefebvre, Abbott & Carver 1989) demonstrate that dispositional optimism is a good predictor of behavioral outcome and affect in stressful situations. On the whole, dispositional optimists have better behavioral and subjective outcomes than do pessimists in times of difficulty. The authors argue that this is because optimists have favorable expectancies which keep them focused on dealing with their problems, rather than lamenting them. They conclude that more research is needed to determine how general this effect is and how broad its applications are.

One critical analysis of this concept (Smith, Pope, Rhodewalt & Poulton 1989) argues that the Life Orientation Test might actually not have any discriminant validity when compared with measures of neuroticism. This is an interesting argument. We suggest that by considering this concept and its functions in the framework of a general theory, the underlying process might become clearer and its relevance more readily assessed.

10.1.4 The Self

Another group of studies on the effects of person factors in explaining reactions to critical life events is concerned with the self. It has become increasingly evident in recent years that self-cognitions are relevant to coping, depression, and mental health issues (Beck 1976; Cantor & Kihlstrom 1987; Higgins, Klein & Strauman 1985; Kuiper & Derry 1981; Linville 1985). We will discuss research on the effects of self-esteem, and self-complexity, in a person's reactions to critical life events.

10.1.4.1 Self-Esteem

Self-esteem is one ingredient of a person's self-concept (Greenwald, Bellezza & Banaji 1988). It has been found to be a key person factor when studying stress resistance and coping processes (Hobfoll & Walfisch 1984; Pearlin, Lieberman, Menaghan & Mullan 1981; Pearlin & Schooler 1978). One explanation of these effects is that those with a positive view of themselves are not overwhelmed by stressful events to the same degree as those with a negative view of themselves. For example, Pearlin, Lieberman, Menaghan, and Mullan (1981) demonstrate that those persons with high self-esteem do not get as depressed when they lose their jobs as persons with low self-esteem. Furthermore, those persons with high self-esteem tend to have a more positive evaluation of their own abilities than low self-esteem persons and this influences the kind of reactions they choose to reduce tension in situations with critical life events.

Originally, the effects of self-esteem were studied in connection with depression. Recently, increasing attention has been paid to such topics as the interaction of self-esteem and receiving social support (Hobfoll, Nadler & Leiberman 1986; DeLongis, Folkman & Lazarus 1988). There is no clear evidence whether having high self-esteem and receiving help leads to higher or lower satisfaction (Nadler & Mayseless 1983). On one hand, it is argued that receiving social support has a negative effect on the well-being of low self-esteem persons because they are more vulnerable to incoming negative information. On the other hand, from a consistency point of view it is argued that high self-esteem persons will feel less good when receiving help, because this would be inconsistent with their self-concept (Hobfoll, Nadler & Leiberman 1986).

This discussion raises an essential point in studying the effects of self-esteem. It is not sufficient to measure self-esteem on one hand and reactions to critical life events on the other hand, because there is no unvarying simple relationship between the two. Instead, we need to understand the psychological processes unfolding in situations with critical life events and the role that self-esteem has in these processes.

10.1.4.2 Self-Complexity

While self-esteem refers primarily to the *kind* of self-cognitions a person has, self-complexity is concerned with the *structure* of the cognitive representations of the self. The issue of understanding the structure of self-cognitions has attracted considerable attention recently (see Cantor & Kihlstrom 1987, for an overview). Linville (1985, 1987a, 1987b) has investigated how the structure of the self influences reactions to stressful events. She defines greater self-complexity as entailing cognitively organizing self-knowledge in terms of a greater number of self-aspects and maintaining greater distinctions among self-aspects. Self-complexity is measured in a sorting task in which the subjects sort thirty-three index cards with positive and negative features about themselves into groups. By analyzing the number of groups a person forms and the overlap of the groups (that is how many cards are put into several groups), Linville (1985, 1987a, 1987b) determines a self-complexity score. The greater the number of groups created and the less redundantly the features are used, the higher is the person's self-complexity score.

Linville (1982, 1985, 1987a, 1987b) reports clear evidence that persons actually do differ in the cognitive complexity of their self. Her basic hypothesis is that greater self-complexity moderates the adverse effects of stressful events on physical and mental health outcomes, and buffers the person against stress-related illness and depression. She finds support for this hypothesis in her empirical research.

Linville's considerations complement the generalized principle of cognitive consistency very usefully, helping clarify our understanding of that part of a person's worldview which concerns the self. This has implications for applying the sum rule to predict the amount of tension arising. The sum of single inconsistencies relative to the sum of consistencies is likely to be smaller if self-complexity is high rather than low. Linville's work also has implications for the kind of reactions a person may choose to reduce tension. If given aspects of the self are relatively distinct, the cognitive availability of behavioral alternatives will be quite different than if these aspects of the self are connected with each other. Thus, it seems worthwhile to consider the structure and not just the contents of a person's self-cognitions and worldview, when analyzing the effects of person factors on reactions to critical life events.

10.1.5 Interactionistic Considerations

The most prominent supporter of an interactionistic approach in research on reactions to critical life events is Lazarus (Lazarus & Folkman 1985; see Caspi, Bolger & Eckenrode 1987, for another approach). He describes his theory as "transactional, mediation, time-oriented and process-oriented" (Lazarus & Launier 1987, p. 321), and assumes that each reaction reflects an interaction between all factors important in such a situation, which includes both person factors and situational factors. He explicitly discusses two person factors, namely commitment and beliefs, and the influence they have on a person's reactions (Lazarus & Folkman 1985, pp. 55ff). Lazarus argues that these two groups of factors influence the appraisal of a critical life event (cf. Wrubel, Benner & Lazarus 1981). Person factors alone are not seen as a sufficient basis to predict reactions to critical life events.

Lazarus (Lazarus & Folkman 1985) postulates that commitment has a cognitive as well as an affective component. It structures a person's thinking and actions, and it motivates the person. At the same time, it also makes the person more vulnerable. If a person has a high commitment to another person or object, then he or she will experience more tension when an event with a negative impact on this relationship occurs, than if the commitment is low.

Beliefs are defined as personally formed or culturally shared cognitive configurations (Wrubel, Benner & Lazarus 1981); they are preexisting notions about reality which structure the perception of reality and shape a person's appraisal. Lazarus holds that control beliefs are especially important.

We pointed out earlier that Lazarus' phenomenological perspective has the advantage of doing justice to the complexity of reality, helping provide a basic sense of what is going on in these situations. But we also argued that it is difficult to deduce testable hypotheses from his theory. This argumentation applies to his considerations on the role of person factors in situations with critical life events. One would like to understand the role these factors play in the appraisal and coping process on the whole, but it is difficult to move from these general considerations to specific predictions for given situations.

10.1.6 Person Factors and Reactions to Critical Life Events—
Evaluating the Research

This chapter started with an overview of the most discussed person factors in research on reactions to critical life events. This seems to be the fastest growing segment of research on reactions to critical life events. But analyzing this research brings to light the fact that there are contradictory findings concerning the contribution of virtually every person factor discussed so far. Furthermore, problems with the measurement of the variables and/or with the explanation of the psychological processes involved are discussed in the literature. It is virtually impossible to produce a summarizing list of the confirmed contributions of person factors to explaining reactions to critical life events.

Nevertheless, an overview of this research contributes to our understanding of this topic in one significant way. It helps us to identify which essential underlying dimensions are tapped by these variables. Such an analysis may help structure future research designed to explain how these factors relate to each other and—even more importantly—how we can understand the psychological processes connected with these variables.

We suggest that these approaches differ along three dimensions. These dimensions are (a) the degree to which a person feels positive or negative toward the critical life event, (b) the kind of control beliefs a person has, and (c) whether the self is explicitly considered or not.

Table 10.1 provides a classification of the person variables discussed so far according to whether they explicitly consider these three dimensions or not. This table makes it evident that these approaches clearly differ in their contents. One might argue about whether each variable has been put in its correct place. But this classification should be interpreted primarily as an attempt to identify which contents are most relevant when analyzing the function of these variables and the underlying psychological processes. It will guide us in exploring the effects that person factors have on reactions to critical life events according to the generalized principle of cognitive consistency.

10.2 The Generalized Principle of Cognitive Consistency and
Person Factors—An Exploration

From the perspective of social psychology, individual differences in personality traits are not of central importance. Nevertheless, this topic is included here for two reasons. First, so much research has been conducted on the effects of person factors on reactions to critical life events, that any book on this topic would be incomplete if this research were not considered. And, second, there is no doubt that persons differ in their experiences and the lessons they learn from these experiences. They develop different expecta-

Table 10.1

Various Approaches to Explaining the Effects of Person Factors on Reactions to Critical Life Events

| | | "Self" explicitly considered: | |
		Yes	No
Positivity/negativity explicitly considered: Yes	Control explicitly considered: Yes		Hardiness
	No	Self-esteem	Optimism/ pessimism; Defensive pessimism
No	Yes	Internal vs. external locus of control; explanatory styles	Type A
	No	self-complexity	--

tions about how the world functions, and build up a repertoire of knowledge and strategies that shapes the way they react to new situations. It is important to understand the role that these preexisting notions play in the psychological process that starts when a critical life event occurs.

Let us explore how person factors help predict the amount of tension arising, the kind of general and specific reactions, and the long-term consequences of having encountered a critical life event.

10.2.1 Person Factors and Amount of Tension

The generalized principle of cognitive consistency is a cognitive theory. Thus, we reinterpret person factors from a cognitive perspective when we examine their role in determining reactions to critical life events within the framework of the generalized principle of cognitive consistency.

The basic hypothesis concerning the amount of tensio
critical life event occurs is referred to as the *sum rule*. It s₁
amount of tension arising in situations with inconsistent even⟨
of the sum of the single inconsistencies between the event and
worldview, relative to the sum of consistencies the person consi⟨
situation.

There are two ways in which person factors can be important ⟨ ⟨ applying this sum rule: person factors have a content-free impact and content-
specific influences on the amount of tension arising after a critical life event
occurred.

Concerning the content-free impact of person factors, it is important to
explore the way in which people differ in the structure of their worldviews.
Our considerations on this point start with Linville's work on the structure
of self-cognitions (Linville 1982, 1985, 1987a, 1987b). Linville pointed out
that persons differ in their degree of self-complexity. The more aspects of
the self a person differentiates, and the less overlap there is between these
aspects, the higher is a person's self-complexity. She argues that the higher
a person's self-complexity, the less stress a person will experience and the
better the person's adjustment will be in a situation with a critical life event.

Let us generalize these considerations from the self to the person's worldview as a whole. We argue that a person's worldview as a whole, as well as
specific parts of the worldview, can be structured very differently. They
differ in the number of aspects a person considers and in the way these
aspects relate to each other. The structure of a person's worldview may be
crucial for understanding which cognitions are salient in a situation with a
critical life event. This contributes to predicting how large the sum of salient
inconsistent relationships between this event and the person's worldview is,
in comparison to the sum of consistent relationships that are salient in this
situation.

The second aspect concerns the content-specific differences in person factors. In predicting the amount of tension arising, it is useful to map the
various person factors onto three dimensions (see Table 10.1), namely (a)
whether they consider explicitly the degree to which a person feels positive
versus negative; (b) whether they explicitly consider control issues; and (c)
whether they consider the self. Using these three dimensions helps us predict
the amount of tension arising as well as which kind of reaction will be used
to reduce this tension.

The degree to which a person focuses on the positive as compared to the
negative aspects of a given situation tells us which aspects of the situation
are salient. This helps assess the amount of inconsistent and consistent relationships that are in the focus of the person's attention. According to the
sum rule, the tension arising is a function of the relationship between the
inconsistent and consistent relations salient in a given situation. We hypoth-

esize that those persons who focus on the positive rather than the negative aspects of given situations will experience less tension than persons who focus on the negative aspects.

The degree to which a person perceives that the outcome in a given situation is controllable does not have a direct effect on the amount of tension arising. But it can have an indirect impact, if we consider which other cognitions are introduced into a situation by perceiving it as controllable versus uncontrollable. If we want to understand whether a certain control belief leads to an increase versus a decrease of tension, we need to analyze the implications that this control belief has in given situations. Specifically, we need to understand whether it makes further inconsistent or consistent relations between the critical life event and the person's worldview salient.

The third dimension refers to whether the self is explicitly considered. We can safely assume that the self is a central part of the person's worldview. In discussing the effects of internal versus external post hoc attributions, we argued that the degree of tension arising will be higher when self-cognitions become salient in these situations. The role of self-complexity in predicting the amount of arising tension has already been discussed. We can now add one further consideration concerning the self: that it is important to consider which specific self cognitions are salient in given situations. Cognitions about the real as well as the ideal self, about the past and the future self may be important in these situations. Understanding the content of a person's self-cognitions should contribute to applying the sum rule.

10.2.2 Person Factors and the Kind of Reaction Used to Reduce Tension

How can person factors contribute to predicting the general and the specific reactions as well as the long-term consequences of having encountered a critical life event?

The *general* reactions used to reduce tension due to a critical life event are predicted by the principle of least effort, which holds that a person will use that reaction that demands the least effort. As pointed out earlier, the amount of effort for a reaction cannot be determined objectively. It depends on the person's evaluation of the situation. This evaluation is influenced by person factors. Different persons have different experiences and different behavioral repertoires; they differ in their attitudes and values as well as in the knowledge of themselves and the environment; and they differ in their self-evaluations and the strategies they use. All of these factors have implications for the amount of effort people perceive as necessary for given reactions.

Concerning the three dimensions which given person factors either consider explicitly or do not consider, contributes to our understanding of the kind of reactions a person is likely to choose in a given situation. A positive outlook on a situation encourages one to perceive less effort as being necessary for direct tension-reduction reactions than does a negative outlook. The perception that outcomes are controllable may also imply that the efforts necessary to directly reduce tension due to a critical life event are smaller than the perception that the outcomes in given situations are uncontrollable. Finally, if the *self* is involved in a situation with a critical life event, it may make the attempt to reduce tension by avoiding that specific part of the person's worldview much more costly than if the self is not considered. These considerations suggest how person factors help predict *general* reactions to critical life events.

Predicting the *specific* reactions used to reduce tension depends on the cognitive availability of given reactions. This is a function of earlier experiences with given reactions and the objective availability of stimuli associated with given reactions. Thus, individual differences in the way persons were socialized are important. The behavior that their role models or peers showed in situations with critical life events as well as differences in the behavior they used in earlier situations with critical life events provides information about the cognitive availability of given reactions. Again, it can be useful to understand whether a person tends to be more positive or more negative towards life, what kind of control beliefs this person has, and this person's self-concept, in order to predict the cognitive availability of given reactions in a person's worldview.

Finally, considering the *long-term consequences* of having encountered a critical life event, leads to the questions discussed in the next chapter. According to the generalized principle of cognitive consistency, human beings are motivated to maintain a consistent worldview. They differ in the ways they use to reestablish consistency, once an inconsistent event has occurred. They may shut out tension due to a critical life event, or they may reduce the tension directly by reestablishing cognitive consistency. We will consider the role individual differences in existential and general beliefs play in this life long process of establishing consistency.

It seems clear that person factors influence reactions to critical life events. We are far from completely understanding the psychological processes leading to these effects, but it seems helpful to use a general theory about reactions to critical life events as a framework when investigating these factors and their possible effects.

Chapter 11

The Significance of Life Philosophies

One major interest of social psychologists is how attitudes change, and what the relationship is between attitudes and behavior. But despite this overwhelming interest in social cognitions, relatively little social psychological research has investigated their role in situations with critical life events. This chapter suggests that by considering a person's attitudes, beliefs, and values—which we will refer to as a person's life philosophy—we may learn how individual differences influence reactions to critical life events.

11.1 Relevance of Life Philosophies in Situations with Critical Life Events—An Overview

The term *life philosophy* is defined as the sum of a person's attitudes, beliefs, and values about how the world functions, including social cognitions about oneself, as well as one's social and objective environment.

Why do we devote a chapter to this topic? We argue that although most human beings cannot readily articulate their life philosophy, they nevertheless do have attitudes, beliefs, and values that influence their reactions to life in general and to critical life events in particular. Moreover, we argue that these elements of a person's life philosophy are organized in an elaborate network that obeys the rules of consistency. This does not mean that all cognitions are necessarily consistent with one another. Humans are able to compartmentalize inconsistent parts of their worldviews. But in given situations, the person's worldview provides the basis for judging incoming information and choosing the correct response.

11.1.1 Relevance of Life Philosophies—General Consideration

A tremendous amount of social psychological research deals with attitudes;

many studies investigate the role of beliefs in everyday life and sometimes even in situations with critical life events (see Gorsuch 1988, for an overview of research on religious beliefs; see McIntosh & Spilka 1990, for an overview of the literature on religion and health; see Chapter 10 for a review of the literature on control beliefs). Moreover, some psychological research has focused on values (for example, Rokeach 1973; Bond 1988). All of this work primarily analyzes one part of a person's life philosophy; it does not examine the general question of how life philosophies in general influence human behavior.

Instead of focusing exclusively on one type of belief or value, social psychologists might profitably consider the larger network of cognitions in which given beliefs are embedded and the processes in which they are involved. Relevant research includes Harvey, Hunt, and Schroder's (1961) work on "self systems," Bowlby's (1969, 1973, 1980) "working models" of the world, Hall's (1986) "cosmologies," and Janoff-Bulman's (1989) "assumptive worlds." All of these authors are interested in the organization of a person's assumptions and beliefs about the world.

In this monograph we are primarily interested in investigating the role of beliefs in situations with critical life events.

11.1.2 Relevance of Life Philosophies in Situations with Critical Life Events

Table 11.1 provides an overview of ways in which existing research on aspects of a person's life philosophy may be relevant when studying reactions to critical life events. It is useful to differentiate between the role of beliefs for the reaction of (a) the person directly involved, (b) persons indirectly involved, and (c) outside observers. Different questions arise for each of these three groups of persons, and different aspects of one's life philosophy will be relevant in answering these questions.

Some interesting research deals with the role of beliefs in shaping one's reaction when others encounter an event that is inconsistent with one's own worldview. Tension usually arises and must be reduced. Two aspects of the person's life philosophy investigated in previous research are relevant here: (a) "just world" beliefs (Lerner 1980), and (b) a person's general and existential beliefs.

Research on "just world" beliefs starts with the assumption that human beings want to live in a just world, in which people get what they deserve and deserve what they get. If something happens that violates this just world belief, people reevaluate the situation in order to make it fit the just world belief. One possible reaction is to blame the person directly involved, for example to hold a rape victim responsible for what happened (see Lerner 1980, for an overview of the research on the just world hypothesis). There is empirical evidence that observers assume that raped women provoked the

Table 11.1
Life Philosophies in Situations with Critical Life Events

Person	Question	Part of life philosophy involved
(a) directly involved	Why did it happen?	--- search for meaning; self-cognitions
	How bad is it?	--- social comparisons; values; primary appraisal
	What can be done?	--- control beliefs; existential beliefs; secondary appraisal
(b) indirectly involved	see above	--- all of the above plus
	see below	--- all of the below
(c) observing	how could this happen? will it happen to me?	--- just world belief; --- general / existential beliefs

rapists (e.g., Lerner & Miller 1978; Miller & Porter 1983; Borgida & Brekke 1985), that abused wives provoked their husbands (Summers & Feldman 1984), that poor persons caused their own poverty (Furnham & Gunter 1984), and that sick people were responsible for their illnesses (Gruman & Sloan 1983).

These findings all make sense in the context of the generalized principle of cognitive consistency. If just world beliefs are part of a person's worldview, then inconsistency arises when these beliefs seem contradicted by given events. The least effortful reaction to reduce this inconsistency would be to blame the victim for his or her fate in this specific case, rather than changing one's own belief that the universe is just, which would require reorganizing a major part of one's worldview. Blaming the victim helps reestablish consistency in a relatively parsimonious fashion.

The second group of studies that relates life philosophies to critical life events is research on beliefs. People differ in their beliefs and these differences influence their evaluation of events. One demonstration of this point is provided by a laboratory study of the impact of moral conservatism on evaluations of rape victims (Inglehart & McDonald, under review). We prescreened 1073 undergraduates with the Sexual Attitude Scale (Hudson, Murphy & Nurius 1983), a measure of sexual liberalism versus conservatism. Randomly selected subjects from the top and the bottom ten percent of the distribution of scores in this pretest then participated in the main experiment. These subjects read two rape descriptions and were then asked to evaluate the rapist's behavior, the victim's behavior, and the situation in general. The answers were clearly a function of the person's beliefs: Conservatives indicated that the rape victim experienced significantly less pain, but significantly more pleasure in this situation, than did liberal respondents. The conservatives were also far more likely to conclude that the victim had encouraged the rapist with her actions and the way she dressed, had made less effort to stop the rapist, was less respectable, and got more or less what she deserved.

These findings concerning the role of a just world belief and of beliefs in general on a person's reactions when observing a person encountering an inconsistent event, suggest that it is useful to investigate the relevance of life philosophies in their whole complexity in these situations.

Let us now examine how a directly involved person's life philosophy influences his or her reactions. We differentiate between two types of situations: (a) those in which inconsistent events occur over a long period of time, such as when a person has a chemotherapy treatment after a cancer operation, or has a newborn baby, and (b) situations in which a critical life event occurs at one point in time as when a person is raped or burglarized.

The relevance of life philosophies in situations with critical life events of protracted duration is well documented in the literature on life during World War II. Viktor Frankl (1946, Engl. translation 1984) describes his experiences as a prisoner in a Nazi concentration camp, which made him aware of how important a sense of meaning is in such existentially threatening situations. DesPres (1976) conducted intensive research on the survivors of World War II camps. His description of life in these camps forcefully conveys the significance that the survivors' political and religious beliefs had for helping them survive in these situations.

Such studies provide ample evidence of the importance of a person's beliefs when victimized as a prisoner in a concentration camp. Another body of research aims at understanding those civilians who went out of their way during World War II to save people in danger, even though they endangered themselves. Impressive documentation of such behaviors appears in Rossiter's book on women in the French Resistance (Rossiter 1986) that describes women whose existential beliefs led them to risk their lives to save people during this time. Another insightful analysis of the psychological processes underlying rescuing behavior—in this case oriented towards rescuing Jews— is provided by Fogelman (1987). Investigating what kinds of persons rescued Jews during the Holocaust, Fogelman found that one group of rescuers were persons with clearly defined life philosophies. Their ethical beliefs forced them to actively stand up against injustice despite the tremendous risks involved.

At this point, let us turn again to Table 11.1, which lists the questions arising for the person directly involved in a critical life event. Such persons would want to understand why this event happened, how good or bad it actually is, and what can be done about it. Research on the importance of a person's search for meaning (see Taylor 1983) and on the role of self-cognitions, especially self-blame (see Janoff-Bulman 1979; Shaver 1985) are relevant in answering the first question. For example, Taylor (1983) reports that 95 percent of the women who survived a breast cancer operation had thought about the sense that this event had for their lives. Acklin, Brown, and Mauger (1983) also point to the significance of life philosophies for making sense of situations with cancer; and Silver, Boon, and Stone (1983) investigated this issue in a study of women who had been victims of incest in their childhood. McIntosh, Silver, and Wortman (under review) analyzed the role of religious beliefs in adjusting to the loss of a child.

A body of research in clinical psychology—the research conducted in connection with Frankl's logotherapy (Frankl 1983)—focuses specifically on the search for meaning. This theory is based on the assumption that a psychologically healthy person is one who has found meaning in life. Frankl provides numerous case descriptions of persons who encountered a critical life event at an earlier point in time and who struggle in therapy to make sense out of this event and find meaning in it (compare, for example, Frankl 1984, pp. 135, 139).

The answer to the second question, how good or bad a given event is, partly depends on social comparisons with other persons in similar situations (see Taylor 1983), but also on the person's expectations and values. In this connection, we should recall Lazarus' hypotheses about primary and secondary appraisal in general, and his ideas about the importance of existential beliefs in these processes in specific (see Lazarus & Folkman 1985, pp. 77ff.).

The answer to the question, what can be done about the event, is tied to those parts of a person's life philosophy with control beliefs and other beliefs about the costs of certain reactions.

If a critical life event occurs, an indirectly involved person will partly experience this as a critical life event for him or herself, and thus be concerned with the questions a directly involved person would ask. At the same time, the issues connected with observers of critical life events are applicable to these persons also.

11.2 The Generalized Principle of Cognitive Consistency and Life Philosophies

11.2.1 General Consideration

In the first part of this chapter, we argued that instead of focusing exclusively on one type of beliefs or values, social psychologists might profitably consider the larger network of cognitions in which single beliefs are embedded and the processes in which they are involved. The sum of a person's attitudes, beliefs, and values about the social and the objective world was referred to as a person's life philosophy.

Two considerations seem to be of crucial importance here. The first concerns whether it makes sense to think about the *content* of a person's life philosophy. The second issue concerns the *structure* of a person's worldview.

Shall we try to assess the contents of a person's life philosophy? We suggest that it is not practical to deal with each specific content, but that it is useful to understand how the specific beliefs of a person's worldview map onto the three general content areas, identified in the preceding chapter. The main issues were (a) the positivity/negativity, (b) control beliefs, and (c) self-related beliefs (see Table 10.1). We argue that these three crucial dimensions may apply when we deal with life philosophies. People's life philosophy may vary in the degree to which they are positive versus negative toward life, the kind of control beliefs they incorporate, and their self-related cognitions. Furthermore, we suggest that the role of specific beliefs such as religious beliefs, just-world beliefs, or political beliefs can only be understood if their meaning in regard to these three underlying dimensions is clear. To understand the role of a person's beliefs in specific situations, we need to know how these beliefs map onto the three general dimensions.

To illustrate this point, let us consider a person with strong religious beliefs. It is useless to ask whether strong religious beliefs per se will lead to specific outcomes in a given situation, because the contents of people's religious beliefs vary enormously. Instead we argue that it is useful to analyze the degree to which these specific beliefs reflect the person's positivity towards life, and what kind of control and self-related beliefs they entail. If we know these pieces of information, we can predict certain outcomes: for example, that the more positive the person's religious beliefs are, and the more they reflect an internal locus of control and positive self-cognitions, the better the outcome should be.

The second issue of importance here is the question of how life philosophies are structured. McIntosh, Inglehart, and Pacini (under review), argue that a differentiated and flexible belief system tends to be beneficial for reacting to life changes, finding supporting evidence for this hypothesis from a study of 514 undergraduates.

Life philosophies have another interesting feature: They influence the person's cognitions about the future—specifically, those about possible selves and goals. These cognitions are consistent with the person's life philosophy, but they are inconsistent with that part of the person's worldview that represents the present reality. This causes tension, and one way to reduce this tension is to work toward realizing positive goals or positive possible selves and toward avoiding negative goals or negative possible selves.

These considerations were explored in the research conducted by Inglehart, Markus, and Brown (1989) described in Chapter 8. This study demonstrated that the academic achievement in medical school is a clear function of the person's possible selves of becoming an M.D. Furthermore, Inglehart, Wurf, Brown, and Moore (1987) and Inglehart, Malanchuk, and Brown (1988) demonstrated that the strength with which one focused on one possible self had a clear impact on the subjective well-being of the person after realizing this possible self.

These findings indicate that life philosophies help structure long-term behavioral sequences as well as the emotional reactions connected with them, by influencing one's goals and one's possible selves. The inconsistencies between these future cognitions and the present world lead to tension that needs to be reduced. In this way, behavior oriented toward the future is initiated, structured, and energized. It is useful to consider this dynamic when investigating the role of life philosophies in situations with critical life events according to the generalized principle of cognitive consistency.

11.2.2 The Generalized Principle of Cognitive Consistency and the Role of Life Philosophies in Situations with Critical Life Events

Life philosophies have an impact on both the amount of tension arising in a situation with a critical life event as well as on the reactions used to reduce this tension. They determine the amount of tension arising by influencing how many aspects of the person's worldview are inconsistent and consistent with a critical life event. For example, let us imagine a person with strong, traditional Roman Catholic beliefs facing a divorce. We would expect this person to experience more tension in this event than an atheist or a person with a liberal value system, because for the Catholic, a divorce is likely to be inconsistent with more aspects of his or her worldview than is the case for the liberal or atheist. As this example suggests, knowledge of life philosophies can provide a clearer idea of how many inconsistencies versus consistencies are likely to arise in a given situation.

The generalized principle of cognitive consistency suggests that life philosophies can also help answer the question of which *general* reaction will be used to reduce tension due to a critical life event. Life philosophies provide ideas about the relative effort required for these reactions. If having a successful professional life is a central part of a person's life philosophy, then a sudden loss of employment is more likely to lead to a tension-reduction reaction, because a tension-avoidance reaction is relatively costly for a person who is so highly involved in the professional domain. Accordingly, we would not expect that this person would withdraw from the tension in the professional domain by focusing on a happy family life for example; instead we would expect this person to try to reduce the tension in the professional domain directly, for example by looking for another position. The importance of control beliefs as one part of life philosophies deserves emphasis here, because they provide us with information about the relative costs of different reactions.

Life philosophies also influence which kind of *specific* reaction a person will use to reduce tension due to a critical life event. A person's life philosophy influences which topics and behavioral alternatives are likely to be cognitively available. This will influence which specific reaction will be used to reduce tension due to a critical life event.

Let us imagine two different persons who become unemployed and who try to directly reduce the resulting tension. Person A's life philosophy holds that a job offers a chance for intellectual stimulation and challenge, while person B's life philosophy implies that a job offers a way of helping other human beings. A direct tension-reduction reaction for Person A might consist of looking for more professional training, while a tension-reduction reaction for Person B might consist of taking a lower-paying job if this job offers a chance to fulfill the person's goal to help others.

Finally, let us consider whether life philosophies influence the long-term consequences of having encountered such an event. Two aspects are of interest here: (a) the long-term consequences of encountering a specific event, and (b) whether experiences with one critical life event influence the person's reactions to another critical life event in a positive or in a negative way.

A life philosophy may not only provide a person with a way to explain why a critical life event occurred, but can also lead to a positive evaluation and a consistent integration of this event as part of the person's worldview. If this is the case, the amount of tension arising when a new critical life event occurs will be lower than in a situation in which avoided inconsistencies exist and are reintroduced by encountering the new inconsistency.

Furthermore, once a person has used a life philosophy to reduce tension from a critical life event, this can influence the kind of reaction chosen later, both in a content specific and in a content unspecific way. For example, a content unspecific influence would be that a person who reduced tension caused by a critical life event by interpreting it as a chance to mature, might approach a new critical life event with a more positive life philosophy than a person who still mourns about the old experiences. In a content specific way, given reactions to earlier life events that were tied to the person's life philosophy might lead to repeating the same reactions to a later critical life event.

11.3 Final Evaluation of the Significance of Life Philosophies

We must always consider two sets of things when predicting reactions to critical life events. First, we must consider the theoretical considerations about the general psychological process, such as the hypotheses that there is a need for consistency, the sum rule, the principle of least effort, and the hypothesis about the importance of the cognitive availability of certain reactions. This first aspect could be viewed as the computer program used to analyze data. The second set of things consists of the specific conditions under which these theoretical considerations work. This component can be viewed as the data that are fed into the computer program in order to come up with exact predictions. Life philosophies are an essential part of the assumptions that a person provides and which the theoretical considerations must take into account when concrete predictions should be made.

As long as a theoretical concept cannot be investigated empirically, it will not be used in social psychology. A good instrument for measuring a concept can have a very positive effect on stimulating research on such a concept (see, for example, Rotter's internal versus external locus of control scale and the large number of studies stimulated by it; see Lefcourt 1981, 1983a, 1984, for overviews). Life philosophies are complex and difficult to measure. Hence, it is not surprising that the early theoretical attempts to investigate the psychological relevance of life philosophies (see, for example, Allport 1955) did not stimulate much subsequent research. We believe that social psychology has now reached a stage of development at which it can and should address such complex issues.

Life philosophies are important determinants of a person's behavior, both in general and in connection with reactions to critical life events. Thus far, we have only studied pieces of them. We need to understand them in their full complexity. A first attempt at learning more about the structure of life philosophies and the question whether they actually are structured along the three dimensions positivity/negativity, control beliefs, and self-related beliefs was undertaken in a study of the influence of undergraduates' life philosophies on their psychological health (Inglehart, McIntosh & Pacini, in prep.). The three general dimensions were measured with Carver and Scheier's Life Orientation Test (Carver & Scheier 1987), Rotter's Locus of Control Scale (Rotter 1966) and Levenson's Control Scale (Levenson 1981), and with the Texas Social Behavior Inventory (Helmreich, Stapp & Erwin 1974). As domain specific parts of a person's life philosophy, we included measures of religious beliefs (Gorsuch & McPherson 1989; Kojetin 1988), just world beliefs (Lerner, 1980), and values (Inglehart 1977; Rokeach 1973). We predict that these specific beliefs do not directly influence our outcome variables, but do indirectly exert an influence through the three general dimensions. Three aspects of a person's psychological health were considered, namely subjective well-being (Bradburn 1969), social functioning, and productivity (measured with questions concerning the undergraduates' social support system and academic achievement).

Analysis of the influence of the *structure* of the person's belief system on subjective well-being and academic achievement indicated that a differentiated and central belief system relates positively to these outcome variables (McIntosh, Inglehart & Pacini, under review). Two other analyses investigated the relationships between separate parts of these life philosophies: (a) the relationship between postmaterialistic values and religious beliefs (Ingle-hart, McIntosh & Pacini 1990a), and (b) the relationship between postmate-rialistic values and intrinsic control beliefs (Inglehart, McIntosh & Pacini 1990b). These results are a first step in unraveling the organization of life philosophies.

We have only begun to analyze the influence of life philosophies on psy-chological health. This seems to be an interesting and fruitful topic, but much remains to be done, in moving to understand the functions of life philosophies.

Chapter 12

The Generalized Principle of Cognitive Consistency and Reactions to Critical Life Events—Exploring Practical Implications

The introduction to this book argued that one of the more problematic issues in social psychology is the lack of connection between basic and applied research. Lewin's statement that nothing is more useful than a good theory does not seem supported by reality. One reason for the striking gap between the highly specialized theoretical social psychology on one hand and applied social psychology on the other hand may lie in the specificity of the theories that have been developed thus far. Reality is complex and theories with a general domain seem more likely to do justice to the complexity of the real world.

The generalized principle of cognitive consistency is just such a general theory. This book demonstrates that it can be applied to predict reactions to critical life events. We argued that this generalized principle can provide answers to the questions an adequate theory of reactions to critical life events should be able to answer; and that it has implications for reinterpreting the findings of variable-centered research on reactions to critical life events. This final chapter investigates the practical implications of this theory concerning what can and should be done when encountering persons in situations with critical life events.

12.1 The Generalized Principle of Cognitive Consistency and Reactions to Critical Life Events—Practical Implications for Counseling

The generalized principle of cognitive consistency can be useful for professionals who interact with persons in situations with critical life events, and are involved in the treatment of persons who show withdrawal reactions from problems by using mood-altering substances or (in the most extreme case) suicide.

With persons encountering critical life events, the generalized principle of cognitive consistency can provide insights in two ways. First, it can help to understand the psychological processes unfolding in these situations. Second, this understanding can be used as a basis for evaluating how interactions with these persons should be structured. These two implications can be helpful for both private and professional interactions with persons in these situations.

12.1.1 General Implications for Counseling Persons Encountering Critical Life Events

The generalized principle of cognitive consistency provides a conceptual framework to understand the reactions of persons encountering critical life events. Three general considerations concerning private or professional interactions with these persons will be discussed: (a) the emotions arising, (b) the cognitive processes unfolding, and (c) the behaviors planned and performed in these situations.

Human beings encountering a critical life event experience intense feelings. They may be deeply desperate when losing a spouse; they may be overwhelmed by strong anxieties when surviving a traffic accident or a cancer operation; they may be overwhelmed with feelings of gratitude or awe when seeing their newborn baby.

The generalized principle of cognitive consistency does not offer any explanations about why and how specific emotions *arise*; but it has implications concerning *changing* the intensity of these emotions. If we assume that the strength of emotions is, generally speaking, a positive function of the amount of tension arising, it follows that by reducing the amount of tension in a situation, we can also decrease the intensity of the emotions.

How can we reduce the amount of tension according to the generalized principle of cognitive consistency? According to the sum rule, we argue that the tension can be reduced by changing the ratio of inconsistent to consistent relations in this situation. This concretely means that we need to provide the person with ways to either (a) increase the number of consistent relationships, or (b) decrease the number of inconsistent relationships. In order to do so, we can point out consistent parts of the person's worldview which are untouched by the critical life event or are even consistent with it. We might introduce considerations into the situation which can be used to reduce existing inconsistencies. And we can try to suggest how inconsistent relationships can be directly changed into consistent relationships.

This last suggestion leads us to the cognitive processes unfolding in these situations. Persons encountering critical life events sooner or later make verbal statements that mirror cognitive processes. These verbal statements contain valuable information for a person interacting with the directly involved person, because they provide a picture of the inconsistencies in the person's worldview. Taking these questions seriously—even if the answers seem self-evident—and helping the person find satisfying answers to these questions can reduce the amount of tension in such a situation considerably.

We must stress that these questions are cognitive representations of inconsistencies in a person's worldview. They are subjective and, therefore, we are not looking for objectively correct answers. It is crucial to help the directly involved person to find the subjectively acceptable and subjectively consistent answer in this situation. No one else but the directly involved person will be able to reestablish cognitive consistency, because no one else knows this person's worldview as completely as that person.

For concrete interactions with persons in situations with critical life events, we need to support these people to verbalize these questions rather than suppress them. By doing so, the person may actually begin to identify the inconsistencies, which may be a first step toward directly reducing the tension. Furthermore, we must realize that we will never know the other person's worldview completely. This should make the interacting person aware that their answers to these questions may not make sense in the other person's worldview. The counselor's task should be to encourage the directly involved persons to find answers to their own questions that are appropriate in their worldview—even though they may not be the answers we would give according to our worldview. The actual work done to answer these questions must be performed by the directly involved person. The person interacting with the directly involved person can only assist in this process by (a) helping the directly involved person to stay in the tension loaded domain and concentrate on the issue, (b) introducing aspects into the situation that might not be seen by the directly involved person, and (c) making salient to the person whenever a cognitive change occurred that reduced tension.

The third aspect of a person's reactions that a counselor may want to consider are present and planned actions in situations with critical life events. The structuring component of the generalized principle of cognitive consistency has implications for this point.

Counseling concerning the *general* reaction used to reduce tension must consider the principle of least effort. The main goal should be to provide the person with a chance to develop a clearer understanding of the costs that given reactions involve. One might encourage the directly involved person to explicitly consider the effort the possible reactions would involve and to explicitly compare these estimates with each other.

Counseling concerning the *specific* reaction used to reduce tension must consider the cognitive availability of different behavioral alternatives. A counselor can introduce new behavioral alternatives into the situation, for example by pointing out role models. He or she might also help the person to understand why certain behavioral alternatives are so highly available for this specific person. The goal concerning the directly involved person's specific reactions must be to help this person (a) to realize that many alternative ways to react are available, and (b) to explore whether their own most cognitively available reaction is actually the best possible way to react, whether it is only chosen because of earlier experiences with this reaction, or because concrete aspects of the situation make this reaction salient.

Counseling concerning the long-term consequences has one major goal: to consider whether specific reactions used to reduce tension in a situation might have tension-producing, long-term consequences. A counselor might have a broader view of the situation than a directly involved person who is struggling to reestablish cognitive consistency and by doing so, focuses on nothing but the immediate situation. To point out that a given reaction might produce tension in the long run is one aspect of prevention work that counselors should do. Especially important is a counselor's intervention in a situation in which the reaction chosen to reduce the tension is self-destructive in the long run. Such reactions include alcohol and drug abuse, or suicide attempts.

12.1.2 Specific Implications for Counseling Persons Using Self-Destructive Tension-Avoidance Reactions

The generalized principle of cognitive consistency suggests that alcohol abuse, drug abuse, and suicide attempts can be interpreted as reactions used to avoid tension caused by a critical life event. The literature on these topics is vast (concerning suicide, see the bibliographies complied by Lester 1972, 1983; McIntosh 1985; concerning alcohol and drug abuse, see for example Bennett, Vourakis & Woolf 1983; Galanter 1986; Shiffman & Wills 1985), and it is beyond the scope of this book to review the state of research concerning these topics. Instead, we present some practical implications that the generalized theory of cognitive consistency offers for counseling persons using these self-destructive tension-avoidance reactions.

How would a person turn to alcohol or drug abuse, or suicide attempts as specific reactions? The generalized principle of cognitive consistency offers four considerations on this question. First, inconsistencies may have occurred, leading to a high level of tension. Internal or general attributions for the event may contribute, by introducing many cognitions into the situation that are inconsistent with the event.

Second, once a high level of tension existed, the person evaluated direct tension-reduction reactions as requiring a higher amount of effort than that required for tension-avoidance reactions, thus choosing a tension-avoidance reaction as the general reaction.

Third, in opting for a tension-avoidance reaction, the cognitive availability of alcohol abuse, drug abuse, or suicide was high. This might be due to prior experiences with these reactions (for example, observing family members or friends) or due to situational aspects (alcohol or drugs are available; suicide is made cognitively available by the media; see, for example, Phillips

1986, who describes the impact of published suicide attempts on the rate of suicides performed following these publications).

Fourth, when these self-destructive avoidance reactions are used in the long run, high tension is likely to reoccur. This is due to (a) the fact that situational aspects may reintroduce the avoided tension, and (b) the fact that these behaviors themselves or behaviors associated with these self-destructive reactions are likely to be inconsistent with normal patterns of behavior in Western industrialized societies, which introduces new inconsistencies into the situation.

This brief description of the explanations of these reactions in the framework of the generalized principle of cognitive consistency raises the question of what a counselor can do. Several practical implications can be derived. Starting with the energizing component of this situation, we argue that the amount of tension needs to be decreased. This can be done by changing internal or general post hoc attributions for problems into external or specific post hoc attributions, by introducing consistent cognitions, and by changing inconsistent to consistent relations. These changes will decrease the amount of tension arising.

One example of a tension-reduction technique would be to refer to drug addiction and alcoholism as a disease. Such a perspective is likely to alleviate self-blame and thus lead to a more positive image of the self.

Concerning the structuring component of the reactions, the first step should be to change the evaluations of efforts necessary for reactions to reduce tension in such a way that the effort for a direct tension-reduction reaction is evaluated as being smaller than the effort for a tension-avoidance reaction. This could be achieved by changing stable or chronic a priori attributions for problematic events into unstable and acute a priori attributions. One way that Alcoholics Anonymous and similar programs achieve such a reevaluation of efforts involved in coping with the problem is to focus on one day at a time. If an alcoholic or a drug addict focuses on just one day, the efforts of coping do not seem to be so overwhelmingly high that tension avoidance reactions will be chosen.

Furthermore, if a person realizes that tension-avoidance reactions are actually more costly than tension-reduction reactions, a start is made toward finding appropriate tension-reduction reactions. For a drug addict or an alcoholic, "hitting bottom" may be the moment at which they realize that their preferred way to alter their mood and to shut out tension is actually costing them everything they value in their lives. At this point they may realize that the reactions necessary to reduce tension directly might actually be less costly than the tension-avoidance patterns they have been using. They may be at a loss at this point, because appropriate reactions cognitively may not be available. Moreover they do not have the habits connected with these reactions. This is the point at which counselors can fill a crucial role in making a repertoire of tension-reduction reactions cognitively available; and at the same time, counselors must try to prevent tension-avoidance reactions from becoming cognitively available. How can they do so? The generalized principle of cognitive consistency emphasizes the importance of (a) preventing past experiences from becoming salient, and of (b) preventing the objective availability of drug and alcohol related cues. Avoiding contact with persons the addict used drugs with, or places and situations in which alcohol and drugs are available, are concretizations of these two general statements.

If it is not possible to encourage the person to evaluate the tension-avoidance reaction as more effortful, then a counselor might aim at making less self-destructive tension-avoidance reactions cognitively available. Getting involved in a regimen of strenuous exercise can be such a way of using a potentially healthy reaction as a way to shut out tension and to alter one's mood. If a counselor thinks about finding a less destructive way to avoid tension for a patient or client, he or she might consider one more aspect of this situation. This involves the dynamic that might get started with such a nondestructive reaction. If this reaction would actually enhance the person's self-esteem and/or his or her subjective well-being—as might be the case with an exercising program—then this might in turn help the person reevaluate the efforts needed for a tension-reduction reaction and help bring about changes in the direction of directly reducing tension.

Alcoholism, drug abuse, and suicide are behaviors that clearly fall in the domain of clinical psychologists. The considerations offered here should be understood as aimed at grasping the dynamic of these self-destructive reactions.

Many of the suggestions made here are part of treatment programs for alcoholics and drug addicts. In the context of the generalized principle of cognitive consistency, they fit together and make sense. The generalized principle of cognitive consistency provides a theoretical basis for understanding how concrete treatment techniques, such as the Twelve Step Program, work.

12.2 The Generalized Principle of Cognitive Consistency and Reactions to Critical Life Events—Practical Implications for Prevention

Four hundred billion dollars are currently being spent annually on health care in the United States (Taylor 1990). While infectious diseases have decreased systematically over the last eighty years, such "preventable" disorders as lung cancer, cardiovascular disease, and drug and alcohol abuse have increased steadily (Matarazzo 1982). Probably no other task has as much practical importance for psychologists concerned with stress and reactions to critical life events, as understanding how prevention programs can be implemented.

It is surprising how little preparation for handling inconsistent life events in general or in specific situations, is given to children in their homes or schools. Psychological knowledge is usually not introduced until students enter college. In a world in which human beings are more than ever before confronted with inconsistent life events, and in which they have too many options for self-destructive activities around them, this is unfortunate. If people are to make wise lifestyle decisions and be able to react to critical life events in nondestructive ways, they need a basic understanding of human functioning. Education about preventing self-destructive behavior must start early, and psychology can take a leading role in it.

Many situations with critical life events are clearly predictable: inconsistent life events are not necessarily unexpected. Many events such as starting college, getting divorced, or starting a new job can be anticipated well before the actual life change occurs. Accordingly, people can be given a fair amount of preparation before they face such situations.

For some critical life events, particularly for the positive ones, people actually do prepare themselves. One good example involves expectant parents. A huge number of books are on the market concerning pregnancy and childrearing, and Lamaze and child-care classes are increasingly popular. But it is much harder to get persons involved in preparation for negative critical life events. Such preparation could be very beneficial. On one level it could simply provide people with knowledge about the upcoming events. It could also include discussing the objective changes that occur in connection with a critical life event, and the emotions, thoughts, and actions that are likely to occur in connection with these changes. Such preparation could also include concrete training concerning reactions that are useful in these situations. Such preparation should aim at preventing tension from arising, and teaching nondestructive reactions that are useful to reduce the tension if it arises.

Psychologists need to find out how persons can be motivated to engage in preventive activities for situations with *negative* events, and how these preventive activities can be integrated with people's normal activities.

12.3 Final Evaluation

When we want to build a bridge, we need architectural plans with statistical calculations and exact measurements. We also need a great deal of practical knowledge about how to turn the bridge on paper into an actual bridge. Reviewing the practical implications offered by the generalized principle of cognitive consistency for interacting with persons in situations with critical life events, provides a preliminary sketch of how this work will look. To turn this sketch into the real world interaction and make it work is another task. We hope that persons with the necessary knowledge to build the bridge may find our rough drawing of it useful.

We see critical life events as essential parts of each human being's life. Therefore, we do not see reactions to critical life events as belonging to the domain of clinical psychology alone. We are convinced that psychologists outside the clinical area can contribute to our understanding of these processes and hope that this book will help in this task.

This book is based on the assumption that the generalized principle of cognitive consistency captures a crucial phenomenon. Hundreds of publications have been written on this topic. We believe that this issue should be considered in research on reactions to critical life events and that it may be a central issue in these situations. Research on cognitive consistency may have dwindled in recent years, partly because researchers realized there are many important psychological processes besides cognitive consistency. This is undoubtedly true. But cognitive consistency remains important—and in situations with critical life events it may be central, although in other situations the desire for *differentiation* may be virtually as important as the desire for consistency. In a situation with a critical life event, people's activities seem to be focused overwhelmingly on reducing inconsistencies, with little energy left to be spent on differentiating one's worldview. This book was written with the hope that the generalized principle of cognitive consistency may demonstrate the continuing relevance of previous research on consistency and attribution by integrating it in a broader theoretical perspective.

This work was also motivated by the belief that theoretical psychology can offer something of value to applied psychologists. A great deal of applied work concerns people's reactions to critical life events. Our goal was to investigate whether these theoretical considerations can provide useful guidance for working in concrete settings.

References

Abelson, R. P. 1983. Whatever became of consistency theory? *Personality and Social Psychological Bulletin* 9: 37–54.

Abelson, R. P., and M. J. Rosenberg. 1958. Symbolic psycho-logic: A model of attitudinal cognition. *Behavioral Science* 3: 1–13.

Abelson, R. P., E. Aronson, W. J. McGuire, T. M. Newcomb, M. J. Rosenberg and P. H. Tannenbaum, eds. 1968. *Theories of cognitive consistency: A Sourcebook.* Chicago: Rand McNally and Company.

Abramson, L. Y., ed. 1988. *Social cognition and clinical psychology.* New York: Guilford Press.

Abramson, L. Y., M.E.P. Seligman, and J. Teasdale. 1978. Learned helplessness in humans: critique and reformulation. *Journal of Abnormal Psychology* 87: 49–74.

Abramson, L. Y., J. Garber, and M.E.P. Seligman. 1980. Learned helplessness in humans: An attributional analysis. In *Human helplessness—Theory and application* 3–34, edited by J. Garber and M.E.P. Seligman. New York: Academic Press.

Acklin, M. W., E. C. Brown, and P. A. Mauger. 1983. The role of religious values in coping with cancer. *Journal of Religion and Health* 22: 322–333.

Allport, G. W. 1950. *The individual and his religion.* New York: Macmillan.

———. 1955. *Becoming. Basic considerations for a psychology of personality.* New Haven: Yale University Press.

———. 1960. *Religion and prejudice in personality and social encounter.* Boston: Beacon Press.

———. 1966. Traits revisited. *American Psychologist* 21: 1–10.

Antonucci, T. C. 1985. Personal characteristics, social support and social behavior. In *Handbook of Aging and the Social Sciences*, 94–128, edited by R. H. Binstock & E. Shanas. New York: VanNostrand Reinhold Company.

Antonucci, T. C., and H. Akiyami. 1987. An examination of sex differences in social support among older men and women. *Sex Roles* 17: 737–749.

Baker, G. W., and D. W. Chapman, eds. 1962. *Man and society in disaster.* New York: Basic Books.

Baltes, M. M., and P. B. Baltes, eds. 1986. *The psychology of control and aging*. Hillsdale, N.J.: Erlbaum.

Bammer, K., and B. Newberry, eds. 1981. *Stress and cancer*. Toronto: Hogrefe Verlag.

Bandura, A. 1977. Self-efficacy: Toward a unifying theory of behavioral change. *Psychological Review* 84: 191–215.

———. 1982. Self-efficacy mechanism in human agency. *American Psychologist* 37: 122–147.

Bass, C. 1984. Type A behavior pattern in patients with chest pain: Test-retest reliability and psychometric correlates of Bortner Scale. *Journal of Psychosomatic Research* 28: 289–300.

Baumeister, R. F. 1986. *Public self and private self*. New York: Springer Verlag.

Beck, A. T. 1976. *Cognitive therapy and the emotional disorders*. New York: International Universities Press.

Beckmann, J. 1984. *Kognitive Dissonanz—Eine handlungstheoretische Perspektive*. Berlin: Springer Verlag.

Bem, D. J. 1967. Self-perception: An alternative interpretation of cognitive dissonance phenomena. *Psychological Review* 74: 183–200.

———. 1972. Self-perception theory. In *Advances in experimental social psychology*, Vol. 6, edited by L. Berkowitz. New York: Academic Press.

Bennett, G., C. Vourakis, and D. S. Woolf, eds. 1983. *Substance Abuse*. Somerset, N.J.: John Wiley & Sons.

Bentler, P. M., and D. G. Bonett. 1980. Significance tests and goodness of fit in the analysis of covariance structures. *Psychological Bulletin* 88: 588–606.

Bergman, M. V., and M. E. Jucovy, eds. 1982. *Generations of the Holocaust*. New York: Basic Books.

Berkman, L. F., and S. L. Syme. 1979. Social networks, host resistance and mortality. A 9-year follow up study of Alameda County residents. *American Journal of Epidemiology* 109: 188–204.

Bohner, G., H. Bless, N. Schwarz, and F. Strack. 1988. What triggers causal attributions? The impact of valence and subjective probability. *European Journal of Social Psychology* 18: 335–345.

Bolger, N., A. DeLongis, R. C. Kessler, and E. A. Schilling. 1989. Effects of daily stress on negative mood. *Journal of Personality and Social Psychology* 57: 808–818.

Bond, M. H. 1988. Finding universal dimensions of individual variation in multicultural studies of values: The Rokeach and the Chinese Value Surveys. *Journal of Personality and Social Psychology* 55: 1009–1015.

Borgida, E., and N. Brekke. 1985. Psychological research on rape trials. In *Rape and sexual assault: A research handbook*, edited by A. W. Burgess. New York: Garland.

Bortner, R. W. 1969. A short rating scale as a potential measure of Pattern A Behavior. *Journal of Chronical Disease* 22: 87–91.

Bowlby, J. 1946. *Forty-four juvenile thieves: Their characters and home life*. London: Bailliere, Tindall & Cox.

———. 1961. Processes of mourning. *International Journal of Psychoanalysis* 42: 317–340.

———. 1969. *Attachment and loss: Attachment*, Vol. 1. New York: Basic Books.

———. 1973. *Attachment and loss*, Vols. 1 and 2. New York: Basic Books.

————. 1980. *Attachment and loss: Loss, sadness and depression*, Vol. 3. New York: Basic Books.

————. 1990. Biography. *American Psychologist* 45: 451–453.

Bradburn, N. M. 1969. *The structure of psychological well-being*. Chicago: Aldine.

Brehm, J. W. 1966. *A theory of psychological reactance*. New York: Academic Press.

————. 1972. *Responses to loss of freedom: A theory of psychological reactance*. Morristown, N.J.: General Learning Press.

Breznitz, S., ed. 1985. *The denial of stress*. New York: International Universities Press.

Brown, J. D., and K. L. McGill. 1989. The cost of good fortune: When positive life events produce negative health consequences. *Journal of Personality and Social Psychology* 57: 1103–1110.

Brunson, B. I., and K. A. Matthews. 1981. The Type A coronary-prone behavior pattern and reactions to uncontrollable stress: An analysis of performance strategies, affect, and attributions during failure. *Journal of Personality and Social Psychology* 40: 906–918.

Bulman, R. J., and C. B. Wortman. 1977. Attributions of blame and coping in the "Real World": Severe accident victims react to their lot. *Journal of Personality and Social Psychology* 35: 351–363.

Burchfield, S. R., ed. 1985. *Stress: Psychological and physiological interactions*. Washington, D.C.: Hemisphere.

Burgess, A. W., and L. L. Holmstrom. 1976. Coping behavior of the rape victim. *American Journal of Psychiatry* 133: 413–418.

————. 1978. Recovery from rape and prior life stress. *Research in Nursing and Health* 1: 165–174.

————. 1979. Adaptive strategies and recovery from stress. *American Journal of Psychiatry* 136: 1278–1282.

Burns, M. O., and M.E.P. Seligman. 1989. Explanatory style over the life span: Evidence for stability over 52 years. *Personality and Social Psychology* 56: 471–477.

Cannon, W. B. 1929. *Bodily changes in pain, hunger, fear, and rage*. Boston: C. T. Branford.

Cantor, N., and J. F. Kihlstrom. 1987. *Personality and social intelligence*. Englewood Cliffs, N.J.: Prentice-Hall Inc.

Cantor, N., J. K. Norem, P. M. Niedenthal, C. A. Langston, and A. M. Brower. 1987. Life tasks, self-concept ideals, and cognitive strategies in a life transition. *Journal of Personality and Social Psychology* 53: 1178–1191.

Carver, C. S., and M. F. Scheier. 1987. "Dispositional optimism, coping, and stress." Paper presented at the American Psychological Association Meeting, New York.

Cascallar, E. C., R. C. Cervantes, C. DeZan, and T. Gates. 1986. "Multivariate analysis of stress factors following Mexico City's 1985 earthquake." Paper presented at the meetings of the American Psychological Association, Washington, D.C.

Caskey, B. J., and B. A. Gates. 1988. "Caregiver burden: A comparison of Alzheimer's with other chronic disorders." Paper presented at the Midwestern Psychological Association Meeting, Chicago.

Caspi, A., N. Bolger, and J. Eckenrode. 1987. Linking person and context in the daily stress process. *Journal of Personality and Social Psychology* 52: 184–195.

Cassel, J. 1976. The contribution of the social environment to host resistance. *American Journal of Epidemiology* 104: 107–123.

Cattell, R. B. 1946. *The description and measurement of personality*. New York: World.

Coates, D., C. B. Wortman, and A. Abbey. 1979. Relations to victims. In *New Approaches to social problems*, 21–52, edited by I. H. Frieze, D. Bar-Tal & J. S. Carroll. San Francisco: Jossey-Bass.

Cobb, S. 1976. Social support as a moderator of life stress. *Psychosomatic Medicine* 38: 300–314.

Coelho, G. V., D. A. Hamburg, and J. E. Adams, eds. 1974. *Coping and adaptation*. New York: Basic Books.

Cohen, S., and S. L. Syme, eds. 1985. *Social support and health*. Orlando, Fla.: Academic Press.

Cohen, S., and T. A. Wills. 1985. Stress, social support, and the buffering hypothesis. *Psychological Bulletin* 98: 310–357.

Cole, C. S., and J. C. Coyne. 1977. Situational specificity of laboratory induced learned helplessness. *Journal of Abnormal Psychology* 86: 615–623.

Collins, R. L., S. E. Taylor, and L. A. Skokan. Under review. A better world or a shattered vision? Changes in life perspectives.

Cooper, J., and R. H. Fazio. 1984. A new look at dissonance theory. In *Advances in experimental social psychology*, Vol. 17, 229–266, edited by L. Berkowitz. New York: Academic Press.

Coyne, J. C., and I. H. Gotlib. 1983. The role of cognition in depression: A critical appraisal. *Psychological Bulletin* 94: 472–505.

Coyne, J. C., C. B. Wortman, and D. Lehman. 1985. "The other side of support: Emotional overinvolvement and miscarried helping." Paper presented at the American Psychological Association Meeting, Los Angeles.

Dakof, G. A., and S. E. Taylor. 1990. Victims' perceptions of social support: What is helpful from whom? *Journal of Personality and Social Psychology* 58: 80–89.

Darley, J. M., and B. Latane. 1968. Bystander intervention in emergencies: Diffusion of responsibility. *Journal of Personality and Social Psychology* 8: 377–383.

DeLongis, A., J. C. Coyne, G. Dakof, S. Folkman, and R. S. Lazarus. 1982. Relationship of daily hassles, uplifts, and major life events to health status. *Health Psychology* 1: 119–136.

DeLongis, A., S. Folkman, and R. S. Lazarus. 1984. "The impact of everyday hassles on health and well-being." Paper presented at the American Psychological Association Meeting, Los Angeles.

DeLongis, A., S. Folkman, and R. S. Lazarus. 1988. The impact of daily stress on health and mood: Psychological and social resources as mediators. *Journal of Personality and Social Psychology* 54: 486–495.

Derogatis, L. R. 1982. Self-report measures of stress. In *Handbook of stress—Theoretical and clinical aspects*, 270–294, edited by L. Goldberger and S. Breznitz. New York: The Free Press.

DesPres, T. 1976. *The survivor*. New York: Oxford University Press.

Dewey, R., and W. J. Humber. 1951. *The development of human behavior*. New York: Macmillan.

Dimsdale, J. E., ed. 1980. *Survivors, victims, and perpetrators: Essays on the Nazi Holocaust*. Washington, D.C.: Hemisphere.

Dinardo, Q. 1971. "Psychological adjustment to spinal cord injury." Doctoral dissertation, University of Houston.

Dobos, R. 1979. The price of adapting to work. *Human Nature* 2: 29–35.

Dohrenwend, B. P., and P. E. Shrout. 1985. "Hassles" in the conceptualization and measurement of life stress variables. *American Psychologist* 40: 780–785.

Dohrenwend, B. S., B. P. Dohrenwend, M. Dodson, and P. E. Shrout. 1984. Symptoms, hassles, social supports, and life events: Problem of confounded measures. *Journal of Abnormal Psychology* 93: 222–230.

Downey, G., R. C. Silver, and C. B. Wortman. In press. Reconsidering the attribution-adjustment relation following a major negative event: Coping with the loss of a child. *Journal of Personality and Social Psychology*.

Duck, S., and R. C. Silver, eds. 1990. *Personal relationships and social support*. London, Newbury Park: Sage.

Dunkel-Schetter, C., S. Folkman, and R. S. Lazarus. 1984. "A contextual and multidimensional view of support received in stressful episodes." Paper presented at the meetings of the American Psychological Association, Los Angeles.

Dunkel-Schetter, C., and C. B. Wortman. 1981. Dilemmas of social support: Parallels between victimization and aging. In *Aging: Social change*, edited by S. Kiesler and J. March. New York: Academic Press.

———. 1982. The interpersonal dynamics of cancer: Problems in social relationships and their impact on the patient. In *Interpersonal issues in health care*, edited by H. S. Friedman and M. R. DiMatteo. New York: Academic Press.

Durkheim, E. 1897. English translation: 1951. *Suicide*. New York: Free Press.

Endler, N. S. 1982. Whence interactional psychology? In *Social behavior in context*, edited by A. Furnham and M. Argyle. Boston: Allyn & Bacon.

Endler, N. S., and D. Magnusson. 1976. *Interactional psychology and personality*. New York: John Wiley & Sons.

Endler, N. S., and J. Edwards. 1982. Stress and personality. *Handbook of stress—Theoretical and clinical aspects*, 36–48, edited by L. Goldberger and S. Breznitz. New York: Free Press.

Fazio, R. H., and J. Cooper. 1983. Arousal in the dissonance process. In *Social psychophysiology*, edited by J. T. Cacioppo and R. E. Petty. New York: Guilford Press.

Fazio, R. H., M. P. Zanna, and J. Cooper. 1977. Dissonance and self-perception: An integrative view of each theory's proper domain of application. *Journal of Experimental Social Psychology* 13: 464–479.

Festinger, L. 1957. *A theory of cognitive dissonance*. Stanford: Stanford University Press.

Figley, C. R., and E. Leventman, eds. 1980. *Strangers at home: Vietnam veterans since the war*. New York: Praeger.

Fiske, S. T., and S. E. Taylor. 1983. *Social cognition*. Reading, Mass.: Addison-Wesley Publishing Company.

Fitzgerald, R. C. 1970. Reactions to blindness: An exploratory study of adults with recent loss of sight. *Archives of General Psychiatry* 22: 370–379.

Fleming, R., A. Baum, and J. E. Singer. 1984. Toward an integrative approach to the study of stress. *Journal of Personality and Social Psychology* 46: 939–949.

Fogelman, E. 1987. "The rescuers: A socio-psychological study of altruistic behavior during the Nazi Era." Doctoral dissertation, City University of New York.

Folkman, S. 1984. Personal control and stress and coping processes: A theoretical analysis. *Journal of Personality and Social Psychology* 46: 839–852.

Folkman, S., and R. S. Lazarus. 1980. An analysis of coping in a middle-aged community sample. *Journal of Health and Social Behavior* 21: 219–239.

Frankl, V. E. 1946. *Ein Psychologe erlebt das Konzentrationslager*. Oesterreich.

———. 1959. *Man's search for meaning*. Boston: Beacon Press.

———. 1983. *Theorie und Therapie der Neurosen: Einfuehrung in Logotherapie und Existenzanalyse*. Muenchen: Reinhardt Verlag.

———. 1984. *Man's search for meaning*. New York: Washington Square Press.

———. 1985. *The unconscious God*. New York: Washington Square Press.

Freud, S. 1959. *Collected papers*, Vols. 1–4. New York: Basic Books.

Friedman, H. S., and S. Booth-Kewley. 1987. Personality Type A behavior and coronary heart disease: The role of emotional expression. *Journal of Personality and Social Psychology* 53: 783–792.

———. 1988. Validity of the Type A Construct: A reprise. *Psychological Bulletin* 104: 381–384.

Friedman, H. S., and M. R. DiMatteo. 1989. *Health Psychology*. Englewood Cliffs, N.J.: Prentice-Hall Inc.

Friedman, M., and R. H. Rosenman. 1959. Association of specific overt behavior pattern with blood and cardiovascular findings. *Journal of the American Medical Association* 169: 1286–1296.

———. 1974. Type A Behavior and Your Heart. New York: Knopf.

Friedman, R., and D. Ulmer. 1984. *Treating Type A Behavior and your heart*. New York: Knopf.

Funk, S. C., and B. K. Houston. 1987. A critical anlaysis of the Hardiness Scale's validity and utility. *Journal of Personality and Social Psychology* 53: 572–578.

Furnham, A., and B. Gunter. 1984. Just world beliefs and attitudes towards the poor. *British Journal of Social Psychology* 23: 265–269.

Galanter, M., ed. 1986. *Recent developments in alcoholism*, Vol. 4. New York: Plenum Press.

Glass, D. C. 1977. *Behavior patterns, stress and coronary disease*. Hillsdale, N.J.: Erlbaum.

Glick, I. O., R. S. Weiss, and C. M. Parkes. 1974. *The first year of bereavement*. New York: John Wiley & Sons.

Goetz-Marchand, B., J. Goetz, and M. Irle. 1974. Preference of dissonance reduction modes as a function of their order, familiarity and reversibility. *European Journal of Social Psychology* 2: 201–228.

Goldband, S., E. S. Katkin, and M. A. Morell. 1979. Personality and cardiovascular disorder: Steps toward demystification. In *Stress and anxiety*, Vol. 6, edited by I. G. Sarason and C. D. Spielberger. New York: John Wiley & Sons.

Gorsuch, R. L. 1988. Psychology of religion. *Annual Review of Psychology* 39: 201–222.

Gorsuch, R. L., and S. E. McPherson. 1989. Intrinsic/extrinsic measurement: I/E-revised and single item scales. *Journal for the Scientific Study of Religion* 28: 348–354.

Gottlieb, B. H., ed. 1981. *Social networks and social support*. Beverly Hills: Sage.

Green, B. L., J. P. Wilson, and J. D. Lindy. 1985. Conceptualizing Post-traumatic

Stress disorder: A psychosocial framework. In *Trauma and its wake*, 54–69, edited by C. Figley. New York: Brunner/Mazel.

Greenwald, A. G., F. S. Bellezza, and M. R. Banaji. 1988. Is self-esteem a central ingredient of the self-process? *Personality and Social Psychology Bulletin* 14: 34–45.

Grinker, R. R., and J. P. Spiegel. 1945. *Men under stress*. New York: McGraw-Hill.

Gruen, R., S. Folkman, and R. S. Lazarus. 1984. "The role of personal vulnerabilities in recurrent stressors." Paper presented at the American Psychological Association Meeting, Los Angeles.

Gruman, J. C., and R. P. Sloan. 1983. Disease as justice: Perceptions of the victims of physical illness. *Basic and Applied Social Psychology* 4: 39–46.

Guilford, J. P. 1959. *Personality*. New York: McGraw-Hill.

Gullo, S. V., D. J. Cherico, and R. Shadick. 1974. Suggested stages and response styles in life-threatening illness: A focus on the cancer patient. In *Anticipatory Grief*, edited by B. Schoenberg, A. C. Carr, A. H. Kutscher, D. Peretz and I. K. Goldberg. New York: Columbia University Press.

Haan, N. 1977. *Coping and defending: Processes of self-environment organization*. New York: Academic Press.

Hahn, M. E. 1966. *California Life Goals Evaluation Schedule*. Palo Alto, Calif.: Western Psychological Services.

Hall, C. M. 1986. Cosmology and therapy. *Journal of Religion and Health* 25: 254–263.

Hamilton, S., and B. I. Fagot. 1988. Chronic stress and coping styles: A comparison of male and female undergraduates. *Journal of Personality and Social Psychology* 55: 819–823.

Hanusa, B. H., and R. Schulz. 1977. Attributional mediators of learned helplessness. *Journal of Personality and Social Psychology* 35: 602–611.

Harary, F. 1983. Consistency theory is alive and well. *Personality and Social Psychology Bulletin* 9: 60–64.

Harvey, J. H. 1989. Fritz Heider (1896–1988). *American Psychologist* 44: 570–571.

Harvey, J. H., W. J. Ickes, and R. F. Kidd. 1976. *New directions in attribution research*, Vol. 1. Hillsdale, N.J.: Erlbaum.

Harvey, O. J., D. E. Hunt, and H. M. Schroeder. 1961. *Conceptual systems and personality organization*. New York: John Wiley & Sons.

Heider, F. 1944. Social perception and phenomenal causality. *Psychological Review* 51: 358–374.

———. 1946. Attitudes and cognitive organization. *Journal of Psychology* 21: 107–112.

———. 1958. *The psychology of interpersonal relations*. New York: John Wiley & Sons.

———. 1960. The Gestalt theory of motivation. In *The Nebraska Symposium on Motivation*, 145–172, edited by M. R. Jones. Lincoln, Nebr.: University of Nebraska Press.

———. 1976. A conversation with Fritz Heider. In *New directions in attribution research*, Vol. 1, 3–18, edited by J. H. Harvey, W. J. Ickes and R. F. Kidd. Hillsdale, N.J.: Erlbaum.

———. 1983. *The life of a psychologist*. Kansas City: University Press of Kansas.

Heider, F., and M. Simmel. 1944. An experimental study of apparent behavior. *American Journal of Psychology* 57: 243–259.

Helmreich, R. L., R. Stapp, and B. Erwin. 1974. Texas Social Behavior Inventory

(TSBI): An objective measure of self-esteem or social competence. *JSAS Catalogue of Selected Documents in Social Psychology* 4: 79.

Henderson, A. S. 1984. Interpreting the evidence on social support. *Social Psychiatry* 19: 49–52.

Herrmann, C. 1988. Die Rolle von Attributionen im Bewaeltigungsgeschehen. In *Belastung und Bewaeltigung: Trends in der Bewaeltigungsforschung*, edited by L. Bruederl. Muenchen: Juventa.

Heyduk, R. G., and A. Fenigstein. 1984. Influential works and authors in psychology: A survey of eminent psychologists. *American Psychologist* 39: 556–559.

Higgins, E. T., R. Klein, and T. Strauman. 1985. Self-concept discrepancy theory: A psychological model for distinguishing among different aspects of depression and anxiety. *Social Cognition* 3: 51–76.

Hinkle, L. E., Jr. 1977. The concept of "stress" in the biological and social sciences. In *Psychosomatic medicine: Current trends and clinical implications*, edited by Z. J. Lipowski, D. R. Lipsitt, and P. C. Whybrow. New York: Oxford University Press.

Hiroto, D. S. 1974. Locus of control and learned helplessness. *Journal of Experimental Psychology* 102: 187–192.

Hobfoll, S. E., ed. 1986. *Stress, social support, and women*. New York: Hemisphere.

Hobfoll, S. E., and S. Walfisch. 1984. Coping with a threat to life: A longitudinal study of self-concept, social support, and psychological distress. *American Journal of Community Psychology* 12: 87–100.

Hobfoll, S. E., A. Nadler, and J. Leiberman. 1986. Satisfaction with social support during crisis: Intimacy and self-esteem as critical determinants. *Journal of Personality and Social Psychology* 51: 296–304.

Holmes, T. H., and R. H. Rahe. 1967. The social readjustment rating scale. *Journal of Psychosomatic Research* 11: 213–218.

Horowitz, M. J. 1976. *Stress response syndromes*. New York: Aronson.

———. 1985. Disasters and psychological responses to stress. *Psychiatric Annals* 15: 161–167.

Horowitz, M. J., and N. B. Kaltreider. 1980. Brief psychotherapy of stress response syndromes. In *Specialized techniques in individual psychotherapy*, 162–183, edited by T. Karasu and L. Bellak. New York: Brunner/Mazel.

House, J. S. 1981. *Work stress and social support*. Reading, Mass.: Addison-Wesley Publishing Company.

House, J. S., C. Robbins, and H. L. Metzner. 1982. The association of social relationships and activities with mortalities: Prospective evidence from the Tecumseh Community Health Study. *American Journal of Epidemiology* 116: 123–140.

House, J. S., K. R. Landis, and D. Umberson. 1988. Social relationships and health. *Science* 241: 540–545.

Hudson, W. W., G. J. Murphy, and P. S. Nurius. 1983. A short-form scale to measure liberal vs. conservative orientations toward human expression. *The Journal of Sex Research* 19: 258–272.

Hull, J. G., R. R. Van Treuren, and S. Virnelli. 1987. Hardiness and health: A critique and alternative approach. *Journal of Personality and Social Psychology* 53: 518–530.

Inglehart, M. R. 1987. Das Prinzip der kognitiven Konsistenz und der Prozess der

Attribution—Versuch einer Integration. In *Beitraege zum Kongress der Deutschen Gesellschaft fuer Psychologie in Heidelberg 1986*, Vol. 2, 479–488, edited by M. Amelang. Goettingen: Hogrefe Verlag.

Inglehart, M. 1988. *Kritische Lebensereignisse—eine sozialpsychologische Perspektive*. Stuttgart: Kohlhammer Verlag.

———. Under review. Post hoc versus a priori attributions and their consequences: Theoretical considerations and empirical evidence for the area of critical life events.

Inglehart, M., E. Wurf, D. Brown, and W. Moore. 1987. "Possible selves and satisfaction with career choice—A longitudinal analysis." Paper presented at the American Psychological Association Meeting, New York.

Inglehart, M., D. R. Brown, and W. Moore. 1988. "Attitude changes in early adulthood—Reactions to life's inconsistencies?" Paper presented at the Midwestern Psychological Association Meeting, Chicago.

Inglehart, M., H. Markus, and D. Brown. 1989. The effect of possible selves on academic achievement: A panel study. In *Recent advances in social psychology: An international perspective*, 469–477, edited by J. P. Forgas and J. M. Innes. North Holland: Elsevier Science Publ.

Inglehart, M. R., O. Malanchuk, and D. R. Brown. 1988. "Accepting versus creating possible selves and subjective well-being; A longitudinal analysis." Paper presented at APA Meeting, Washington, D.C.

Inglehart, M., and P. Kondoff. In preparation. Reactions to positive and negative inconsistent information—an empirical investigation.

Inglehart, M., D. McIntosh, and R. Pacini. 1990a. "Postmaterialism, terminal values and control beliefs." Paper presented at the American Psychological Society, Dallas.

———. 1990b. "Postmaterialism and religiosity: An empirical investigation." Paper presented at the International Society for Political Psychology, Washington, D.C.

———. In preparation. Life philosophy and psychological health.

Inglehart, M., and M. McDonald. Under review. The influence of sexual attitudes on evaluating rape—a new look at Lerner's Just World hypothesis.

Inglehart, M., and S. Schur. In preparation. Processing inconsistent information—an experimental investigation.

Inglehart, R. F. 1977. *The silent revolution*. Princeton: Princeton University Press.

———. 1990. *Culture shift in advanced industrial society*. Princeton: Princeton University Press.

Irle, M. 1975. *Lehrbuch der Sozialpsychologie*. Goettingen: Hogrefe Verlag.

Jackson, D. N. 1974. *Personality Research Form Manual*. Goshen, N.Y.: Research Psychologists Press.

Janis, I. L. 1983. The role of social support in adherence to stressful decisions. *American Psychologist* 38: 143–160.

Janis, I. L., and L. Mann. 1977. *Decision making*. New York: Free Press.

Janoff-Bulman, R. 1979. Characterological versus behavioral self-blame: Inquiries into depression and rape. *Journal of Personality and Social Psychology* 37: 1798–1809.

———. 1989. Assumptive worlds and the stress of traumatic events: Applications of the schema construct. *Social cognition* 7: 113–136.

Janoff-Bulman, R., and I. H. Frieze. 1983. A theoretical perspective for understanding reactions to victimization. *Journal of Social Issues* 39: 1–17.

Janoff-Bulman, R., and C. Timko. 1986. Coping with traumatic life events: The role
of denial in light of people's assumptive worlds. In *Coping with negative life
events: Clinical and social psychological perspectives*, edited by C. R. Synder and
C. Ford. New York: Plenum.

Jenkins, C. D., R. H. Rosenman, and M. Friedman. 1967. Development of an objective psychological test for the determination of the coronary-prone behavior
pattern in employed men. *Journal of Chronic Diseases* 20: 371–379.

Jenkins, C. D., S. J. Zyzanski, and R. H. Rosenman. 1976. Risk of new myocardial
infarction in middle-aged men with manifest coronary heart disease. *Circulation*
53: 342–347.

Jenkins, C. D., and S. J. Zyzanksi. 1980. Behavioral risk factors and coronary heart
disease. *Psychotherapy and Psychosomatics* 34: 149–177.

Joereskog, K. G., and D. Soerbom. 1984. *LISREL VI; Analysis of linear structural
relationships by the method of maximum likelihood.* Mooresville, Ind.: Scientific
Software Inc.

Jones, E. E. 1987. The seer who found attributional wisdom in naivety. *Contemporary
Psychology* 32: 213–216.

Jones, E. E., and K. E. Davis. 1965. From acts to dispositions: The attribution
process in person perception. In *Advances in experimental social psychology*, Vol.
2, 219–266, edited by L. Berkowitz. New York: Academic Press.

Kanner, A. D., J. C. Coyne, C. Schaefer, and R. S. Lazarus. 1981. Comparisons
of two modes of stress measurement: Daily hassles and uplifts versus major
life events. *Journal of Behavioral Medicine* 4: 1–39.

Kasl, S. V., and S. Cobb. 1979. Some mental health consequences of plant closing
and job loss. In *Mental health and the economy*, 255–299, edited by L. A. Ferman
and J. P. Gordus. Kalamazoo, Mich.: W. E. Upjohn Institute.

Kaylor, J. A., D. W. King, and L. A. King. 1987. Psychological effects of military
service in Vietnam: A meta-analysis. *Psychological Bulletin* 102: 257–271.

Kelley, H. H. 1967. Attribution theory in social psychology. In *Nebraska Symposium
on Motivation*, 192–240, edited by D. Levine. Lincoln, Nebr.: University of
Nebraska.

———. 1971a. Attribution in social interaction. In *Attribution: Perceiving the causes of
behavior*, 1–26, edited by E. E. Jones et al. Morristown, N.J.: General Learning
Press.

———. 1971b. Causal schemata and the attribution process. In *Attribution: Perceiving
the causes of behavior*, 151–174, edited by E. E. Jones et al. Morristown, N.J.:
General Learning Press.

Kelly, W. E., ed. 1985. *Post-traumatic stress disorder and the war veteran patient.* New
York: Bruner/Mazel.

Kessler, R. C., and J. D. McLeod. 1985. The cost of sharing. In *Social support theory,
research and application*, edited by I. G. Sarason and B. R. Sarason. The Hague:
Martinus Nijhof.

Kessler, R. C., J. D. McLeod, and E. Wethington. 1986. The costs of caring. In
Social support: Theory, research and applications, edited by I. G. Sarason and B. R.
Sarason. The Hague: Martinus Nijhof.

Kimball, C. P. 1969. Psychological responses to the experience of open-heart surgery. *American Journal of Psychiatry* 126: 96–107.

Klinger, E. 1975. Consequences of commitment to and disengagement from incentives. *Psychological Review* 82: 1–25.

———. 1977. *Meaning and void: Inner experience and the incentives in people's lives.* Minneapolis: University of Minnesota Press.

Klosterhalfen, W., and S. Klosterhalfen. 1983. A critical analysis of the animal experiments cited in support of learned helplessness. *Psychologische Beitraege* 25: 436–458.

Kobasa, S. C. 1979. Stressful life events, personality and health: An inquiry into hardiness. *Journal of Personality and Social Psychology* 37: 1–11.

———. 1982a. Hardiness Measurement. Manuscript. Department of Behavioral Sciences, University of Chicago, Chicago, Ill.

———. 1982b. Commitment and coping in stress—resistance among lawyers. *Journal of Personality and Social Psychology* 42: 707–717.

Kobasa, S. C., S. R. Maddi, and S. Courington. 1981. Personality and constitution as mediators in the stress-illness relationship. *Journal of Health and Social Behavior* 22: 368–378.

Kobasa, S. C., S. R. Maddi, and S. Kahn. 1982. Hardiness and health: A prospective study. *Journal of Personality and Social Psychology* 42: 168–177.

Kobasa, S. C., S. R. Maddi, and M. C. Puccetti. 1982. Personality and exercise as buffers in the stress-illness relationship. *Journal of Behavioral Medicine* 5: 391–404.

Kobasa, S. C., S. R. Maddi, and M. A. Zola. 1983. Type A and hardiness. *Journal of Behavioral Medicine* 6: 41–51.

Kobasa, S. C., and M. C. Puccetti. 1983. Personality and social resources in stress resistance. *Journal of Personality and Social Psychology* 45: 839–850.

Kojetin, B. A. 1988. "Separating the seekers from the doubters." Presented at the Convention of the Society for the Scientific Study of Religion, Chicago.

Kruglanski, A. W. 1980. Lay epistemologic process and content. *Psychological Review* 87: 70–87.

———. 1989. *Lay epistemics and human knowledge: Cognitive and motivational biases.* New York: Plenum Press.

Kruglanski, A. W., and T. Freund. 1983. The freezing and unfreezing of lay inferences: Effects on impression primacy, ethnic stereotyping, and numerical anchoring. *Journal of Experimental Social Psychology* 19: 448–468.

Kruglanski, A. W., and Y. Klar. 1987. A view from a bridge: Synthesizing the consistency and attribution paradigms from a lay epistemic perspective. *European Journal of Social Psychology* 17: 211–242.

Kuebler-Ross, E. 1969. *On death and dying.* New York: Macmillan.

———. 1982. *Working it through.* New York: Collier Books.

Kuiper, N. A., and P. A. Derry. 1981. The self as a cognitive prototype: An application to person perception and depression. In *Personality, cognition, and social interaction*, 215–232, edited by N. Cantor and J. F. Kihlstrom. Hillsdale, N.J.: Erlbaum.

LaGaipa, Y. Y. 1990. The negative effects of informal support systems. In *Personal relationships and social support*, 122–139, edited by S. Duck and R. C. Silver. London, Newbury Park: Sage.

Last, U., and H. Klein. 1984. Impact of parental Holocaust traumatization on off-springs' reports of parental child-rearing practices. *Journal of Youth and Adolescence* 13: 267–283.

Lazarus, R. S. 1966. *Psychological stress and the coping process.* New York: McGraw-Hill.

————. 1975. The self regulation of emotion. In *Emotions: Their parameters and measurement,* edited by L. Levi. New York: Raven.

————. 1980. Cognitive behavior therapy as psychodynamics revisited. In *Psychotherapy process: Current issues and future directions,* edited by J. Mahoney. New York: Plenum.

————. 1982. Thoughts on the relations between emotion and cognition. *American Psychologist* 37: 1019–1024.

————. 1983. The costs and benefits of denial. In *The denial of stress,* 1–33, edited by S. Breznitz. New York: International University Press.

————. 1984. On the primacy of cognition. *American Psychologist* 39: 124–129.

————. 1990. Biography. *American Psychologist* 45: 455–457.

Lazarus, R. S., and E. Alfert. 1964. The short-circuiting of threat. *Journal of Abnormal and Social Psychology* 69: 195–205.

Lazarus, R. S., J. R. Averill, and E. M. Opton, Jr. 1970. Toward a cognitive theory of emotions. In *Feelings and emotions,* edited by M. Arnold. New York: Academic Press.

Lazarus, R. S., J. R. Averill, and E. M. Opton, Jr. 1974. The psychology of coping: Issues of research and assessment. In *Coping and adaptation,* edited by G. V. Coelho, D. A. Hamburg and J. E. Adams. New York: Basic Books.

Lazarus, R. S., and J. B. Cohen. 1977. Environmental stress. In *Human behavior and the environment: Current theory and research,* edited by I. Altman and J. F. Wohlwill. New York: Plenum.

Lazarus, R. S., and A. DeLongis. 1983. Psychological stress and coping in aging. *American Psychologist* 38: 245–254.

Lazarus, R. S., and S. Folkman. 1984. *Stress, appraisal, and coping.* New York: Springer Publishing Company.

Lazarus, R. S., A. DeLongis, S. Folkman, and R. Gruen. 1985. Stress and adaptational outcomes—The problem of confounded measures. *American Psychologist* 40: 770–779.

Lazarus, R. S., and S. Folkman. 1987. Transactional theory and research on emotions and coping. *European Journal of Personality* 1: 141–169.

Lazarus, R. S., and R. Launier. 1978. Stress-related transactions between person and environment. In *Perspectives in interactional psychology,* 287–327, edited by L. A. Pervin and M. Lewis. New York: Plenum.

Lazarus, R. S., J. C. Speisman, A. M. Mordkof, and L. A. Davison. 1962. A laboratory study of psychological stress produced by a motion picture film. *Psychological Monographs* 76: 34, 553.

Lefcourt, H. M. 1973. The function of the illusion of control and freedom. *American Psychologist* 28: 417–425.

————. ed. 1981. *Research with the locus of control construct—Assessment methods.* New York: Academic Press.

————. ed. 1983a. *Research with the locus of control construct—Developments and problems.* New York: Academic Press.

———. 1983b. The locus of control as a moderator variable: stress. In *Research on the locus of control construct—developments and problems*, 253–279, edited by H. M. Lefcourt. New York: Academic Press.

———. 1984. *Research with the locus of control construct—extensions and limitations.* New York: Academic Press.

Lefcourt, H. M., R. A. Martin, and W. E. Saleh. 1984. Locus of control and social support: Interactive moderators of stress. *Journal of Personality and Social Psychology* 47: 378–389.

Lehman, D. R., J. H. Ellard, and C. B. Wortman. 1986. Social suppport for the bereaved: Recipients' and providers' perspectives on what is helpful. *Journal of Clinical and Consulting Psychology* 54: 438–446.

Lehman, D. R., and S. E. Taylor. 1987. Date with an earthquake: Coping with a probable, unpredictable disaster. *Personality and Social Psychology Bulletin* 13: 546–555.

Lehman, D. R., C. B. Wortman, and A. F. Williams. 1987. Long-term effects of losing a spouse or child in a motor vehicle crash. *Journal of Personality and Social Psychology* 52: 218–231.

Leighton, A. H. 1963. Psychiatric findings of the Sterling County Study. *American Journal of Psychiatry* 119: 1021–1026.

Lerner, M. J. 1980. *The belief in a just world: A fundamental delusion.* New York: Plenum.

Lerner, M. J., and D. T. Miller. 1978. Just world research and the attribution process: Looking back and ahead. *Psychological Bulletin* 85: 1030–1051.

Lester, D. 1972. *Why people kill themselves. A summary of research findings on suicidal behavior.* Springfield, Ill.: Charles C. Thomas.

———. 1983. *Why people kill themselves.* A 1980s summary of research findings on suicidal behavior. Springfield, Ill.: Charles C. Thomas.

Levenson, H. 1981. Differentiating among internality, powerful others and chance. In *Research with the locus of control construct*, Vol. 1, edited by H. M. Lefcourt. New York: Academic Press.

Lieberman, M. A. 1982. The effects of social supports on responses to stress. In *Handbook of stress*, 764–783, edited by L. Goldberger and S. Breznitz. New York: Free Press.

Lifton, R. J. 1963. *Thought reform and the psychology of totalism: A study of "brainwashing" in China.* New York: W. W. Norton.

Lin, N., and A. Dean. 1984. Social support and depression. A panel study. *Social Psychiatry* 19: 83–91.

Lin, N., A. Dean, and W. M. Ensel. 1986. *Social support, life events and depression.* New York: Academic Press.

Linville, P. W. 1982. Affective consequences of complexity regarding the self and others. In *Affect and cognition*, 79–110, edited by M. S. Clark and S. T. Fiske. Hillsdale, N.J.: Erlbaum.

———. 1985. Self-complexity and affective extremity: Don't put all your eggs in one cognitive basket. *Social Cognition* 3: 94–120.

———. 1987a. Self-complexity as a cognitive buffer against stress-related illness and depression. *Journal of Personality and Social Psychology* 52: 663–676.

———. 1987b. "Cognitive Complexity and Coping." Invited Address at the Midwestern Psychological Association Meeting, Chicago.

Litwak, E., and I. Szelenyi. 1969. Primary group structures and their functions: Kin, neighbors, and friends. *American Sociological Review* 34: 465–481.

Long, T. E., and W. C. Richard. 1986. Community post-tornado support groups: Conceptual issues and personal themes. American Psychological Association Meeting, Washington, D.C.

Lootens, A. L., and M. J. Strube. 1985. Daily Hassles, social support, and psychological well-being. American Psychological Association Meeting, Los Angeles.

Lucas, R. A. 1969. *Men in crisis*. New York: Basic Books.

Maddi, S. R., S. C. Kobasa, and M. Hoover. 1979. An alienation test. *Journal of Humanistic Psychology* 19: 73–76.

Maddison, D., and W. L. Walker. 1967. Factors affecting the outcome of conjugal bereavement. *British Journal of Psychiatry* 113: 1057–1067.

Maier, S. F., and M.E.P. Seligman. 1976. Learned helplessness: Theory and evidence. *Journal of Experimental Psychology: General* 105: 3–46.

Malmo, R. B. 1986. Obituary. Hans Hugo Selye (1907–1982). *American Psychologist* 41: 92–93.

Manne, S., and A. J. Zautra. 1987. "Negative and positive interactions, coping and adjustment to arthritis." Paper presented at the American Psychological Association Meeting, New York.

Markus, H., and P. Nurius. 1986. Possible Selves. *American Psychologist* 41: 954–969.

Markus, H., and E. Wurf. 1987. The dynamic self-concept: A social psychological perspective. *Annual Review of Psychology* 38: 299–337.

Markus, H., and R. B. Zajonc. 1985. The cognitive perspective in social psychology. In *Handbook of social psychology*, Vol. 1, 137–230, edited by G. Lindzey and E. Aronson. New York: Random House.

Maslach, C. 1978. The client role in staff burn-out. *Journal of Social Issues* 34: 111–124.

Maslow, A. H. 1968. *Toward a psychology of being*. New York: Van Nostrand Reinhold Company.

Mason, J. W. 1975. A historical view of the stress field: Part I and Part II. *Journal of Human Stress* 1: 6–12 and 22–36.

Matarazzo, J. D. 1982. Behavioral health: A 1990 challenge for the health science professions. In *Behavioral Handbook of Health: A Handbook of Health Enhancement and Disease Prevention*, edited by J. D. Matarazzo, N. E. Miller, and S. M. Wyers. New York: John Wiley & Sons.

Matthews, K. A. 1979. Efforts to control by children and adults with the Type A coronary-prone behavior pattern. *Child Development* 50: 842–847.

———. 1982. Psychological perspectives on the Type A behavior pattern. *Psychological Bulletin* 81: 291–323.

———. 1988. Coronary heart disease and Type A behaviors: Update on and alternative to the Booth-Kewley and Friedman (1987) Quantitative Review. *Psychological Bulletin* 104: 373–380.

Matthews, K. A., and S. G. Haynes. 1986. Type A behavior pattern and coronary disease risk: Update and critical evaluation. *American Journal of Epidemiology* 123: 923–960.

McDaniel, J. W., and A. W. Sexton. 1970. Psychendocrine studies of patients with spinal cord lesions. *Journal of Abnormal Psychology* 76: 117–122.

McFerran, J. R., and L. J. Breen. 1978. A bibliography of research on learned helplessness prior to introduction of the reformulated model (1978). *Psychological Reports* 45: 311–325.

McIntosh, D. N., M. R. Inglehart, and R. Pacini. Under review. The structure of belief systems and adjustment to life changes.

McIntosh, D. N., R. C. Silver, and C. B. Wortman. Under review. Religion's role in adjustment to a negative life event: Coping with the loss of a child.

McIntosh, D. N., and B. Spilka. 1990. Religion and physical health: The role of personal faith and control beliefs. *Research in the Social Scientific Study of Religion*, Vol. 2, 167–194.

McIntosh, J. L. 1985. *Research on suicide: A bibliography*. Westport, Conn.: Greenwood Press.

Mead, G. H. 1934. *Mind, self, and society*. Chicago: University of Chicago Press.

Menninger, K. 1963. *The vital balance: The life process in mental health and illness*. New York: Viking.

Metalsky, G. I., L. Y. Abramson, M.E.P. Seligman, A. Semmel, and C. Peterson. 1982. Attributional styles and life events in the classroom: Vulnerability and invulnerability to depressive mood reactions. *Journal of Personality and Social Psychology* 43: 612–617.

Meyer, C. B., and S. E. Taylor. 1986. Adjustment to rape. *Journal of Personality and Social Psychology* 50: 1226–1234.

Miller, D. T., and C.A.A. Porter. 1983. Self-blame in victims of violence. *Journal of Social Issues* 39: 139–152.

Miller, I. W., III, and W. H. Norman. 1979. Learned helplessness in humans: A review and attribution-theory model. *Psychological Bulletin* 86: 93–118.

Miller, S. M. 1980. When is a little information a dangerous thing? Coping with stressful life-events by monitoring vs. blunting. In *Coping and health*, 145–169, edited by S. Levine and H. Ursin. New York: Plenum.

———. 1981. Predictability and human stress: Towards a clarification of evidence and theory. In *Advances in experimental social psychology*, Vol. 14, 203–256, edited by L. Berkowitz. New York: Academic Press.

———. 1987. Monitoring and blunting: Validation of a questionnaire to assess styles of information seeking under threat. *Journal of Personality and Social Psychology* 52: 345–353.

———. 1988. "Styles of coping with threat: To see or not to see." Invited address at the Midwestern Psychological Association Meeting, Chicago.

———. 1989. Cognitive informational styles in the process of coping with threat and frustration. *Advances in Behavioral Research* M: 223–234.

Miller, S. M., and D. S. Brody. 1985. "Styles of coping with threat: Implications for health." Paper presented at the American Psychological Association Meeting, Los Angeles.

Miller, S. M., D. S. Brody, and J. Summerton. 1988. Styles of coping with threat: Implications for health. *Journal of Personality and Social Psychology* 54: 142–148.

Miller, S. M., E. R. Lack, and S. Asroff. 1982. "Preference for control and the Type A coronary-prone behavior pattern." Paper presented at the Association for the Advancement of Behavior Therapy Meeting, Toronto.

Miller, S. M., and C. E. Mangan. 1983. The interacting effects of information and coping style in adapting to gynecologic stress: Should the doctor tell all? *Journal of Personality and Social Psychology* 45: 223–236.

Miller, S. M., and W. Mischel. 1986. "A cognitive social learning approach to information seeking styles under threat." Manuscript, Temple University, Philadelphia.

Mischel, W. 1968. *Personality and assessment.* New York: John Wiley & Sons.

———. 1973. Toward a cognitive social learning reconceptualization of personality. *Psychological Review* 80: 252–283.

———. 1985. Looking for personality. In *A century of psychology as science,* 515–526, edited by S. Koch and D. E. Leary. New York: MacGraw-Hill.

Moentmann, V., and E. Irle. 1978. Bibliographie der wichtigen seit 1956 erschienenen Arbeiten zur Theorie der kognitiven Dissonanz. In *Leon Festinger. Theorie der kognitiven Dissonanz,* 366–413, edited by M. Irle and V. Moentmann. Bern: Huber Verlag.

Monat, A., and R. S. Lazarus, eds. 1985. *Stress and coping: An Anthology,* 2nd ed. New York: Columbia University Press.

Moos, R. H. 1976. *Human adaptation: Coping with life crises.* Lexington, Mass.: D. C. Heath.

———. Ed. 1986. *Coping with life crises: An integrated approach.* New York: Plenum.

Murphy, L. B. 1962. *The widening world of childhood.* New York: Basic Books.

———. 1974. Coping, vulnerability, and resilience in childhood. In *Coping and Adaptation,* edited by G. V. Coelho, D. A. Hamburg, and J. E. Adams. New York: Basic Books.

Musante, L., J. M. McDougall, and T. M. Dembroski. 1984. The Type A behavior pattern and attributions for success and failure. *Personality and Social Psychology Bulletin* 10: 544–553.

Nadler, A., and O. Mayseless. 1983. Recipient self-esteem and reactions to help. In *New directions in helping,* Vol. 1, 167–188, edited by J. D. Fisher, A. Nadler and B. M. DePaulo. New York: Academic Press.

Nolen-Hoeksema, S., J. S. Girgus, and M.E.P. Seligman. 1986. Learned helplessness in children: A longitudinal study of depression, achievement and explanatory style. *Journal of Personality and Social Psychology* 51: 435–442.

Norem, J. K., and N. Cantor. 1986a. Defensive Pessimism: Harnessing anxiety as motivation. *Journal of Personality and Social Psychology* 51: 1208–1217.

———. 1986b. Anticipatory and post-hoc cushioning strategies: Optimism and defensive pessimism in "risky" situations. *Cognitive Therapy and Research* 10: 347–362.

Northouse, L., and C. B. Wortman. Under review. Models of helping and coping in cancer cure.

Notman, M. T., and C. C. Nadelson. 1976. The rape victim: Psychodynamic considerations. *American Journal of Psychiatry* 133: 408–412.

Oettingen, G., and M.E.P. Seligman. 1990. Pessimism and behavioral signs of depression in East versus West Berlin. *European Journal of Social Psychology* 20: 207–220.

Osgood, C. E., and P. H. Tannenbaum. 1955. The principle of congruity in the prediction of attitude change. *Psychological Review* 62: 42–55.

Overmier, J. B., and M.E.P. Seligman. 1967. Effects of inescapable shock upon subsequent escape and avoidance responding. *Journal of Comparative and Physiological Psychology* 63: 28–33.

Pargament, K. I., J. Kennell, W. Hathaway, N. Grevengoed, J. Newman, and W.

Jones. 1988. Religion and the problem-solving process: Three styles of coping. *Journal for the Scientific Study of Religion* 27: 90–104.

Parkes, C. M. 1972. *Bereavement*. New York: International Universities Press.

Parkes, K. R. 1984. Locus of control, cognitive appraisal, and coping in stressful episodes. *Journal of Personality and Social Psychology* 46: 655–668.

Pearlin, L. I. 1980. Life strains and psychological distress among adults. In *Themes of work and love in adulthood*, edited by N. J. Smelser and E. H. Erikson. Cambridge, Mass.: Harvard University Press.

Pearlin, L. I., M. A. Lieberman, E. G. Menaghan, and J. T. Mullan. 1981. The stress process. *Journal of Health and Social Behavior* 22: 337–356.

Pearlin, L. I., and C. Schooler. 1978. The structure of coping. *Journal of Health and Social Behavior* 19: 2–21.

Peck, A. 1972. Emotional reactions to having cancer. *American Journal of Roentgenology, Radium Therapy, and Nuclear Medicine* 114: 591–599.

Pennebaker, J. W. 1989. Confession, inhibition and disease. In *Advances in experimental social psychology*, Vol. 22, edited by L. Berkowitz. New York: Academic Press.

Peterson, C. 1986. "Explanatory style as a risk factor for illness." Paper presented at the American Psychological Association Meeting, Washington, D.C.

———. 1988. Explanatory style as a risk factor for illness. *Cognitive Therapy and Research* 12: 119–132.

Peterson, C., and L. C. Barrett. 1987. Explanatory style and academic performance among university freshman. *Journal of Personality and Social Psychology* 53: 603–607.

Peterson, C., L. Luborsky, and M.E.P. Seligman. 1983. Attributions and depressive mood shifts: A case study using the symptoms-context method. *Journal of Abnormal Psychology* 92: 96–103.

Peterson, C., and M.E.P. Seligman. 1984. Causal explanations as a risk factor for depression: Theory and evidence. *Psychological Review* 91: 347–374.

Peterson, C., M.E.P. Seligman, and G. E. Vaillant. 1988. Pessimistic explanatory style is a risk factor for physical illness: A thirty-five-year longitudinal study. *Journal of Personality and Social Psychology* 55: 23–27.

Peterson, C., A. Semmel, C. von Baeyer, L. Y. Abramson, G. I. Metalsky, and M.E.P. Seligman. 1982. The attributional style questionnaire. *Cognitive Therapy and Research* 6: 287–299.

Phillips, D. P. 1986. Natural experiments on the effects of mass media violence on fatal aggression: Strengths and weaknesses of a new approach. In *Advances in Experimental Social Psychology*, Vol. 19, 207–250, edited by L. Berkowitz. New York: Academic Press.

Piaget, J. 1936, Engl. translation 1953. *The origins of intelligence in the child*. London: Routledge and Kegan Paul.

———. 1947, Engl. translation 1950. *The psychology of intelligence*. London: Routledge and Kegan Paul.

Pierce, G. R., B. R. Sarason, and L. G. Sarason. 1990. Integrating social support perspectives: Working models, personal relationships, and situational factors. In *Personal relationships and social support*, 173–189, edited by S. Duck and R. C. Silver. London, Newbury Park: Sage.

Pyszczynski, T. A., and J. Greenberg. 1981. Role of disconfirmed expectancies in the instigation of attributional processing. *Journal of Personality and Social Psychology* 40: 31–38.

Rhodewalt, F., and J. B. Zone. 1989. Appraisal of life change, depression, and illness in hardy and nonhardy women. *Journal of Personality and Social Psychology* 56: 81–88.

Rich, V. L., and A. R. Rich. 1985. "Personality hardiness and burnout in female staff nurses." Paper presented at the American Psychological Association Meeting, Los Angeles.

Robins, C. J. 1988. Attributions and depression: Why is the literature so inconsistent? *Journal of Personality and Social Psychology* 54: 880–889.

Rodin, J. 1986. Aging and health: Effects of the sense of control. *Science* 237: 4770–4773.

Rodin, J., and E. Langer. 1977. Long-term effects of a control-relevant intervention with the institutionalized aged. *Journal of Personality and Social Psychology* 35: 897–902.

Rokeach, M. 1973. *The nature of human values*. New York: Free Press.

Rosch/Inglehart, M. 1981. Die Integration von Aussiedlern aus Polen in das politische Leben in der Bundesrepublik Deutschland. In Politische Psychologie, edited by H. D. Klingemann and M. Kaase. Sonderheft 12 der *Politischen Vierteljahresschrift* 22: 306–319.

———. 1983. *Konsistenzprinzip und Attributionsgeschehen—Versuch einer Integration*. Habilitationsschrift. Universitaet Mannheim.

———. 1985a. Rueckzug oder Coping? Eine Analyse des Kontaktverhaltens von Spaetaussiedlern. In *Auslaendische Arbeitnehmer und Immigranten—Sozialwissenschaftliche Beitraege zur Diskussion eines aktuellen Problems*, 239–257, edited by M. Rosch/Inglehart. Weinheim: Beltz Verlag.

———. 1985b. Einstellung und Verhalten bei auftretenden Lebensproblemen—eine "als-ob" Untersuchung. In *Bericht ueber den 34. Kongress der Deutschen Gesellschaft fuer Psychologie*, 502–503, edited by D. Albert. Goettingen: Hogrefe.

———. 1985c. Verhalten im sozialen Kontext: Soziale Foerderung und Unterdrueckung von Verhalten. In *Theorien der Sozialpsychologie: Gruppen- und Lerntheorien*, Vol. 2, 11–38, edited by D. Frey and M. Irle. Bern: Huber Verlag.

Rosch/Inglehart, M., D. Dickenberger, M. Irle, and V. Moentmann. 1981. *Tabellenband zur Laengsschnittstudie zur ersten Direktwahl zum Europaeischen Parlament*. Report SFB 24, University of Mannheim, West Germany.

Rosch/Inglehart, M., and M. Irle. 1983. Immigration as a role transition—A cognitive analysis of its impact on health. In *Role transition*, 97–108, edited by V. Allen and E. van de Vliert. London: Plenum.

Rosch/Inglehart, M., and R. Rohrlach. 1981. "Vorhersagen zur Art der Dissonanzreduktion und ihre Abhaengigkeit von der Verankerung der beteiligten Kognitionen." Paper presented at the 23rd meeting of German Experimental Psychologists, Berlin.

Rosch/Inglehart, M., and P. Schmidt. 1981. Modelle kognitiver Veraenderungen vor einer Wahl. In Politische Psychologie, edited by H. D. Klingemann and M. Kaase. Special Issue of the *Politische Vierteljahresschrift* 22: 240–262.

Rosenberg, M. J., and Abelson, R. P. 1960. An analysis of cognitive balancing. In *Attitude organization and change*, 112–163, edited by M. J. Rosenberg, C. I.

Hovland, W. J. McGuire, R. P. Abelson, and J. W. Brehm. New Haven: Yale University Press.

Rosenman, R. H., R. J. Brand, C. D. Jenkins, M. Friedman, R. Strauss, and M. Wurm. 1975. Coronary heart disease in the Western Collaborative Group Study: Final follow-up experience of 8 1/2 years. *Journal of the American Medical Association*, 233: 872–877.

Rosenmann, R. H., M. Friedman, R. Strauss, M. Wurm, R. Kositchek, W. Hahn, and N. T. Werthessen. 1964. A predictive study of coronary heart disease. *Journal of the American Medical Association* 189: 15–22.

Rossiter, M. 1986. *Women in the Resistance*. New York: Praeger.

Roth, D. L., D. J. Wiebe, R. B. Fillingim, and K. A. Shay. 1989. Life events, fitness, hardiness, and health: A simultaneous analysis of proposed stress-resistance effects. *Journal of Personality and Social Psychology* 57: 136–142.

Rotter, J. B. 1954. *Social learning and clinical psychology*. Englewood Cliffs, N.J.: Prentice-Hall Inc.

———. 1966. Generalized expectancies for internal versus external control of reinforcement. *Psychological Monographs: General and Applied* 80: 1, No. 609.

———. 1975. Some problems and misconceptions related to the construct of internal versus external control of reinforcement. *Journal of Consulting and Clinical Psychology* 43: 56–67.

———. 1989. Citation. *American Psychologist* 44: 625–626.

———. 1990. Internal vs. external control of reinforcement: A case history of a variable. *American Psychologist* 45: 489–493.

Rotter, J. B., M. Seeman, and S. Liverant. 1962. Internal vs. external locus of control of reinforcement: A major variable in behavior theory. In *Decisions, values, and groups*, edited by N. F. Washburne. London: Pergamon.

Rowlison, R. T., and R. D. Felner. 1988. Major life events, hassles, and adaptation in adolescence: Confounding in the conceptualization and measurement of life stress and adjustment revisited. *Journal of Personality and Social Psychology* 55: 432–444.

Sarafino, E. P. 1990. *Health psychology*. New York: John Wiley & Sons.

Schachter, S. 1964. The interaction of cognitive and physiological determinants of emotional state. In *Advances in experimental social psychology*, Vol. 1, 49–80, edited by L. Berkowitz. New York: Academic Press.

———. 1971. *Emotion, obesity and crime*. New York: Academic Press.

Schachter, S., and J. E. Singer. 1962. Cognitive, social and physiological determinants of emotional states. *Psychological Review* 69: 379–399.

Scheier, M. F., and C. S. Carver. 1985. Optimism, coping, and health: Assessment and implications of generalized outcome expectancies. *Health Psychology* 4: 219–247.

Scheier, M. F., and C. S. Carver. 1987. Dispositional optimism and physical well-being: The influence of generalized outcome expectancies on health. *Journal of Personality* 55: 169–210.

Scheier, M. F., K. A. Matthews, J. F. Owens, G. J. Magovern, R. C. Lefebvre, R. A. Abbott, and C. S. Carver. 1989. Dispositional optimism and recovery from coronary artery bypass surgery: The beneficial effects on physical and psychological well-being. *Journal of Personality and Social Psychology* 57: 1024–1040.

Scher, S. J., and J. Cooper. 1989. Motivational basis of dissonance: The singular role of behavioral consequences. *Journal of Personality and Social Psychology* 56: 899–906.

Schlosser, M. B., and L. A. Sheeley. 1985. "The hardy personality: Females coping with stress." Paper presented at the American Psychological Association Meeting, Los Angeles.

Schwarzer, R. ed. 1984. *The self in anxiety, stress and depression*. New York: Elsevier Science Publisher.

Seligman, M.E.P. 1972. Learned helplessness. *Annual Review of Medicine* 23: 407–412.

———. 1975. *Helplessness: On development, depression and death*. San Francisco: Freeman Press.

Seligman, M.E.P., L. Y. Abramson, A. Semmel, and C. von Baeyer. 1979. Depressive attributional style. *Journal of Abnormal Psychology* 88: 242–247.

Seligman, M.E.P., and S. F. Maier. 1967. Failure to escape traumatic shock. *Journal of Experimental Psychology* 74: 1–9.

Seligman, M.E.P., C. Peterson, N. J. Kaslow, R. L. Tannenbaum, L. B. Alloy, and L. Y. Abramson. 1984. Attributional style and depressive symptoms among children. *Journal of Abnormal Psychology* 83: 235–238.

Seligman, M.E.P., and P. Schulman. 1986. Explanatory style as a predictor of productivity and quitting among life insurance sales agents. *Journal of Personality and Social Psychology* 50: 832–838.

Selye, H. 1936. A syndrome produced by diverse nocuous agents. *Nature* 138: 32.

———. 1946. The general adaptation syndrome and diseases of adaptation. *Journal of Clinical Endocrinology* 6: 117–230.

———. 1956. *The stress of life*. New York: McGraw-Hill.

———. 1976. *Stress in health and disease*. Reading, Mass.: Butterworths.

Shaver, P., ed. 1985. Self, situations, and social behavior. *Review of Personality and Social Psychology*, Vol. 6. Beverly Hills: Sage.

Shiffman, S., and T. A. Wills, eds. 1985. *Coping and substance use*. Orlando: Academic Press.

Shontz, F. C. 1965. Reactions to crisis. *Volta Review* 67: 364–370.

———. 1975. *The psychological aspects of physical illness and disability*. New York: Macmillan.

Silver, R. L. 1982. *Coping with an undesirable life event: A study of early reactions to physical disability*. Doctoral dissertation, Northwestern University, Evanston, Ill.

Silver, R. L., C. Boon, and M. H. Stone. 1983. Searching for meaning in misfortune: Making sense of incest. *Journal of Social Issues* 39: 81–102.

Silver, R. L., and C. B. Wortman. 1980. Coping with undesirable life events. In *Human helplessness—Theory and applications*, 279–340, edited by J. Garber and M.E.P. Seligman. New York: Academic Press.

Silver, R. L., and C. B. Wortman. 1987. "The role of positive emotions in the coping process." Manuscript. University of Waterloo, Waterloo, Canada.

Silver, R. L., C. B. Wortman, and D. S. Klos. 1982. Cognitions, affect and behavior following uncontrollable outcomes: A response to current human helplessness research. *Journal of Personality* 50: 480–514.

Singer, P. S., and A. R. Rich. 1985. "Personality hardiness in college students:

Failure to cross-validate." Paper presented at the meetings of the American Psychological Association, Los Angeles.

Smelser, N. J. 1963. *Theory of collective behavior*. New York: Free Press.

Smith, T. W., M. K. Pope, F. Rhodewalt, and J. L. Poulton. 1989. Optimism, neuroticism, coping, and symptom reports: An alternative interpretation of the Life Orientation test. *Journal of Personality and Social Psychology* 56: 640–648.

Snyder, C. R., and B. K. Houston, eds. 1988. *Type A behavior pattern: Research, theory and interventions*. Somerset, N.J.: John Wiley & Sons.

Snyder, J. J. 1989. *Health psychology and behavioral medicine*. Englewood Cliffs, N.J.: Prentice-Hall Inc.

Solkoff, N. 1981. Children of survivors of the Nazi Holocaust: A critical review of the literature. *American Journal of Orthopsychiatry* 51: 29–42.

Speisman, J. C., R. S. Lazarus, A. M. Mordkoff, and L. A. Davison. 1964. Experimental analysis of a film used as a threatening stimulus. *Journal of Consulting Psychology* 28: 23–33.

Steele, C. M. 1988. The psychology of self affirmation: Sustaining the integrity of the self. In *Advances in experimental social psychology*, Vol. 21, edited by L. Berkowitz. New York: Academic Press.

Strack, S., C. S. Carver, and P. H. Blaney. 1987. Predicting successful completion of an aftercare program following treatment for alcoholism: The role of dispositional optimism. *Journal of Personality and Social Psychology* 53: 579–584.

Stroebe, M. S., and W. Stroebe. 1983. Who suffers more? Sex differences in health risks of the widowed. *Psychological Bulletin* 93: 279–301.

Strube, M. J. 1990. A self-appraisal model of the Type A behavior pattern. In *Perspectives in personality: Theory, measurement and interpersonal dynamics*, Vol. 3, edited by R. Hogan and W. H. Jones. Greenwich, Conn.: JAI Press.

Strube, M. J., J. M. Berry, B. Goza, and D. Fennimore. 1985. Type A behavior, age, and psychological well-being. *Journal of Personality and Social Psychology* 49: 203–218.

Strube, M. J., S. M. Boland, P. A. Manfredo, and A. Al-Falaij. 1987. Type A behavior pattern and the self evaluation of abilities: Empirical test of the self-appraisal model. *Journal of Personality and Social Psychology* 52: 956–975.

Suls, J., and C. K. Wan. 1989. The relation between Type A behavior and chronic emotional distress: A meta-analysis. *Journal of Personality and Social Psychology* 57: 503–512.

Summers, G., and N. S. Feldman. 1984. Blaming the victim versus blaming the perpetrator: An attributional analysis of spouse abuse. *Journal of Social and Clinical Psychology* 2: 339–347.

Sutherland, S., and D. Scherl. 1970. Patterns of response among victims of rape. *American Journal of Orthopsychiatry* 40: 503–511.

Taylor, S. E. 1979. Hospital patient behavior: Reactance, helplessness, or control? *Journal of Social Issues* 35: 156–184.

———. 1982a. The availability bias in social perception and social interaction. In *Judgment under uncertainty: Heuristics and biases*, edited by D. Kahneman, P. Slovic, and A. Tversky. New York: Cambridge University Press.

———. 1982b. Social cognition and health. *Personality and Social Psychology Bulletin* 8: 549–562.

————. 1983. Adjustment to threatening events: A theory of cognitive adaptation. *American Psychologist* 38: 1161–1173.

————. 1986. *Health Psychology*. New York: Random House.

————. 1990. Health psychology: The science and the field. *American Psychologist* 45: 40–50.

Taylor, S. E., and J. D. Brown. 1988. Illusions and well-being: Some social psychological contributions to a theory of mental health. *Psychological Bulletin* 103: 193–210.

Taylor, S. E., B. P. Buunk, and L. G. Aspinwall. 1990. Social comparison, stress, and coping. *Personality and Social Psychology Bulletin* 16: 74–89.

Taylor, S. E., J. Crocker, and J. D'Agostino. 1978. Schematic bases of social problem solving. *Personality and Social Psychological Bulletin* 94: 447–451.

Taylor, S. E., and G. A. Dakof. 1988. Social support and the cancer patient. In *The social psychology of health*, 95–118, edited by S. Spacapan and S. Oskamp. Newbury Park, Calif.: Sage.

Taylor, S. E., and S. T. Fiske. 1978. Salience, attention, and attribution: Top of the head phenomena. In *Advances in Experimental Social Psychology*, Vol. 11, edited by L. Berkowitz. New York: Academic Press.

Taylor, S. E., R. R. Lichtman, and J. V. Wood. 1984. Attributions, beliefs about control, and adjustment to breast cancer. *Journal of Personality and Social Psychology* 46: 489–502.

Taylor, S. E., and M. Lobel. 1989. Social comparison activity under threat: Downward evaluation and upward contact. *Psychological Review* 96: 569–575.

Taylor, S. E., and S. C. Thompson. 1982. Stalking the elusive "vividness" effect. *Psychological Review* 89: 155–181.

Taylor, S. E., J. V. Wood, and R.R. Lichtman. 1983. It could be worse: Selective evaluation as a response to victimization. *Journal of Social Issues* 39: 19–40.

Tennen, H., and S. J. Eller. 1977. Attributional components of learned helplessness and facilitation. *Journal of Personality and Social Psychology* 35: 265–271.

Thompson, S. C. 1981. Will it hurt less if I can control it? A complex answer to a simple question. *Psychological Bulletin* 90: 89–101.

Turkington, C. 1985. What price friendship? The darker side of social support. *APA Monitor* February: 38–41.

Vaillant, G. E. 1977. *Adaptation to life*. Boston: Little, Brown.

Walker, L. A. 1987. What comforts AIDS families. *The New York Times Magazine* June 21: 16–78.

Ward, S., and H. Leventhal. 1986. "Social support: Reciprocity, the negatives and the person with cancer." Paper presented at the American Psychological Association Meeting, Washington, D.C.

Weber, M. 1904. Die protestantische Ethik und der Geist des Kapitalismus. *Archiv fuer Sozialwissenschaft und Sozialpolitik* 20: 1–54; 1905: 21, 1–110.

Weiner, B. 1972. *Theories of motivation. From mechanisms to cognition*. Chicago: Markham.

————. 1984. An attributional interpretation of expectancy—value theory. In *Cognitive views of human motivation*, 51–70, edited by B. Weiner. New York: Academic Press.

————. 1985a. "Spontaneous" causal thinking. *Psychological Bulletin* 97: 74–84.

————. 1985b. An attributional theory of achievement motivation and emotion. *Psychological Review* 92: 548–573.

Weiner, B., and A. Kukla. 1970. An attributional analysis of achievement motivation. *Journal of Personality and Social Psychology* 15: 1–20.

White, R. H. 1974. Strategies of adaptation: An attempt at systematic description. In *Coping and adaptation*, 47–68, edited by G. V. Coelho, D. A. Hamburg, and J. E. Adams. New York: Basic Books.

Wicklund, R. A., and D. Frey. 1981. Cognitive consistency: Motivational vs. non-motivational perspectives. In *Social cognition. Perspectives on everyday understanding*, 141–164, edited by J. P. Forgas. London: Academic Press.

Wilson, J. P., W. K. Smith, and S. K. Johnson. 1985. A comparative analysis of PTSD among various survivor groups. In *Trauma and its wake*, 142–172, edited by C. Figley. New York: Brunner/Mazel.

Wolff, H. G. 1953. *Stress and disease*. Springfield, Ill.: Charles C. Thomas.

Wong, P.T.P., and B. Weiner. 1981. When people ask "why" questions, and the heuristics of attributional search. *Journal of Personality and Social Psychology* 40: 650–663.

Wood, J. V., S. E. Taylor, and R. R. Lichtman. 1985. Social comparison in adjustment to breast cancer. *Journal of Personality and Social Psychology* 49: 1169–1183.

Wortman, C. B. 1976. Causal attributions and personal control. In *New directions in attribution research*, Vol. 1, edited by J. H. Harvey, W. J. Ickes, and R. F. Kidd. Hillsdale, N.J.: Erlbaum.

Wortman, C. B., and J. W. Brehm. 1975. Responses to uncontrollable outcomes: An integration of reactance theory and the learned helplessness model. In *Advances in experimental social psychology*, Vol. 8, 278–336, edited by L. Berkowitz. New York: Academic Press.

Wortman, C. B., and T. L. Conway. 1985. The role of social support in adaptation and recovery from physical illness. In *Social support and health*, 281–302, edited by S. Cohen and S. L. Syme. New York: Academic Press.

Wortman, C. B., and L. Dintzer. 1978. Is an attributional analysis of the learned helplessness phenomenon viable? A critique of the Abramson—Seligman—Teasdale reformulation. *Journal of Abnormal Psychology* 87: 75–90.

Wortman, C. B., and D. R. Lehman. 1985. Reactions to victims in life crises. Support attempts that fail. In *Social support: Theory, research and applications*, edited by I. G. Sarason and B. R. Sarason. Dordrecht, The Netherlands: Martinus Nijhof.

Wortman, C. B., and R. C. Silver. 1987. Coping with irrevocable loss. In *Cataclysms, crises, and catastrophes: Psychology in action*, Master Lecture Series, Vol. 6, 189–235, edited by G. R. VandenBos and B. K. Bryant. Washington, D.C.: American Psychological Association.

————. 1989. The myths of coping with loss. *Journal of Consulting and Clinical Psychology* 57: 349–357.

————. Under review. Searching for meaning following loss.

Wright, L. 1988. The Type A behavior pattern and coronary artery disease: Quest for the active ingredients and the elusive mechanism. *American Psychologist* 43: 2–14.

Wrubel, J., P. Brenner, and R. S. Lazarus. 1981. Social competence from the perspective of stress and coping. In *Social competence*, edited by J. Wine and M. Syme. New York: Guilford.

Zahourek, R., and J. S. Jensen. 1973. Grieving and the loss of the newborn. *American Journal of Nursing* 73: 836–839.

Zajonc, R. B. 1980. Feeling and thinking: Preferences need no inferences. *American Psychologist* 35: 151–175.

———. 1990. Leon Festinger (1919–1989). *American Psychology* 45: 661–662.

———. 1983. Discussion of Abelson's Talk on Cartwright's Founders' Day. *Personality and Social Psychology Bulletin* 9: 55–59.

Zajonc, R. B., S. T. Murphy, and M. R. Inglehart. 1989. Feeling and facial efference: Implications of the vascular theory of emotion. *Psychological Review* 96: 395–416.

Zanna, M. P., and J. Cooper. 1974. Dissonance and the pill: An attribution approach to studying the arousal properties of dissonance. *Journal of Personality and Social Psychology* 29: 703–709.

———. 1976. Dissonance and the attribution process. In *New directions in attribution research*, Vol. 1, 199–218, edited by J. H. Harvey, W. J. Ickes, and R. F. Kidd. New York: Erlbaum.

Zarit, S. H., K. E. Reeves, and J. Bach-Peterson. 1980. Relatives of the impaired elderly: Correlates of feeling of burden. *The Gerontologist* 20: 649–655.

Zarski, J. J. 1984. Hassles and health: A replication. *Health Psychology* 3: 243–251.

Zullow, H., G. Oettingen, C. Peterson, and M.E.P. Seligman. 1988. Pessimistic explanatory style in the historical record: Lyndon B. Johnson, Presidential Election, and East vs. West Berlin. *American Psychologist* 43: 673–682.

Author Index

Abbey, A., 146
Abbott, R. A., 162
Abelson, R. D., 59, 65, 66, 70, 73, 92
Abramson, L. Y., 38–41, 43, 44, 47, 51, 52, 159
Acklin, M. W., 175
Adams, J. E., 7
Ainsworth, M., 19
Akiyami, H., 146
Al-Falaij, A., 154
Alfert, E., 28
Alloy, L. B., 40
Allport, G., 153, 179
Antonucci, T. C., 146, 147
Aronson, E., 65
Aspinwall, L. G., 49
Asroff, S., 160
Averill, J. R., 7, 34

Bach-Peterson, I., 145
Baker, G. W., 12, 189
Baltes, M. M., 155
Bammer, K., 13
Banaji, M. R., 162
Bandura, A., 39, 155
Barrett, L. C., 41
Bass, C., 154
Baum, A., 18
Baumeister, R. F., 63
Beck, A. T., 162

Beckman, J., 65
Bellezza, F. S., 162
Bem, D. J., 86, 89
Bennett, G., 184
Bentler, P. M., 112, 113, 121, 123
Bergman, M. V., 133
Berkman, L. F., 143
Berry, J. M., 154
Blaney, P. H., 161, 162
Bless, H., 88
Bohner, G., 88
Boland, S. M., 154
Bolger, N., 33, 164
Bond, M. H., 172
Bonett, D. G., 112, 113, 121, 123
Boon, C., 13, 175
Booth-Kewley, S., 154, 155
Borgida, E., 173
Bortner, R. W., 154
Bowlby, J., 17
Bradburn, N. M., 179
Brand, R. J., 154
Breen, L. J., 38
Brehm, J., 37, 39, 42–45, 47, 48, 51, 52, 57
Brekke, N., 173
Brenner, P., 164
Breznitz, S., 134
Brody, D. S., 160
Brower, A. M., 161

Brown, D., 98, 100, 176, 177
Brown, E. C., 175
Brown, J. D., 51, 107
Brunson, B. I., 154, 155
Bulman, R. J., 13
Burchfield, S. R., 57
Burgess, A. W., 13
Burns, M. O., 41
Buunk, B. P., 49

Cannon, W. B., 7, 12
Cantor, N., 158, 161–163
Carver, C. S., 161, 162, 179
Cascaller, E. C., 13
Casky, B. J., 145
Caspi, A., 164
Cassel, R. B., 142
Cattell, J., 153
Cervantes, R. C., 13
Chapman, D. W., 12
Cherico, D. J., 19
Coates, D., 146
Cobb, S., 13, 142, 143
Coelho, G. V., 7
Cohen, J. B., 33
Cohen, S., 143, 144, 146
Cole, C. S., 39
Collins, R. L., 49, 50
Conway, T. L., 146
Cooper, J., 65, 86, 87
Courington, S., 14, 157
Coyne, J. C., 6, 28, 33, 35, 39, 146,
    159
Crocker, J., 48

D'Agostino, J., 48
Dakof, G. A., 6, 28, 33, 49, 147
Darley, J. M., 141
Davis, K. E., 63, 80–83
Davison, L. A., 28
Dean, A., 144
DeLongis, A., 6, 28, 33, 35, 144, 163
Dembroski, T. M., 154
DePres, T., 14, 133, 174
Derogatis, L. R., 154
Derry, P. A., 162
Dewey, R., 153
Dezan, C., 13

Dickenberger, D., 104, 128
DiMatteo, M. R., 56
Dimsdale, J. E., 13
Dinardo, Q., 26
Dintzer, L., 43–45, 47
Dobos, R., 13
Dohrenwend, S. P., 35
Downey, G., 44, 45
Duck, S., 14, 142
Dunkel-Schetter, C., 34, 145, 150
Durkheim, E., 12, 142

Eckenrode, J., 164
Edwards, J., 153
Ellard, J. H., 45, 145
Endler, N. S., 153
Ensel, W. M., 144
Erwin, B., 179

Fagot, B. I., 159
Fazio, R. H., 65, 86, 87
Feldman, N. S., 17
Felner, R. D., 36
Fenigstein, A., 79
Fennimore, D., 154
Festinger, L., 59, 63, 65–70, 79, 88, 89
Figley, C. R., 133
Fillingham, R. B., 158
Fiske, S. T., 48, 63
Fitzgerald, R. C., 19
Fleming, R., 18
Fogelman, E., 174
Folkman, S., 7, 11, 13, 15, 28–35, 57,
    144, 155–158, 163, 164, 175
Frankl, V. E., 13, 174, 175
Freud, S., 153
Freund, T., 87, 88
Frey, D., 86
Friedman, H. S., 56, 155
Friedman, M., 154
Friedman, R., 14
Frieze, I. H., 50
Funk, S. C., 157
Furnham, A., 173

Galanter, M., 184
Garber, J., 39
Girgus, J. S., 41, 159

Glass, D. C., 154, 155
Glick, I. O., 26
Goetz, J., 74
Goetz-Marchand, B., 74
Goldband, S., 154
Gorsuch, R. L., 172, 179
Gotlib, I. H., 159
Gottlieb, B. H., 142
Goza, B., 154
Green, B. L., 13
Greenberg, J., 88
Greenwald, A. G., 162
Grinker, R. R., 6, 13
Gruen, R., 33–35
Gruman, J. C., 173
Guilford, J. P., 153
Gullo, S. V., 19
Gunter, B., 173

Haan, N., 55
Hahn, M. E., 157
Hahn, W., 154
Hall, C. M., 172
Hamburg, D. A., 7
Hamilton, S., 159
Hanusa, B. H., 38
Harary, F., 65
Harvey, J. H., 79, 86
Harvey, O. J., 172
Haynes, S. G., 155
Heider, F., 2, 59, 63–66, 68, 70, 79–
    83, 86, 88, 89, 91
Heimreich, R. L., 179
Henderson, A. S., 142
Herrmann, C., 109, 159
Heyduk, R. G., 79
Higgins, E. T., 162
Hinkle, L. E., 7
Hiroto, D. S., 38
Hobfoll, S. E., 146, 147, 162, 163
Holmes, T. H., 6
Holmstrom, L. L., 13
Hoover, M., 157
Horowitz, M. I., 19, 21
House, J. S., 143, 144, 147
Houston, B. K., 155, 157
Hudson, W. W., 173
Hull, J. G., 157

Humber, W. J., 153
Hunt, D. E., 172

Ickes, W. J., 86
Inglehart, M. R., 65, 98, 100, 104–106,
    110, 113, 118, 122, 124, 126, 130,
    176, 177, 179, 180
Irle, E., 65
Irle, M., 65, 66, 74, 104, 110, 128, 131

Jackson, D. N., 157
Janis, I. L., 7, 151
Janoff-Bulman, R., 50, 172, 175
Jenkins, C. D., 154
Jensen, J. S., 19
Joereskog, K. C., 110, 120
Johnson, S. K., 13
Jones, E. E., 63, 66, 80–83
Jucovy, M. E., 133

Kahn, S., 157
Kaltreider, N. B., 21
Kanner, A. D., 28, 33, 35
Kasl, S. V., 13
Kaslow, N. J., 40
Katkin, E. S., 154
Kaylor, J. A., 6, 13
Kelley, H. H., 2, 59, 63, 80, 81, 83
Kelley, W. E., 133
Kessler, R. C., 33, 146, 147
Kidd, R. F., 86
Kihlstrom, J. F., 162, 163
Kimball, C. P., 21, 26
King, D. W., 6, 13
King, L. A., 6, 13
Klar, Y., 87, 95
Klein, H., 133
Klein, R., 162
Klinger, E., 17, 22–26, 56
Klos, D. S., 44, 45, 47
Klosterhalfen, S., 37
Klosterhalfen, W., 37
Kobasa, S. C., 14, 145, 146, 155, 157,
    158
Kojetin, B. A., 179
Kondoff, P., 104, 106
Kositcher, R., 154
Kruglanski, A. W., 83, 87, 88, 95

Kuebler-Ross, E., 8, 14, 17, 20, 21, 25,
    26, 56
Kuiper, N. A., 162
Kukla, A., 84

Lack, E. R., 160
LaGaipa, Y. Y., 146
Landis, K. R., 144
Langer, E., 155
Langston, C. A., 160, 161
Lasut, U., 1, 133
Latane, B., 141
Launier, R., 28, 32, 164
Lazarus, R. S., 6, 7, 11, 13, 15, 18,
    27–36, 57, 145, 156–158, 163, 164,
    175
Lefcourt, H. M., 145, 146, 155, 156,
    179
Lefebvre, R. C., 162
Lehman, D., 45, 50, 145, 146
Leiberman, J., 163
Leighton, A. H., 142
Lerner, M. J., 172, 173, 179
Lester, D., 184
Levenson, H., 179
Leventhal, H., 145
Leventman, E., 133
Lichtman, R. R., 6, 13, 49, 50
Lieberman, M. A., 148, 162
Lifton, R. J., 14
Lin, N., 144
Lindy, J. D., 13
Linville, P. W., 108, 162, 163, 167
Litwak, E., 142
Lobel, M., 49
Long, T. E., 13
Lootens, A. L., 147, 154
Luborsky, L., 40
Lucas, R. A., 12

Maddi, S. R., 14, 157
Maddison, D., 146
Magnusson, D., 153
Magovern, G. I., 162
Maier, S. F., 37, 38
Malanchuk, O., 177
Malmo, R. B., 17
Mangan, C. E., 160

Mann, L., 6
Manne, S., 151
Markus, H., 86, 91, 98, 176
Martin, R. A., 145, 146
Maslach, C., 146
Maslow, A. H., 142
Mason, J. W., 7, 18
Matarazzo, J. D., 186
Matthews, K. A., 154, 155, 162
Mauger, P. A., 175
Mayseless, O., 163
McDaniel, J. W., 21, 26
McDonald, M., 173
McDougall, J. M., 154
McFerran, J. R., 38
McGill, K. L., 107
McGuire, W. J., 65
McIntosh, D. N., 45, 175, 176, 179,
    180
McIntosh, J. L., 184
McLeod, J. D., 146, 147
McPherson, S. E., 179
Mead, G. H., 153
Menaghan, E. G., 162
Menninger, K., 55
Metalsky, G. I., 40, 41
Metzner, H. L., 143, 144
Meyer, C. B., 49
Miller, D. T., 173
Miller, I. W., 37
Miller, S. M., 158, 159, 160
Mischel, W., 153, 160
Moentmann, V., 65, 104, 128
Monat, A., 7
Moore, W., 100, 177
Moos, R. H., 7, 55
Mordkoff, A. M., 28
Morell, M. A., 154
Mullan, J. T., 162
Murphy, G. J., 173
Murphy, L. B., 7
Mustante, L. J., 154

Nadelson, C. C., 26
Nadler, A., 146, 162
Newcomb, T. M., 65, 189
Niedenthal, P. M., 161
Nolen-Hoeksema S., 41, 159

Norem, J. K., 158, 160
Norman, W. H., 37
Northouse, L., 145
Notman, M. T., 26
Nurius, P. S., 98, 173

Oettingen, G., 41
Opton, E. M., Jr., 7, 34
Osgood, C. E., 65–67, 69, 70
Overmier, J. B., 37
Owens, J. F., 162

Pacini, R., 176, 179, 180
Parkes, C. M., 19, 26
Parkes, K. R., 156
Pearlin, L. I., 162
Peck, A., 26
Pennebaker, J. W., 134, 149
Peterson, C., 40, 41, 44, 47, 51, 159
Phillips, D. P., 184
Piaget, J., 19
Pierce, G. R., 144
Pope, M. K., 162
Porter, C. A. A., 173
Poulton, J. L., 162
Puccetti, M. C., 145, 146, 157
Pyszczynski, T. A., 88

Rahe, R. H., 6
Reever, K. F., 145
Rhodewalt, F., 157, 162
Rich, A. R., 157, 158
Rich, V. L., 158
Richard, W. C., 13
Robbins, C., 143, 144
Robins, C. J., 159
Rodin, J., 41, 155
Rohrlach, R., 104, 105, 130
Rokeach, M., 172, 179
Rosch/Inglehart, M., 13, 65, 104–106,
    110, 120, 122, 128, 130, 131
Rosenberg, M. J., 59, 65, 66, 69, 70,
    73, 92
Rosenman, R. H., 154, 155
Rossiter, M., 14, 174
Roth, D. L., 158
Rotter, J. B., 153, 155, 179
Rowlison, R. T., 33, 36

Saleh, W. E., 145, 146
Sarafino, E. P., 56
Sarason, B. R., 144
Sarason, L. G., 144
Schachter, S., 80, 81, 83, 84, 95
Schaefer, C., 6, 28, 33, 35
Scheier, M. F., 161, 162, 179
Scher, S. J., 65
Scherl, D., 19
Schilling, E. A., 33
Schlosser, M. B., 157
Schmidt, P., 104, 105, 128
Schooler, C., 162
Schroeder, H. M., 172
Schulman, P., 41, 52, 159
Schulz, R., 39
Schur, S., 130
Schwarz, N., 88
Seligman, M. E. P., 27, 37–44, 47, 48,
    51, 52, 57, 159
Selye, H., 7, 12, 15, 17, 18, 25, 27,
    56, 142
Semmel, A., 40, 41
Sexton, A. W., 21, 26
Shadick, R., 19
Shaver, P., 175
Shay, K. A., 158
Sheeley, L. A., 157
Shiffman, S., 184
Shontz, F. C., 19, 21
Shrout, P. E., 35
Simmel, M., 80
Singer, J. E., 18, 80, 81
Singer, P. S., 157, 158
Sloan, R. P., 173
Smelser, N. J., 7
Smith, T. W., 162
Smith, W. K., 13
Snyder, C. R., 155
Snyder, J. J., 56
Soerbom, D., 110, 120
Solkoff, N., 133
Speisman, J. C., 28
Spiegel, J. P., 6, 13
Spilka, B., 162
Stapp, R., 179
Steele, C. M., 104
Stone, M. H., 13, 175

Strack, F., 88
Strack, S., 161, 162
Strauman, T., 162
Strauss, R., 154
Stroebe, M. S., 6, 13
Stroebe, W., 6, 13
Strube, M. J., 147, 154, 155
Suls, J., 155
Summers, G., 173
Summerton, J., 160
Sutherland, S., 19
Syme, S. L., 143, 144

Tannenbaum, P. H., 65–67, 69, 70
Tannenbaum, R. L., 40
Taylor, S. E., 6, 13, 14, 27, 37, 48–52, 56, 57, 63, 76, 109, 147, 175, 186
Teasdale, J., 38–40, 43, 44, 47, 51, 52, 57, 159
Tennen, H., 38
Thompson, S. C., 48, 155, 156
Timko, C., 50
Turkington, C., 144, 146

Ulmer, D., 14, 154
Umberson, D., 144

Vaillant, G. E., 41, 55
VanTreuren, R. R., 157
Virnelli, S., 157
von Baeyer, C., 40, 41
Vourakis, C., 184

Walfisch, S., 162
Walker, L. A., 141

Walker, W. L., 146
Wan, C. K., 141, 146
Ward, S., 155
Weiner, B., 145
Weiss, R. S., 2, 59, 63, 80, 81, 83, 84, 88, 89, 95, 134
Werthessen, N. T., 154
Wethington, E., 146, 147
White, R. H., 7
Wicklund, R. A., 86
Wiebe, D. J., 158
Williams, A. F., 45, 50
Wills, T. A., 144, 146, 184
Wilson, J. P., 13
Wolff, H. G., 12
Wong, P. T. P., 81
Wood, J. V., 6, 13, 49, 50
Woolf, D. S., 184
Wortman, C. B., 13, 21, 26, 27, 37, 38, 42–48, 50–52, 56, 57, 145, 146, 150, 175
Wright, L., 154, 155
Wrubel, J., 164
Wurf, E., 91, 177
Wurm, M., 154

Zahourek, R., 19
Zajonc, R. B., 63, 65, 86
Zanna, M. P., 87
Zarit, S. H., 145
Zarski, J. J., 33
Zautra, A. J., 151
Zola, M. A., 157
Zone, J. B., 157
Zullow, H., 41
Zyzanski, S. J., 154

Subject Index

Acceptance, 20
Accidents, 45
Achievement, 80, 84, 99, 154, 177
Adaptation, 14, 48–50
AIDS, 141, 145
Alameda County Study, 143, 144
Alcohol, 102, 131–133, 161–162, 184–186
Alzheimer's Disease, 145
Anger, 20, 26, 42
Appraisal, 23, 30, 42, 156; primary, 30, 175; secondary, 30, 175
Attachment, 19–20
Attitude, 65, 69
Attribution, 37, 39–40, 43, 47, 48, 63, 79–89; a priori, 93, 121–127, 185; external, 81, 90, 184; internal, 81, 90, 108, 184; post hoc, 91–93, 108–117, 185
Attributional style, 40–42, 158–159
Availability, 74, 93, 131, 178

Balance theory, 64, 66, 86, 88
Bargaining, 20
Beliefs, 51, 76, 138, 164, 171–177; just world belief, 172, 179; religious, 175, 179, 180
Blindness, 19
Blunter, 159–161

Bortner Scale, 154
Burnout, 146

Cancer, 48–50, 145, 175
Catastrophes, 13–14
Choice, 100–102
Cognitive Congruency. *See* Cognitive consistency
Cognitive consistency, 59, 63–71, 85–88
Cognitive dissonance. *See* Cognitive consistency
Commitment, 23, 164
Comparisons; social, 49
Concentration camp, 13–14, 133, 174
Confounded indicators, 35–36
Control, 48, 126–127, 155–158, 165
Coping, 27, 31; definition, 7; direct actions, 31; palliative actions, 7, 31; stage-centered, 8
Coping modes, 31–32
Coping styles, 159–161
Coronary artery disease, 26, 154, 162

Daily hassles, 32–36, 147
Death, 13, 14, 19–21, 55
Defensive pessimism, 161
Denial, 20, 28
Depression, 20, 23, 40, 42, 46, 102, 155, 162, 163

Developmental issues, 55
Divorce, 13
Drugs, 102, 184–186

Election, 104–105, 128–130
Emotions, 80, 81, 137
Employment loss, 13
Energizing component, 9
Events: importance, 6, 103, 120; nega-
   tive, 6, 103–108, 133–134; positive,
   6, 103–108, 133–134; threatening, 14,
   37, 48–52; uncontrollable, 38, 43; un-
   expected, 81
Expectations, 38

Framingham Type A Scale, 154
Freedom, expectation of, 42

Gender differences, 146, 157
General adaptation syndrome, 18
Generalized principles of cognitive consistency, 2, 15, 57–59, 62, 79, 88–98,
   166, 176–180, 182–188

Hardiness, 14, 155–158
Health, 41, 46, 56, 107, 120–121, 142–
   144, 157–159, 163, 186
Helping behavior, 141–142
Helplessness, 155; symptoms, 38; the-
   ory of, 37–42

Illusions, 50–51
Immigration, 13, 110–113, 122–124
Incentive-disengagement theory, 17,
   22–24
Incest, 13
Inconsistency, 65
Individual differences. See Personality
   variables
Interpersonal relations, 80, 82
Invigoration, 23

Jenkins Activity Scale (JAS), 154
Just world belief. See Beliefs

Lay-epistemology, 87–88
Life Orientation Test (LOT), 161–162,
   179

Life philosophy, 171–180
Locus of control, 155–156, 179
Long-term consequences. See Reaction,
   long-term
Loss, 19–20, 45–47, 52, 175

Mastery. See Control
Meaning, 48–51, 174
Miller Behavioral Style Scale, 160
Miscarriage, 19, 72
Monitors, 159–161

Need for evaluation, 80–81

Optimism, 41, 161–162

Past experiences, 74
Personality variables, 14, 32–33, 145–
   147, 153–169
Person perception, 80, 82
Pessimism, 41, 161–162
Politics, 41
Prevention, 186–188
Principle of least effort, 69, 73, 85, 178
Psychoanalytic approaches, 55, 153

Rape, 13, 19, 48, 109, 172–174
Reactance, 37, 42–43
Reaction: energizing component, 10,
   56; general, 9–10, 25, 56, 73, 92–93,
   96, 121–131, 150–151, 168, 177, 183;
   long-tern, 9–11, 25–26, 32, 46, 56,
   75–76, 93–96, 133–134, 169, 178,
   184; specific, 9–11, 25, 56, 74, 93,
   96, 131–133, 151, 169, 178, 183;
   structuring component, 10, 56
Religion, 172
Research: applied, 1, 102, 181–188;
   basic, 1, 63; event-centered, 13–14,
   55; theory centered, 15, 55; variable-
   centered, 14–15, 55, 137
Retirement, 55

Self, 91, 162–165; complexity, 163–164,
   167; enhancement, 48; esteem, 47,
   162–163; image, 107; possible, 98,
   100
Self perception, theory of, 86–87
Separation, 19–20
Sexual Attitude Scale, 173

Social Readjustment Rating Scale, 6
Social support, 14, 32–34, 141–151, 163
Spinal cord injury, 26, 45
Stage theories, 15, 17–26
Stress, definition, 7, 18, 30
Structured interview, 154
Sudden Infant Death Syndrome, 45
Suicide, 102, 142, 182, 184–186
Sum rule, 66, 68, 72, 85, 89–90, 109, 149, 167, 178

Tecumseh Community Health Study, 144

Tension, 7, 68, 75, 86, 89, 95, 108–121, 148–150, 166, 182; avoidance reactions, 8, 69–70, 151, 184–186; reduction reactions, 8, 69–70, 151, 185
Type A behavior pattern, 154–155

Values, 171–172, 179, 180
Ventilation, 150

War, 13, 133
Worldview, 118–121, 127–131, 163, 167, 171, 177, 183

ABOUT THE AUTHOR

MARITA R. INGLEHART is Assistant Professor of Psychology and Senior Research Associate at the Center for Research on Teaching and Learning at the University of Michigan, Ann Arbor. She has contributed articles to scholarly journals, including the *Journal of the American Medical Women's Association*, *Psychological Review*, and several German journals.